WITH THE TIBETANS
IN
TENT AND TEMPLE

TIBETAN WOMAN AND SON

WITH THE TIBETANS
IN
TENT AND TEMPLE

NARRATIVE OF FOUR YEARS' RESIDENCE ON THE TIBETAN BORDERS, AND OF A JOURNEY INTO THE FAR INTERIOR

SUSIE CARSON RIJNHART

FOURTH EDITION

ISBN : 978-93-5324-533-7 (HB)

First Published, London, 4th edn, 1904

Published, 2020

Published by

Facsimile Publisher
12 Pragati Market
Ashok Vihar, Ph-2
Delhi-110052
E-mail: books@facsimilepublisher.com

Printed at: G. Print Process, Delhi.

With the Tibetans
in
Tent and Temple

Author: Susie Carson Rijnhart

With the Tibetans in Tent and Temple

NARRATIVE OF FOUR YEARS' RESIDENCE ON THE TIBETAN BORDER, AND OF A JOURNEY INTO THE FAR INTERIOR

BY

SUSIE CARSON RIJNHART, M.D.

Fifth Edition

CHICAGO NEW YORK TORONTO
FLEMING H. REVELL COMPANY
LONDON & EDINBURGH
1904

TO THE MEMORY OF MY
HUSBAND, WHOSE HEART
AND LIFE WERE GIVEN
TO THE TIBETANS, THIS
VOLUME IS DEDICATED

PREFACE

In the following pages I have attempted to narrate briefly the events of four years' residence and travel among the Tibetans (1895-1899). The work does not aim at literary finish, for it has been written under the stress of many public engagements. It is sent forth in response to requests and suggestions received from friends in all parts of the United States and Canada.

If I may succeed in perpetuating and deepening the widespread interest in the evangelization of Tibet, already aroused by the press and platform accounts of the missionary pioneering herein described, I shall be glad. To this end I have incorporated in the narrative as many data concerning the customs, beliefs and social conditions of the Tibetans as space would allow. My close contact with the people during four years has enabled me to speak with confidence on these points, even when I have found myself differing from great travelers who, because of their brief sojourn and rapid progress, necessarily received some false impressions. The map accompanying the book shows the route of the last journey undertaken in 1898 by my husband, myself and our little son, and of which I am the sole survivor. Leaving Tankar on the northwestern frontier of Chinese or Outer Tibet, crossing the Ts'aidam Desert, the Kuenlun and Dang La Mountains, we entered the Lhasa district of Inner Tibet, reaching Nagch'uk'a, a town about one hundred and fifty miles from the capital. In describing this journey, such portions of Mr. Rijnhart's diary as I was able to preserve, and also his accurate geographical notes, have been of inestimable value to me.

My thanks are due to Rev. Mr. Upcraft, Baptist missionary at Ya Cheo, China, for photographs from which some of the illustrations were made. And I am especially grateful to Prof. Charles T. Paul, of Hiram College, who placed at my disposal the fruits of his many years' study of *Tibetiana*, and rendered me invaluable assistance in the preparation of the manuscript.

SUSIE C. RIJNHART.

Chatham, Ontario, Canada.

CONTENTS

CONTENTS

CONTENTS

LIST OF ILLUSTRATIONS

WITH THE TIBETANS

CHAPTER I

TO THE TIBETAN BORDER

Mission in a Buddhist Lamasery—Preparation for the Journey—Across China—Impressions by the Way.

On the slopes of two hills in the province of Amdo, on the extreme northwestern Chino-Tibetan frontier, nestles the great lamasery of Kumbum, famed among the devotees of Buddha as one of the holiest spots on Asiatic soil. As a center of Buddhist learning and worship it is known in the remote parts of China, Manchuria, Mongolia, and in all the Tibetan territories, even to the foot of the Himalayas, and is estimated to be second in rank only to Lhasa, the Tibetan capital. It is the seclusive residence of some four thousand lamas and, at festive seasons, the goal of pilgrimages from all Buddhist countries contiguous to Tibet. Desiring to carry on missionary work among the Tibetans we left America in the autumn of 1894, having Kumbum as our point of destination. We expected to make our home and establish a medical station at Lusar, a village which may be called the secular part of the lamasery, where the lamas do their trading, and which is only about five minutes' walk from the lamasery proper.

The considerations which led us to select Lusar as a basis of operations, besides its proximity to the lamasery, were as follows: My husband, Mr. Petrus Rijnhart, about three years previous had conceived the idea of entering Tibet for missionary purposes, from the Chinese side. From the experiences of Huc and Gabet, the Lazarist fathers, who, following a route through Tartary and China, had gained free access into the forbidden land, he was convinced that the antipathy to foreign intrusion everywhere manifested in the vigilantly guarded passes of the Himalayan frontier south and west did not exist to any extent on the northeastern border between Outer Tibet and China. In this he was right. Crossing the Chinese Empire, he had reached Lusar in 1892, had resided for ten months in the vicinity of the lamasery, had been well received by the priests, who called him a "white lama from the West," and had labored diligently to make known the Gospel. His work had consisted principally of private conversations with the lamas, and of short journeys among the nomads of the surrounding country, preaching and teaching, and wielding what little medical knowledge he possessed in the treatment of the sick. Among his patients were people of high and low degree, lamas from the great monastery, Tibetan and Mongol chiefs of the Koko-nor tribes, officials, merchants, shepherds, and even robbers. The interest with which his ministrations were received gave him great encouragement and deepened the intense longing he had already conceived for the evangelization of the Tibetans. Many with whom he came in contact had never seen a European nor heard the name of Christ. Some of the lamas said the Christian doctrine was too good to be true; others inquired why, if the doctrine were true, the Christians had waited "so many moons" before sending them the glad tidings. During one of his itinerating journeys "a living buddha" with his train of dignitaries came to the tent, having heard, as he said, that a man with a white face had come, and, sitting at the feet of the white stranger, the Buddhist teacher listened with rapt attention to the wonderful story of the world's Saviour. During his sojourn no official, either Chinese or Tibetan, asked for his passport, or questioned him as to his intentions of penetrating to the interior. Thus under circumstances unexpectedly favorable, surrounded by good will and hospitality, and free from that prejudice and espionage with which foreigners approaching the Tibetan border are usually regarded, he had had ample opportunity of studying the life, needs and disposition of the people, and his knowledge gave us assurance of the reception that awaited us at the lamasery village. Again, Lusar was advantageous from a topographical standpoint, being situated near the juncture of several important highways; one leading to China, another to Mongolia, and still another, the great caravan route, leading to Lhasa. Here we could easily receive supplies, and would be likely to come in contact with the people on a large scale, owing to the amount of traffic that passes along the great roads. Also, the surrounding country being inhabited by a cosmopolitan population comprising Mongols, Chinese, Tibetans, and a few Turkestani

Mohammedans, it was a good place in which to become conversant with the languages we should require, looking forward as we were to a life-long sojourn in the regions of Central Asia. We left America for our distant field without any human guarantee of support, for we were not sent out by any missionary society. Although, through Mr. Rijnhart's lectures in Holland, the United States and Canada, considerable interest had been aroused and many friends won to the cause of Tibetan missions, yet our visible resources were limited at best. We went forth, however, with a conviction which amounted to absolute trust that God would fulfil His promise to those who "seek first the Kingdom," and continue to supply us with all things necessary for carrying on the work to which He had called us. From the outset we felt that we were "thrust forth" specially for pioneer work, and although anticipating difficulties and sacrifices we were filled with joy at the prospect of sowing precious seed on new ground.

Our party, consisting of Mr. Rijnhart, his fellow-worker, Mr. William Neil Ferguson, and myself, sailing from the Pacific Coast, had decided to follow substantially the same route across China which Mr. Rijnhart had taken on his former journey. From Shanghai up the Yangtse to Hankow we would go by steamer; thence by house-boat up the Han as far as Fancheng, situated about four hundred miles up the river. The remainder of the journey would be completed overland by cart and mule. We had endeavored, before leaving America, to equip ourselves as well as possible, not only against the long journey, but also, in view of our pros-

NOTES:—The red line shows DR. RIJNHART's route.
The baby died and is buried at the spot indicated by the red circle.
MR. RIJNHART disappeared near TASHI GOMBA, marked by red cross.

pective residence far from civilization, with the possibility of being temporarily cut off altogether, owing to the frequent rebellions that take place in Central China, rendering the passage of mails and supplies uncertain. Our stores were contained in thirteen large, ponderous boxes, and consisted of clothing, culinary utensils, and other portable domestic necessities, medicines, dental and surgical instruments, fire-arms and ammunition, photographic materials, books, including copies of the Scriptures in Tibetan, and stationery, besides compasses, thermometers, a sewing machine and a bicycle. In Shanghai we added drugs, clothing, food for the river journey, Chinese brazen oil lamps, trinkets for bartering, and other articles. Knowing the advantage of traveling in native costume, each of us donned a Chinese suit. It was my first experience with oriental attire, and I shall not soon forget it. After adjusting the unwieldy garments to my own satisfaction, I attended a service in the Union Church, where, to my consternation, I discovered I had appeared in public with one of the under garments outside and dressed in a manner which shocked Chinese ideas of propriety.

Mr. Rijnhart, on account of his thorough knowledge of Chinese, was able to make excellent arrangements for our passage into the interior. As the war with Japan was then raging and the country in an unsettled state, there were difficulties to be anticipated; nor was there anything inviting in the thought of doing two thousand miles in midwinter under such exposure as would be entailed by the primitive modes of oriental travel. Yet, if one holds to progress with any comfort worthy the name, there are reasons for making the journey during the hibernating period of the greater portion of the inhabitants of China, namely, the verminous!

Our first stage up the Yangtse was made in a steamer manned by English officers and a Chinese crew. There was a sense of security, which afterwards we sadly lacked, in the feeling that the great river was but an arm of the gentle Pacific that laved our native shores, stretched far inland as if to assure us of protection. Our first stopping-place was the city of Hankow, an important commercial centre situated at the confluence of the Han and Yangtse rivers, and, following the sinuosities of the Yangtse, distant about eight hundred and fifty miles from the seaboard. The city was full of stir on our arrival. The people were intensely excited over the war, and signs of military activity were on every hand. The spacious harbor at the mouth of the Han presented the appearance of a forest of masts in which all the ships of Tarshish and of the world had congregated in one dense fleet. They were chiefly house-boats and cargo junks that usually ply up and down the river, but conspicuous among them were the high-pooped transports, their decks crowded with blue and red jacketed soldiers on their way to the scene of action.

We took passage for Fancheng in the inevitable house-boat, a long, clumsy-looking scow divided into three compartments; the captain's cabin at the stern, inhabited by himself, his wife and little child; another long cabin for the passengers, situated amidships and separated from the former by a movable partition; and a space at the bow where the crew discharged the functions of eating, sleeping and working. Under each compartment was a hold for the belongings of its occupants. On the rare occasions when the winds were favorable the sails were sufficient to propel the awkward craft; otherwise she was pulled along by the sturdy trackers on the shore. In deep water the captain steered by means of a prodigious rudder; in the shallows he managed with a long, stout bamboo pole. This mode of traveling was not without its amenities. The weather being fine, and the scenery along the river banks charming, we frequently disembarked and went afoot, and occasioned no little commotion as we passed through the villages, a foreign woman being an object of especial interest. Crowding around, the people would handle my clothing and ply me with questions, evincing astonishment at the size of my feet.

The villagers were mostly of the agricultural class, and appeared to be very industrious. The door-yards were tidy, as were also the farms, every available foot of land being cultivated. Everything about the houses betokened an air of freedom, even the pigs and chickens being allowed to go in and out at will. Signs of religious life were not wanting. In one village we came across an old temple mostly in ruins, in the one remaining corner of which were ten idols, some incense bowls and sticks, while near by lay the huge bell, silent and long since fallen from its lofty place. In the evening the people flocked to the old ruin to worship amid the sound of firecrackers and the beating of a huge gong by the attendant priest, and as the weird sounds were carried afar and re-echoed in the cold, still evening air there was about the whole scene a touching picturesqueness not unmingled with solemnity. Christmas day found us still on the house-boat, and with it came many pleasant memories of that glad, festive season in the homeland, and many reflections concerning China's teeming millions to whom the Christ of Bethlehem was still a stranger.

On January 7 we reached Fancheng, none the worse for our river journey. A hearty welcome was given us by the resident Scandinavian missionaries, Mr. and Mrs. Matson, Mr. and Mrs. Woolin, and Mr. Shequist, whom we found engaged in a most valuable work. Besides preaching, they conducted a boys' school, and at the time of our visit were erecting a school for girls. Our stay in Fancheng was brief, just long enough to get through the unenviable and seemingly endless preliminaries to an overland journey by cart. The hiring of the carts was itself no little matter even with the assistance of our Scandinavian friends, but finally the *piao* was signed, by which we secured two carters, with two large carts and a small one, to take us to Signan. By the word "cart" this Chinese vehicle is but faintly described. It consists of a clumsy, bulky frame set on a single axle, innocent of springs, its two wheels furnished with tires several inches in width and in thickness. The frame is covered by an awning of matting to shelter the traveler and his baggage from the heat and rain. The smaller carts, constructed on the same plan, are generally painted and have a cloth covering with windows in the sides. These carts are drawn in China by mules or horses, in Mongolia by camels or oxen. In many of the principal roads deep grooves have been worn by the constant passing of the great wheels, and, the length of the axle differing in the various districts, the grooves are not equidistant on all roads, so that it occasionally happens that at certain junctures all axles have to be changed. At Tung Kuan, for instance, a town situated at the meeting-place of the provinces of Shensi, Shansi and Honan, this operation is necessary.

On January 11 we were ready to start. We had taken the precaution to furnish our cart with a straw mattress, some pillows and comforters, to provide against the jolting which we knew awaited us. Our boxes being already in position, after Scripture reading with the missionaries our little caravan moved off. Two of the missionaries accompanied us outside the city gates to bid us God-speed, and it was only after we had parted ways with them that we realized we had actually set out on the most difficult part of our journey across the Celestial Empire. The road from the start was very uneven, a fall of two feet being not uncommon. I received a severe bump on the head, and experienced so many changes of position and came so frequently and emphatically into collision with various portions of the cart as to have remembered that springs are not a luxury of cart travel in China.

Carters are supposed to make a certain stage each day, and inns are found at the end of each stage for the accommodation of travelers. In order to cover the required distance we were frequently on the way in the middle of the night, and even though traveling from long before daylight until dusk we were not always able to reach an inn. At such times one must either sleep in the cart or put up in a farmhouse. Even the regular inns are by no means inviting. We first stopped in one of these thirty-five miles from Fancheng. It was a flimsy structure, with great crevices gaping in the walls, in which were rude lattice windows with paper panes; the ceilings were composed of bamboo poles nailed across the rafters, from which cobwebs hung in profusion; the sleeping-room had no floor, and the bed was as hard as boards could make it, springless of course, and destitute of covers. But one welcomes any variation from the tedium of a Chinese cart journey, and after the jolting of the first day can rest even in a Chinese inn.

One night, having failed to make the required stage, we sought shelter in a native hut on a hillside and slept on the *k'ang,* an article of furniture which no traveler in Western China soon forgets. The *k'ang* is a sort of elevation built across one end of the room, resembling a hollow platform, the top sometimes covered with flat stones. It serves the purpose of all the principal articles of furniture in an occidental house—chairs, stove, bed and table. It is warmed by a fire placed in the box, and, when the surface is moderately heated, one may recline with comfort; but on this night the *k'ang* was so hot that we soon became uncomfortable, being almost roasted on one side and frozen on the other. We were finally obliged to get up and rake out all the fire, and at last fell asleep from sheer exhaustion and despair.

A foreigner's passport in China enables him to pass free of charge all customs, and also the ferries that are usually found, in lieu of bridges, plying across all the rivers of considerable size which cut the great highways. The ferry which took us across one large river was crowded with people going to market on the other side, paying their passage, some with vegetables, some with cash. The ferryman collected the fee as he sat on the ground in front of his straw wigwam. After congratulating ourselves on the safe passage of the river, one of the wheels of our heaviest cart sank fast in the sand, and two extra mules had to be hitched on to pull it out.

Our carters were interesting fellows, but their knowledge of Chinese politics, as of things in general, was limited. Referring to the war with Japan, one of them informed us that Li Hung Chang had been made Emperor of China. Some of the people through whose territory we passed had heard nothing of the war, and others said that the Emperor's subjects in France had rebelled !

China is favorable soil for the flourishing of the older cults, Buddhism, Confucianism and Taoism standing side by side and being largely intermingled. A Chinaman may with no sense of incongruity profess all these beliefs at once. He would not appreciate Dr. Martin's statement that logically the three are irreconcilable, Taoism being materialism, Buddhism idealism, and Confucianism essentially ethical. Like the state, he makes a unity of them by swallowing a portion of each.* As we journeyed onward the monuments to this complex religious life increased in abundance. Here, passing through a city, we beheld the "gates of virtue," immense, carved stone arches spanning the streets, and erected to the memory of some sage, or pious person; there, on the hillsides, reared to some Buddhist saint, "stones of merit," on the tops of which little bells are fixed so that the wind causes them to ring out the praises of the great man long since passed away. Caves also, formerly the abodes of hermits, were pointed out to us, and colossal statues of the Buddha hewn from the solid rock, gazing down upon us with an air of sublime and majestic calm, still bearing witness to the zeal of the early Buddhist *bhikshus* who wandered forth from India to make known "the Teacher of Nirvana and the Law." In Western China nearly every farm has its contiguous graveyard in which may be seen the tables whereon the people place their offerings to the spirits of the dead. As we reflected on the part that the great non-Christian religions have played in China, and on the deep-grained, age-long impress they have made upon her people, the magnitude of our mission to a people not less religious, more superstitious, and enchained in a denser ignorance and a more blighting system, grew upon us in unwonted realization. Yet our faith did not waver. In much weakness we were going to undertake a stupendous task—not in our own strength but in His who when He commanded His disciples to "go and make

* A Cycle of Cathay, p. 289.

disciples of all the nations," also promised "Lo, I am with you all the days, even unto the end of the world."

Crossing a stone bridge of stately and antique architecture, we reached the city of Signan, the old imperial capital of China, and at present the capital of the province of Shensi. Here our carters made arrangements with other carters to take us on to Lancheo, they themselves returning to Fancheng. Signan is the most important trade centre of the northern interior, the home of the Emperor of a former dynasty, a city of heavy walls, paved streets, stately palaces and handsome governmental buildings. It is the site of the famous Nestorian tablet which bears record of Christian missions in China as early as the seventh century of our era. The surrounding country, relieved by undulating hills, is particularly charming; great roads branch off in all directions, two of the main ones leading to Kansu. The merchants of Signan carry on trade in all the surrounding provinces, and even in Mongolia, Tibet and Turkestan.

With our new carters we set out once more, although unfortunately for us it was the Chinese New Year, and consequently very difficult to buy food, as during that festive season all the shops are closed for days together. However, we did not wish to tarry at Signan. Bright, sunny days and cloudless skies, with nothing more adverse than an occasional wind or dust storm, such as are common in Western China, seemed to us to be favorable conditions for pressing on.

One of the important functions in connection with the celebration of the New Year is the lantern festival observed on the fifteenth of the first moon. Arriving at a large city one night, intending to put up at an inn in the suburbs, we found ourselves in the midst of the festival. The long street was lined on either side with lighted lanterns of exquisite and varied designs. Crowds of people surged up and down, and all was life, movement and jubilation—a weird scene, the moon shining down in icy calmness upon it all. Our horses becoming frightened at the tumult and glare of light and at the passing of a long string of camels with ringing bells, almost upset our carts in their frantic efforts to hide somewhere. We thus attracted attention even against our will, and it was with difficulty that we ourselves avoided being mobbed. Relieved indeed we felt when we reached a miserable inn, which in our thoughts was transformed almost into a palace, as it afforded us a haven of rest and safety from that brilliantly lighted festive street.

It was a happy day for us when we reached Lancheo, the capital of Kansu, for we had looked forward to a few days' respite in that city. Shortly after we had taken up quarters in an inn, Mr. Mason, of the China Inland Mission, came with a message from Mr. and Mrs. Redfern, extending to us a pressing invitation to stop at their home. He had brought the mission cart to transport us, and we soon found ourselves enjoying the hospitality of the missionaries. At Lancheo we formed the acquaintance of Mr. Wu, a Chinaman who had studied eight years in America, making a specialty of telegraphy. He had been up in the new province superintending the laying of telegraph lines, and in com-

BORDER TYPES

pany with his companions in Lancheo, was now returning to Peking. The day before we had arrived he had entertained Messrs. Redfern and Mason at a feast in a restaurant, where, of course, according to Chinese etiquette, ladies could not be present. Wishing to entertain us all, he prepared a second feast, which was served in the sitting-room of the mission house, so that the ladies might with propriety attend. Everything, including dishes, was brought from the restaurant. While on the road we had had considerable practice in using chopsticks, and we thoroughly enjoyed the food, which was dainty to the palate and artistic in appearance. Knowing our views regarding the use of wine as a beverage, Mr. Wu had provided delicious tea in elegantly decorated covered china cups, and sweatmeats by way of compensation. Chinese politeness ruled the feast, each one helping with his own chopsticks another to whom he wished to show courtesy. Among the many delicacies there was a sucking pig cut into little pieces and cooked in a perfect manner, also bamboo sprouts, lily tubers and other dishes of which at the time we did not even know the names. Western people are mistaken who imagine that the only items in the Chinese menu are rice and rats. As cooks the Chinese vie even with the French, and some of the most delicious meals we partook of while abroad were prepared by the Chinese. In acknowledgment of Mr. Wu's hospitality, Mrs. Redfern in turn prepared a feast for him; it was a proper English dinner, with several kinds of dessert; yet we must confess, in point of delicacy the Chinese feast was superior.

After a few days, Mr. Rijnhart and Mr. Ferguson went up the big cart road to Sining with the luggage, while I remained behind with Mr. and Mrs. Redfern, until Mr. Rijnhart, who would go on from Sining to Lusar to rent a house, should return for me. I shall ever gratefully remember the intervening pleasant days spent at Lancheo and the kindness received from the missionaries. Within a few days Mr. Rijnhart came back and announced that he had been successful in leasing a house, but that considerable repairs would be necessary. We left the next day for Sining, Mr. Rijnhart riding on a horse and I on a donkey, both of which had been generously loaned us by Mr. Ridley, of the China Inland Mission of Sining. The two animals had been companions for so long that wherever the horse led the donkey followed, a fact which I appreciated on this, my first donkey ride, as it solved for me the anticipated difficulty of guiding one of these proverbially stubborn animals along steep and difficult paths. Not far from Lancheo we arrived at the branch of the Great Wall which crosses the Yellow River, and found the ancient structure in a very dilapidated condition, broken by great gaps and much worn by the rains of centuries. It was not more than five feet in height, and however effective a defence it once may have been against the incursions of Turks, Mongols and Manchus, it would not be a serious obstacle before a modern army. There are two roads from Lancheo to Sining; one for cart, the other for mule travel. The carts make the journey by the "big road" in ten days; by the "short road" over the mountains, the one we had chosen, mules arrive in half the time.

The Kansu country presents an elevation varying, according to Rockhill's itinerary, from four thousand to nine thousand feet. Hilly ridges run in several directions, sheltering from the cold winds the fruitful valleys, remarkable for their luxuriant production of grapes, melons, peaches, apricots and all kinds of grain. Around the city of Lancheo tobacco is grown in large quantities and forms the basis of the city's industry. Part of our route lay beside the Yellow River, and for a time, also, we followed the rushing waters of the Hsi-ho, one of its tributaries. We saw Mohammedan merchants coming down the river with their cargoes of vegetable oil, destined for the Lancheo market, on rude floats made of inflated cowhides lashed together. How exciting it was to see the skillful boatmen guide one of these heavily laden floats around a sharp bend in the river, where the water boiled and foamed over the shallows. Just when it seemed certain that destruction against some sharp ledge awaited the craft, by a dexterous thrust it would be sent out into the current and carried past the point of danger amid the shouts of all the spectators.

Passing over the ruins of many villages which had been devastated in the Mohammedan rebellion of 1861-74, we came eventually to a narrow gorge of considerable historical importance. Ascending the road that skirts the precipice, we saw the river boiling below, beating itself into foaming rage in protest against its sudden limitation. It was in this pass that the Mohammedans held the Chinese army at bay during that bloody period forever memorable to the inhabitants of Kansu, and where again, in 1895, they placed themselves thousands strong, and sought to repeat the tactic. Little did we think, as we passed along the river edge on a beautiful sunny day, beneath an over-arching sky of cloudless blue, and amid the peaceful solitude of the mountains, broken only by the patter of the animals' hoofs and the low monotonous thud of plunging torrents, that this very place was within a few weeks to be again the scene of military tumult, filled with legions of infuriated, bloodthirsty rebels; and we dreamed even less that the massing of the Mohammedans here to check the advance of the Chinese army, was to be the providential dispensation which would prevent them from sweeping down on Lusar and Kumbum, where they would have found us an easy prey.

The people of Kansu we found to be gentle and obliging. They quite sustained their reputation of being less disagreeable than the natives of other provinces, for they treated us with the utmost kindness and did all in their power to expedite our journey. On the fifth day after our departure from Lancheo the walls of Sining loomed in the distance, and we were within the gates in time for afternoon tea at the China Inland Mission Home, where we were cordially welcomed by Mr. and Mrs. Ridley and Mr. Hall. Fifty *li* westward lay Lusar, where our house had already been secured, and the glittering turrets of the great Buddhist lamasery of Kumbum.

CHAPTER II

AMONG THE LAMAS

Arrival at Lusar—Strange Lama Ceremonies—Medical Work—Our Tibetan Teacher—First Experience With Robber Nomads.

The western portion of the province of Kansu, variously denominated by geographers as part of Chinese or Outer Tibet, is known to the Tibetans as Amdo, and the inhabitants are called Amdo-wa. According to Chinese ethnographers the foreign population of Amdo may be divided into two great classes, the T'u-fan, or "agricultural barbarians," who have a large admixture of Chinese blood, and the Si-fan, or "western barbarians," who are of pure Tibetan stock. The Si-fan live, for the most part, a nomadic life and are organized into a number of bands under hereditary chiefs responsible to the Chinese Amban at Sining, to whom they pay tribute. Chinese authors further say that the present mixed population of Amdo is the progeny of many distinct aboriginal tribes, but there are some elements of it that must be accounted for by later immigrations. Westward from Sining the road leads through a highly cultivated plateau; the farms are watered by a perfect system of artificial irrigation, bearing evidence of the industry and skill of the peasants. The houses in the villages are all built of mud and have flat roofs. On the road one meets groups of merchants, partly Chinese, but bearing a strong resemblance to the Turk and distinguished by a headdress which seems to be a cross between a Chinese cap and a Moslem turban. These are Mohammedans going down to trade in Sining. Next comes creeping along a small caravan of camel-mounted Mongolians or Tibetans, clad in their ugly sheepskin gowns and big fur caps, on their way to see the Amban of Sining, or perhaps going to Eastern Mongolia or Pekin; or one may meet a procession of swarthy faced Tibetan pilgrims returning single file, with slow and stately tread, from some act of worship at Kumbum, to their homes in the valleys north of Sining. The entire western portion of Kansu, so far as its inhabitants are concerned, marks the transition between a purely Chinese population and a foreign people, the Chinese predominating in the larger centers but the villages and encampments being made up largely of foreign or mongrel inhabitants.

Mr. Rijnhart had left me at Sining and had gone on to Lusar to complete the preparation of our house; but I had become impatient, not having too much confidence in masculine ability to set a house in order in a way altogether pleasing to a woman, so I rode up to Lusar with Mr. Hall. Half a day's journey brought us within sight of the hills that surround Kumbum, and as we approached we could see some of the lamas attending to their horses or gathering fuel. But the strangest sight of all was that of Mr. Rijnhart and Mr.

Ferguson in European clothing; so accustomed had our eyes become to oriental attire that they appeared more grotesque even than any of the fantastically arrayed travelers we had met on the road. Assisted by some native carpenters, they had been very busy at the house, but when I arrived I found everything in confusion, just as I had anticipated. Yet I was thankful that our long journey had been completed, not a single accident worthy the name having happened to us since we left the Pacific Coast of America six months before.

Lusar boasts of a single main street with mud-brick flat-roofed buildings on either side, and, at the time of our arrival, contained about one thousand inhabitants, evenly divided between Mohammedans and Chinese, with a sprinkling of Tibetans and Mongols. These different peoples could be distinguished by their general appearance as well as by their speech. The Mongol, with his broad, flat, good-natured countenance and short-cut hair, clad in his long sheepskin robe, with his matchlock thrown over his shoulder, could not be mistaken as he waddled through the street followed by his wife a few paces behind him; the pure Tibetan, likewise robed in sheepskin, heralded his nationality by the sword he carried in his belt. To mistake a Chinaman was, of course, beyond question, while the Mohammedan of Turkestani origin could be recognized by his aquiline nose, slender face and straggling beard or moustache. Being the trading station of the Kumbum lamasery Lusar is visited by merchants from China, Mongolia and various parts of Tibet. Especially during the great religious festivals held from time to time at the lamasery a brisk trade is done in altar-lamps, charm-boxes, idols, prayer-wheels and the other paraphernalia of Buddhist worship. Near the village is a remnant of an old wall which evidently at some time had been used as a rampart of defence. In Huc and Gabet's narrative no mention is made of Lusar for the reason that it probably did not exist when these travelers passed that way, the business of the Kumbum lamasery being done formerly at Shen-ch'un, a few miles distant from Kumbum.

The Chinese carpenters made characteristically slow progress with our house. The noise that accompanied the work was at times almost deafening, the workmen all shouting at once when anything urgent was to be done. The house, situated at the foot of a hill, the façade pointing toward the main street, was a substantial mud-brick structure with flat roof, built entirely according to Chinese ideas of architecture, and after we had the premises put in order the disposition of the apartments was about as follows: The main gate led into an outer courtyard, walled but not roofed; from the outer court a dark, narrow passage led to the central or inner courtyard, around which the rooms were arranged on all sides. In one corner was the kitchen, and diagonally opposite to it a storeroom, and in another corner the stable, while along the sides nearest the entrance were the two guest-rooms, one for men and the other for women, the latter containing a cupboard for drugs. The guest-rooms we destined for the reception of visitors coming for medical treatment or to inquire about spiritual matters. The walls were hung with colored Bible pictures which did us good service in suggesting topics for religious conversation. Many of the pictures represented scenes in the life of Christ and aroused the natives to the asking of questions which opened for us golden opportunities to read the New Testament and to tell them more fully the Gospel story. The furniture was plain and scant, a large table four feet square, a few high, straight-backed and very uncomfortable chairs, and the indispensable *k'ang*. Opposite the guest-rooms were our dining-room, study and bedroom. On the two remaining sides were Mr. Ferguson's apartments, our Chinese servant's bedroom and a sitting-room where we all met for prayer, Bible study and conversation. Access to the flat roof of the house could be had by means of a ladder, and oftentimes when the weather was fine we repaired thither to take our constitutional, or to sit basking in the sun. Behind the house on the hill we afterwards prepared quite a large piece of garden, in which we raised several kinds of vegetables from seeds sent to us by a friend in Canada. Our housekeeping was reduced to simplicity. Han-kia, our Chinese "boy," aged about twenty-two years, soon learned under my tuition to prepare many kinds of food in English or American style, and twice a week he regaled us with *m'ien*. Having no oven in our stove, we extemporized one out of a paraffin tin, in which we could roast meat and bake cookies. Altogether we did not fare badly at Lusar; in the market we could buy mutton, eggs, milk, vegetables, flour and rice. Custom soon introduced us to our new surroundings, and when the carpenters had finished, we were, taking it all in all, as happy in our far-away, isolated home as we possibly could have been in America.

Not long after our arrival we were visited by Mr. and Mrs. Ridley and their little baby Dora. They had come up for the purpose of recuperating their health among the hills, and during their sojourn we witnessed the interesting ceremony of burnt offerings celebrated near the Kumbum lamasery. Crowds of Chinese and Tibetans, men, women and children, had congregated to see the procession of lamas issue from their temple, and, discovering that some foreigners were among the throng, they turned their attention to us, almost overwhelming us with their friendly curiosity. It seemed at times that we would be crushed to death. Being surrounded we could not return home, and we were obliged to devise at once some means of protection. Inviting the native women to sit down beside us we were soon in the midst of a large group squatting tailor-fashion about us, serving as an effective bulwark, preventing the crowd from surging in upon us. Mrs. Ridley drew the women into an interesting conversation, taxed to the utmost all the while to keep them from laying violent hands on her baby.

The Tibetan women were to us an especial object of interest, conspicuous in their long, bright colored dresses fastened around the waist by green or red sashes, their clumsy top-boots and their elaborate head dress. The hair was done up in a number of small plaits which hung down the back and were fastened together with wide strips of gay colored cloth, or by a heavy band of pasteboard or felt covered with silver ornaments, shells and beads, and on top of it all was a hat with white fur brim and red tassels hanging from the pointed crown. From the ears were pendant great rings, to which were attached strings of beads hanging in long loops across the breast. The Chinese women with no hats, their black hair shining with linseed water, their common blue dresses and deformed feet, were not nearly so attractive as their neighbors, the Tibetans.

Presently the sound of horns, cymbals and gongs announced the approach of the procession, and all in confusion rushed off to see the sight. Hundreds of lamas, clad in their flowing robes, issued with solemn tread from the lamasery, some of them carrying large, irregular wooden frames painted red, blue and yellow, and huge bundles of straw. The frames were set up in an open place, the straw arranged around them, and the ceremony of burnt offerings was ready to begin. The lamas fired off guns, chanted some unintelligible incantations, blew deafening blasts on their gigantic horns, and then set fire to the straw. The frames were soon reduced to ashes, and the purpose of the ceremony, we learned, was to ward off the demons of famine, disease and war.

As soon as the people found out that we were prepared to treat their ailments and dispense medicines they came to us quite freely. The Chinese were the first to approach us, but soon the Tibetans came, even the lamas, and it was not long before we had as much medical and resultant guest-room work as we could attend to. As it is impossible to get a crowd of Tibetans to listen to a discourse, our evangelistic work consisted chiefly in conversing upon Christianity with the people who came to see us, and from the very beginning we were able to interest them in the teachings of the New Testament. The Tibetans themselves having no medical science worthy the name, the treatment given by the native doctors generally means an increase of agony to the sufferer. For headache large sticking plasters are applied to the patient's head and forehead; for rheumatics often a needle is buried in the arm or shoulder; a tooth is extracted by tying a rope to it and jerking it out, sometimes bringing out a part of the jaw at the same time; a sufferer with stomachache may be subjected to a good pounding, or to the application of a piece of wick soaked in burning butter grease; or if medicine is to be taken internally it will consist probably of a piece of paper on which a prayer is written, rolled up into the form of a pellet, and if this fails to produce the desired effect another pellet is administered, composed of the bones of some pious priest.

Although the natives appear to have great faith in the native doctors, yet they were quick to bestow their patronage upon us. Among the common ailments we were called upon to treat were diphtheria, rheumatism, dyspepsia, besides many forms of skin and eye disease. One morning a woman brought to us her husband, who was suffering from diphtheria, and asked us to give him medicine. After explaining that the disease was very fatal, and that her husband was so ill that he would probably die, adding that we would not be responsible if he did, we gave him what treatment we could, including some medicine to be taken at home. The next morning his wife came to announce that he could not take the medicine. I then offered to go to the house, purposing to clear away some of the membrane and relieve the sufferer, but on our arrival we found that a lama had pasted a notice on the door forbidding anyone to enter because, he said, a devil had taken possession of the house. We were obliged to turn away and our hearts were saddened to hear two days later that the man and also one of his little children had died.

Since it was our intention to work principally among the Tibetans, we at once faced the problem of acquiring the language, although we might have got along with Chinese alone since all the Tibetans on the frontier speak that language as well as their own; but knowing that the Tibetan language would be to us a means of closer communication with the natives, we set about to find a teacher. As the lamas are the sole possessors of Tibetan letters, the great masses of the lay population being unable either to read or write, they were not over pleased with the thought of communicating their sacred language to "foreign devils," and we had great difficulty in persuading any one to teach us. Finally a young, rather good looking lama, named Ishinima,* consented to give us instruction for a nominal sum, on condition that we would not let it be known, for he seemed very much afraid lest someone might accuse him before the *sung kuan,* or dis-

* Pronounce E-sheé-ne-ma.

ciplinarian of the lamasery, of being on too friendly terms with the foreigners; for of course as yet we were looked upon with more or less reserve and perhaps with a little suspicion. Ishinima was of medium height, well built, and favored the Mongolian type rather than the Tibetan, although he always said that he was of the latter parentage. His face was pockmarked, but not devoid of expression, and when he smiled his whole countenance glowed with good humor. He did not belong to the highest class of lamas, yet, not having to do menial work, he was well dressed, wearing the lama's ordinary habit—a sleeveless red jacket, a full skirt girded around the waist, and a long, wide scarf carelessly, yet always in the same manner, thrown about the shoulders. His garments were dirty, but not ragged. The first money he received in payment for his lessons he invested in cloth at Sining, and I made him garments of it on my sewing machine. He told us that the lamas were not allowed to wear sleeves, trousers or socks except upon special occasions, and added that on this point the lamasery had a code of very strict laws, violation of which entailed severe punishment, sometimes even expulsion. Though Ishinima could read the Tibetan character well, we found to our disappointment that he could not explain it at all, so our lessons took a more practical turn, we giving him Chinese words and phrases which he translated for us into Tibetan. He came to teach us every day except Sunday, on which day he always attended the religious service held in the guest-room.

Tibetan belongs, philologically, to the Turanian

family of languages. It is essentially monosyllabic, resembling in this respect many of the languages of our North American Indians. The verb system is built up on roots with prefixes and affixes, the syntax is comparatively uninvolved and the idioms clear and expressive. The alphabet, adapted from the Sanskrit by Tou-mi-sam-bho-ta, a noted Tibetan scholar and statesman, about 623 A. D., affords a character simple and easily formed, contrasting strongly with the cumbrous glyphics of the Chinese. There are two principal dialects of the language—Lhasa Tibetan, supposed to be the standard of excellence, and Eastern Tibetan, which varies from it to a considerable degree. The Koko-nor Tibetans, in fact, have great difficulty in understanding the speech of Lhasa traders and lamas. For colloquial purposes we were particularly interested in the Eastern Tibetan, though of course if one desires to read, the Lhasa dialect must be learned, as that is the literary language of the country.

Our professor yielded to none in the matter of uncleanliness, hence we made it our endeavor to instill into his mind some idea of hygiene. After some instruction he learned to use the towel and soap, and though the lamas have a rule not to allow scissors to touch their heads when having their hair cut, he allowed his head to be shaved by the clippers, which were an endless source of wonder and interest to the natives. By degrees he took on an appearance of decency, and began to show some signs of interest in new ideas. Being somewhat of an epicure he went freely into the kitchen, supervising the preparation of the dainties for which he had a preference. He taught our Chinese servant to make *oma-ja,* a decoction which the Tibetans drink with great relish. The ingredients are implied in the name—a piece of brick-tea is put into a pot of water and allowed to boil a few minutes, then about half as much milk as water is added, and the whole brought to boiling point again. When later we were without a servant, our boy having gone to enlist as a soldier, Ishinima would make the *m'ien.* Instead of cutting it into strips he would cut it into squares, and add it to water, meat and vegetables, making a palatable and substantial dish. Though we studied hard at our Tibetan and endeavored to understand the people and to communicate with them, we did not make the progress we should have made, the cause of this being that he taught us a mixture of Tibetan and Mongolian, which was to a large extent unintelligible to either people. In this and other things we found him unreliable, and some of his actions bordered on dishonesty.

Soon after we had made his acquaintance, Ishinima invited us to his home in the Kumbum lamasery, and, having set his house in order for our visit, he came to escort us thither. Crossing the ravine which divides Kumbum into two sections, and threading our way along narrow alleys and past rows of whitewashed dwellings, we finally stood before one of the outermost and best houses of the lamasery. The courtyard presented a tidy appearance, and was graced by a flower garden in the center, in which some yellow poppies were in bloom. Several red-robed lamas with bare heads and smiling faces gave us a Mongol welcome, holding out toward us both hands with the palms turned upward, and immediately ushered us through a small room into a still smaller one, of which the *k'ang* covered the entire floor. Upon the door hung a curtain, laden with the dust and grease of ages. The furniture was that usually found in a lama's home. There was the *k'ang* table, about ten inches in height, on which were placed some china basins, a brightly-painted *tsamba* dish, and a wooden plate containing bread fried in oil, none too inviting either by its taste or smell. The walls of the room were adorned with the pictures which we ourselves had given to our host, and which with their western flavor seemed quite out of keeping with the rude interior. During a very pleasant conversation about the great monastery with its revered lamas and sacred traditions, about Lhasa, the home of Buddhist learning, and of the great Dalai Lama, about the doctrines of Christianity, and about the great western world, of which Ishinima knew next to nothing, we drank tea and partook of other refreshments which the latter had prepared with his own hands. According to custom he offered us a large lump of rancid butter, which, had we been as polite as our host, we should have dropped into our cup of tea in lieu of sugar; but knowing Ishinima so well, we refused the dainty morsel, although to have done so under any other circumstances would have been considered little less than insult. He was, moreover, so thoroughly charmed with Mr. Rijnhart's telescope and camera that we might have ignored all Tibetan politeness with impunity.

After tea we were conducted across the courtyard to Ishinima's private chapel, or room containing his household altar and instruments of worship. Upon the altar sat several diminutive but none the less hideous brass and clay idols, representing various Buddhist divinities, before which were burning small butter lamps, also of brass, filled with melted butter, each furnished with a wick and darting up its little flame. Other flat brazen vessels of water, some *khatas* or "scarfs of ceremony"—narrow strips of veil-like cloth, corresponding in use to the western carte-de-visite—, a few musty-looking tomes of Buddhist literature, completed the equipment of this domestic sanctuary. We found Ishinima withal a most genial host, exercising every art within his grasp to make our visit pleasant; yet we were glad when the time came to return to our own clean and airy dwelling at Lusar, and we left conscious that we had done Ishinima good service in ridding him of a generous share of the vermin in his sacerdotal abode. Our battle with this unwelcome company was to begin when we reached home.

Through our friendship with Ishinima we gained a knowledge of Kumbum and all that pertained to it, which otherwise we might long have sought in vain. Shortly after our visit to his home he accompanied us again to the lamasery to witness an elaborate ceremony on the occasion of the ordination of the priest who was to serve as lamasery doctor. Ishinima having some scruples about appearing publicly as our guide, walked about fifty yards ahead of us, never, however, turning a corner until he assured himself that we were following. Having arrived in the courtyard of the temple where the ceremony was to be held, we took our places, Ishinima standing at some distance opposite us and scarcely taking his eye off us from first to last. The walls of the temple court were hung with all manner of fantastic pictures executed in flaming colors by Chinese artists. In the middle of the enclosure was a long narrow table, similar to those often found on American picnic grounds, on which were placed rows of decorated plates and brazen vessels of various shapes and sizes, containing *tsamba,* rice, barley, flour, bread, oil and other eatables. These, we learned, were offerings which had been brought to be sacrificed in honor of the new candidate for the position of medical superintendent. A large crowd of spectators had congregated and were gazing with reverent and longing looks upon the feast prepared for the gods, when suddenly a procession of about fifty lamas broke into the courtyard, arrayed in red and yellow robes, each one carrying in his hand a bell. As soon as they had seated themselves on the stone pavement, the *mamba fuyeh,* or medical buddha, came in and took his place on an elevated wooden throne covered with crimson and yellow cloth. He wore a tall, handsomely embroidered hat and brilliant ceremonial robes, befitting the occasion. The ceremony began by a deafening clatter of discordant bells, each lama vying with the others to produce the most noise from his instrument. The music was followed by the muttering of some cabalistic incantations and the weird chanting of prayers. Immediately in front of the *mamba fuyeh* was a large urn in the bottom of which a fire was smoldering, sending up its vapory clouds of smoke and incense. At a given signal some of the lamas rose and, each one taking up in a ladle a portion of the delicious viands that stood on the table, walked gravely to the urn and dropped it into the fire as an offering in honor of the new *mamba fuyeh,* and finally a stream of liquid which we took to be some kind of holy oil was poured in from a little brass pot. Then there were repetitions of the prayers, incantations and bell-ringing, and it was a long time ere the *mamba fuyeh* was declared duly installed. The position of medical lama is considered one of great importance. The office in the Kumbum lamasery is held for varying periods of time, depending partly on the incumbent's efficiency, but more perhaps on the number of his influential friends.

Like most lamas, Ishinima had many strange tales to tell of the Koko-nor, the blue inland sea, that lies away to the west of Lusar and Kumbum, far up into the grass country. Many an evening he entertained us detailing in reverent tones something of the wealth of legend which tradition and the popular fancy have woven around that body of water. It is known by Tibetans, Mongols and Chinese, each calling it by a different name, but the Mongol name "Koko-nor," meaning "Blue Lake," seems to have gained ascendency. Its religious importance is recognized throughout a large portion of Central Asia. Even the Amban, the Chinese Ambassador or Governor of North-eastern Tibet, who lives at Sining, makes a pilgrimage to it once a year and pays it homage. The immediate effect of Ishinima's representations was to arouse in us an intense desire to visit the lake, to make the acquaintance of the Koko-nor tribes and to ascertain the prospects for missionary work among them. As Ishinima had never seen the lake himself, he seemed overjoyed when we asked him to accompany us. The date for the departure was set in the month of June when the hills had taken on their luxuriant carpeting of green, and all nature seemed to conspire in producing ideal conditions for such an excursion. As W. W. Rockhill, the American traveler, had written about the opposition of the Amban and other Chinese officials to Europeans going into the grass country, all our preparations were very quietly made. We employed a muleteer with four animals, collected stores for the entire journey which, going and returning, we calculated would last about twelve days, and in the highest spirits started off, leaving our home in the care of a servant. Ishinima, perched high on a load consisting of the tent and bale of food, wore a large straw hat with the wide brim of which he carefully concealed his face until we got out of the locality where he was known. Reaching Tankar late in the evening, we pitched our camp outside the gate. Anxious to avoid officials, we arose at daybreak and passed through the town to the west gate, being frequently accosted by men who wanted to drag us before the *lao-yeh* at the *yamen;* but we escaped into the grass country, and passed the monastery of Gomba Soma, although every one we met was looked upon as some official who might possibly forbid us to go any further. Ten miles from

Gomba Soma, and still a long way from the lake, we camped for breakfast near a bend of the Hsi-ho, or Western River, in a beautiful grassy spot studded with pink flowers. On the other side of the river was spread a charming panorama of rolling hills which in the early morning looked like the grey, slumbering tents of some giant army. Never shall I forget the calm of that beautiful day on the oriental plateau far away from the turmoil of civilization, nor within sight or sound of the rudest encampment or settlement of any kind.

But out of this tranquil environment there was to grow a great unrest. While Ishinima was gathering *argols* (the Mongolian word for the dried excreta of animals which the nomads use for fuel, and which must be used in fact by all travelers, as these wild regions are bare of wood) our mules broke away from their tether and had soon scampered out of sight. Mr. Ferguson and the muleteer set out in search of the missing animals. All day Mr. Rijnhart and I waited, wondering how both the mules and pursuers fared. We knew nothing definite until Mr. Ferguson's return at eleven o'clock at night, and he could only announce that no trace of the runaway mules had been found, and added, to our horror, that he had become separated from the muleteer and did not know what fate might have befallen him. He might have lost his way somewhere on the dreary plain or among the winding hills, and there was the graver possibility of his having been eaten by wolves or having fallen into the hands of the redoubtable Tangut robbers who lurk in the ravines ready to pounce upon any prey, great or small. Clouds of anxiety hung on Ishinima's dusky face. He could not sleep. Time and time again he went outside the tent, casting his eyes far and wide over the starlit waste, eager to catch any sign of the lost muleteer, but in vain. His anxiety was not without cause, for if anything should have happened to the muleteer he would have been held responsible. A feeling of insecurity pervaded the whole camp, Ishinima having succeeded in persuading us that the Tanguts might swoop down upon us at any moment. The agony and stillness of that awful night, broken only by the subdued sounds of our own voices, the distant howl of a wolf, and the monotonous babble of the Hsi-ho rapids, were not soon forgotten. At daybreak next morning, just as Ishinima was preparing breakfast, two of the missing mules, quite mule-like, returned of their own accord, and soon after, to our great joy, our muleteer came running into camp. The faithful fellow had continued his fruitless search away into the night, and, having lost his way, had crouched down behind a rock to rest till daybreak; he seemed quite compensated for his trouble on finding that two of the mules had come back. One black animal being still astray, Mr. Ferguson went out again on the search. As he did not return after an unaccountably long time, Mr. Rijnhart took the sweep of the horizon with the telescope to see if there were any trace of him, and, after a short absence, came running to the tent shouting, "Get the guns ready! There are six wild Tibetans after Will!" Excitement reigned supreme and every preparation was made to show the enemy our ability and readiness to defend ourselves and our goods if need be. Mr. Ferguson rode well, outstripping his pursuers all but one, a big Tibetan armed with a spear, who followed closely on his track. We knew that Mr. Ferguson was quite capable of looking after himself, as he carried a revolver, and usually the sight of foreign arms of any kind has a salutary effect on these wild nomads. Soon not only Mr. Ferguson but the six Tibetans had reached our tent, and the latter were preparing to help themselves to our possessions when Ishinima remonstrated, informing them that we had foreign guns, whereupon they threw their rude matchlocks and clumsy spears to the ground, sat down beside them, filled their pipes and smoked and chatted in a very friendly manner. Presently another group of Tibetans came galloping toward our tent. They were ten in number, and as they drew near we espied our lost black mule among their animals. These Tibetans were well dressed in garments of various and gorgeous colors. We did not know their intentions, but they kept assuring us in the name of Buddha that they were good men, and if any proof were wanting they triumphantly added that one of their company was a lama. At the same time the predatory instinct began to manifest itself; the newcomers insisted on having first one thing and then another of our belongings, and were only restrained from looting the entire camp when Mr. Rijnhart threatened to shoot if they laid hands on a thing. After some further altercation we gave them some cash for catching our mule—Ishinima gave them a *mani,* or rosary, of great value, and the entire band rode off. The question now was: should we continue our journey to the Koko-nor or return home? I was ever so grateful when Ishinima declared that the Tibetans who had just left us were Tangut robbers, and that they would most assuredly return presently with reinforcements to attack us, for that announcement led to an immediate decision to turn back. Although later we made the Koko-nor journey with no fear, but with greater experience and knowledge of the grass country and its inhabitants, for the moment the vision of the Blue Lake grew dim, and loading our mules we leaped into our saddles, and were soon galloping toward Tankar, with sweet dreams of the safety and shelter that awaited us in our little home at Lusar.

Deviating a little from the road by which we had come, we arrived at Chang-fang-tai, a Tibetan village nestling on the edge of a small stream. The country hereabout was quite fertile, although in an uncultivated state. Roaming along the bank of the stream, we gathered specimens of ferns, grasses and wild flowers. The inhabitants seemed to be peaceably disposed, coming into our tent and taking tea with us. Here, by the way, I tried my first dish of *tsamba,* the staple article of diet throughout Tibet, taking the place of bread in other countries, and which I had always imagined must be very delicious from the zest with which Ishinima invariably devoured it. *Tsamba* is a kind of meal made from parched barley, which, after being thoroughly kneaded with the fingers in a mixture of tea and butter, is taken out in lumps and eaten from the hand. Though Mr. Rijnhart added sugar to make it more palatable, I could not eat it.

In the midst of our enjoyment at this village we heard the first alarming tidings of the terrible rebellion which shortly broke out in full fury among the Mohammedans of Western Kansu. Faint rumblings of the storm had already been heard, but we had not considered the outlook serious. During the day we had noticed clouds of smoke rising in the distance, and these, a Tibetan courier informed us, marked the scene of the beginning of Mohammedan depredations. A column of the rebel fanatics had swept across the North country and fallen upon a Chinese village, killing all the inhabitants, setting fire to the buildings, and leaving nothing but ashes, smoke and charred corpses. Hastily we pulled up our tent, and, though the night was dark, we rode off toward Kumbum, with great difficulty following the trail which wound in and out among the hills, while every dark object became to our excited imagination a crouching Mohammedan ready to dart his merciless spear. A sigh of relief escaped us as we arrived at the gate of Lusar, yet we knew more serious news awaited us as, contrary to custom, the gate was closed and carefully guarded. The old gate-keeper, whom we knew well, opened to let us in, and informed us of the danger that like a dark cloud had fallen on the village since we left. At any moment the Mohammedans were expected to rush in from some neighboring ambush. But amid the gloomy forebodings that for the moment filled our minds, there was a tremor of joy at the thought of our good fortune in returning to Lusar when we did. The Divine Providence had indeed overshadowed us and directed our movements. Had we gone on to the Koko-nor and attempted to return later, we should have found our way intercepted by the Mohammedan stronghold which a few days afterwards commanded the roads from Tankar to Kumbum.

CHAPTER III

A MOHAMMEDAN REBELLION

Moslem Sects—Beginnings of the Struggle—Our Acquaintance with the Abbot—Refuge in the Lamasery—The Doctrine of Reincarnation.

Among China's four hundred millions the Mohammedan element, though comparatively small, must be counted as a significant factor. Like a fomenting leaven, a hotbed of domestic turmoil within themselves, and ever and anon working to the surface of the national life, the followers of the Prophet have proved a constant source of trouble to the Chinese authorities, especially in the provinces of Shensi, Yunnan and Kansu, where they have planted their most extensive colonies. According to Dr. Martin, there are about ten millions of them throughout the empire, although other authorities place the number much higher. They are known by the general appellation of *Siao-chiao,* that is, adherents of the "small religion," as opposed to the Chinese, who, with their complex cult of ancestor worship, idolatry and incense burning, are of the *Ta-chiao,* or "great religion," the comparative magnitude of the two religions being estimated of course by the relative number of their adherents. The Mohammedans are further distinguished from the Chinese by their abstaining from opium, wine, tobacco, pork and other meats except when killed by a Mohammedan slaughterer who has been specially authorized by the *ahon.* Travelers, for this reason, may always be certain of getting good, clean meat from Mohammedan butchers, whereas the Chinese do not scruple to cut up and offer for sale an animal that has died of disease. Besides being generally clean, the Mohammedans are industrious, making a success of whatever calling they embrace, be it that of a merchant, muleteer, carter, cook, innkeeper, or worker in copper, silver or iron. Their restaurants along the great highways enjoy the liberal patronage of all classes, while on the other hand no Mohammedan will partake of the "ceremonially unclean" dishes of the ordinary innkeeper of the *Ta-chiao* persuasion.

The Mohammedans of the province of Kansu, numbering about one million and a half, constitute one-fourth of its population. In the principal cities, such as Lancheo, the capital, and Sining, they monopolize the suburbs, and whole villages and towns of them are to be found in various parts of the province, even as far west as the Tibetan border. Besides being known under the usual designation of *Siao-chiao,* to distinguish them religiously from the Chinese, they are also called by the latter *Huei-huei,* while the Tibetans and Mongolians speak of them as *K'a-che.* Though now having lost to a considerable extent their racial characteristics through intermarriage with the Chinese, they are still recognized as the descendants of the great migrations which came from Turkestan, Kashmir, and Samarkand nearly five centuries ago. They are divided into two sects, called the "white-capped" and "black-capped," the latter being identical with the Salars, who are much more fanatical and exclusive than the other sect. In the Sining district the two divisions are known as the *Lao-chiao,* or "old religion," and the *Sin-chiao,* or "new religion," the latter being, as far as we could ascertain, the same sect as the Salars, or "black-capped" Mohammedans. They have not merged nearly so agreeably with the Chinese as the former, for, while they are usually ready to rebel, the *Lao-chiao,* as a rule, remain neutral, or even cooperate with the Chinese.

The Salars who boast of their Samarkandi origin are settled around Hocheo, Hsuen-hua-ting, Mincheo and Taocheo, the first mentioned town of thirty thousand inhabitants being their stronghold, where the Chinese have to keep a large body of soldiers, as nearly every year for the most trivial reasons there is trouble. The Salars speak their own language, which is understood by travelers from Kashgar, and when we visited their country in 1897, Rahim, our Tibetan boy, a native of Ladak, was delighted that he could converse in their own tongue, which he had learned on his journeys into Turkestan. The men have a purely foreign look, good figures, oval faces, aquiline noses, and wear the Chinese queue, while the women do not bind their feet, though the Mohammedans around us were as much in love with small feet as were the pure Chinese. They are all supposed to be conversant with

Arabic, but, as a fact, have not usually much knowledge of it, except the *ahons,* some of the latter being Turkestani. Occasionally some great mufti from Mecca or other important Moslem center visits the faithful in Kansu, exhorting them to greater zeal; while the many mosques that tower above the Chinese dwellings, the dogged fidelity with which the devotees perform their religious services, and the death-embracing fanaticism with which in times past they have fought for their faith, all attest the vigorous hold which Mohammedanism has gained in the land of Confucius.

The religious dissimilarities between the two sects are trivial, the lines of cleavage being quite as insignificant as some that divide Christendom. The chief bone of contention is a difference of opinion as to the hour at which the fast may be broken during the Ramadan, and as to the propriety of incense burning. The cause of the dispute which culminated in one of the most sanguinary and disastrous wars that ever took place in Western China was the question as to whether or not a Mohammedan might wear a beard before the age of forty!

It need not be wondered at that terror filled the minds of the people of Lusar and Kumbum, and of all the surrounding villages, when the news spread that the Mohammedan sword was again unsheathed; for fresh in their memories were the terrible atrocities perpetrated during the former uprising, which was one long intermittent period of bloodshed and pillage lasting from 1861 to 1874, both parties, however, assenting to a cessation of hostilities each year during seedtime and harvest. The government troops sent to subdue the rebels had been, on account of their inadequate numbers, hewn down, harrassed and beaten year after year, and only succeeded finally in quelling the outbreak because of a dissension among the Mohammedans themselves as to whether the Koran sanctioned the use of tobacco. Our own little Lusar had in those troublous times been twice destroyed, while before the rebellion Kumbum, the great monastery, had been the residence of 7,000 lamas, hundreds of whom dyed their temple thresholds with their blood, falling in defense of their treasures and their homes, repulsing the rebels barely in time to save their treasure-house, and to keep unholy hands from ravishing their gold-tiled temples. Whenever the lamas look at the bullet-pierced silver bowl which is still in service on one of the altars, they remember that Kumbum's palmiest days ended in that great struggle, for never since has it contained more than four thousand lamas.

Although the Chinese had finally subdued the rebellion, they had not quelled the fanaticism that gave it rise. They forbade the Mohammedans to reside within the towns and cities, but this only led to their gathering in thousands outside the walls or in separate settlements, where they brooded over their lack of freedom, and cherished a hatred towards the Chinese, fanned by the memory of the treachery by which during the war the latter had beguiled them into many a bloody snare; and throughout all the intervening years, up to the time of the fresh outbreak in 1895, the *ahons* had done their part in keeping the fire of hatred and dissatisfaction burning in their hearts. The vague rumors of trouble at a distance that had reached us before our departure for the Koko-nor had caused little alarm in our district, but on our return the reports were distinct and dire enough. The little fire so recently kindled was already assuming uncontrollable proportions. A dissension had occurred in the *Sin-chiao* on account of the beard question already referred to, and swords were drawn; the Chinese, who, while inert enough in most emergencies, seem to be ready to interfere in Mohammedan disputes, stepped in to settle this one, and the progress of the campaign until it reached the immediate vicinity of Kumbum had been, we learned, as follows.

The quarrel between the two sects having broken out eighty English miles from Sining, and the district inhabited by the Salars being governed from that city, a Major Uang had been sent with two hundred soldiers to make peace, which apparently he had succeeded in doing; but suspicions of his failure were aroused when, on the 13th of March, the Tao-tai of Sining was summoned by the Governor-general of Kansu to Lancheo and despatched with more troops to Hsuen-hua-ting, the seat of the trouble. The latter official did a most imprudent thing in seizing and putting to death a prominent chief and three or four others, for to avenge this outrage the Salars, largely forgetting their own differences, rose *en masse* against the Chinese, imprisoning the general and several other officers who had been sent from Hocheo to aid him. Reports that the Salars were advancing and that other Mohammedans were joining them, threw the Chinese of the Sining district into the wildest exicitement, and soldiers were sent into the villages not as yet affected by the rebellion, to inquire into rumors and exhort the Chinese and Mohammedans to live together in peace. By the end of March the truth about Major Uang's defeat was learned. A "white-capped" Mohammedan, a supposed ally of the Chinese, but really in league with the Salars, offered to guide the Major to a position from which he might crush the rebels at a single blow. The Major and his men followed the guide over the treacherous river and along its southern bank, until, arriving at the juncture of two valleys, they camped for the night, the Yellow River on the north of them, and a ridge of high rocky hills on the south. Here, when wholly unprepared, they were surprised by the Salars into whose hands they had been secretly betrayed by the would-be guide, seventy-four of their number being killed, while the others, having given up their rifles on the promise of mercy and freedom, were immediately afterwards shot by their enemies.

The news of this disaster having reached the Governor-General, he issued a proclamation ordering the extermination of the Salar sect, root and branch. Two days later a fresh proclamation was affixed to the city gates, couched in milder terms, saying that a distinction was to be made between good and bad Salars, that only the latter were to be killed. But no reverse tide of second thought could dam back the mighty cataclysm of bloodthirsty revenge which had broken out over the land. This first proclamation had done the work; already the blacksmiths were busy night and day sharpening old swords and making new ones, and people from the villages were flocking into the cities with their families, furniture and grain. Farming was suspended, and a general panic prevailed as it became known that the Salars had risen up in the fulness of their strength, all joining swords from various motives—fear, zeal, revenge, and the hope of gain through success and plunder being the chief ones. Detachments of imperial soldiers came up from Lancheo and Liangcheo, but the Mohammedans had congregated in such overwhelming hordes that the Chinese could not begin to cope with them.

About the end of April the imperial troops had succeeded in taking three Salar villages, but at the same time the operations of the rebels became more extensive. The Chinese government, now realizing the magnitude of their undertaking, appointed to the command of the imperial troops Brigadier-General Teng of Sining, a man of rare decision and military reputation, who, departing for the seat of trouble, defeated the rebels near the city of Hsuen-hua-ting, a victory with which further uprisings in the vicinity of Hocheo were simultaneous; nor was his victory accomplished without extreme difficulty and much bloodshed. The enemy having been apprised of the Brigadier-General's start from Sining, had come to meet him, and but for the timely help of the Tibetans, his army would have been annihilated. It became evident that the rebellion was no longer confined to the "black-capped" sect, and when the news spread that Hocheo, the Mecca of Kansu Moslemism, the site of Moslem colleges and mosques, had become a center of rebel activity, it was felt that the worst had only begun. General Teng with the resources at his command adopted the most vigorous measures. In the beginning of July he inflicted a severe defeat on the enemy, killing 700 of them, but its glory was dimmed by the ominous rumor that 10,000 Mohammedans in the suburbs of Sining were about to join the rebels.

As the reports that reached Lusar and Kumbum became more and more alarming, the people were thoroughly aroused, lamas and laymen joining heart and hand in offensive and defensive measures to be employed against the rebels, whom they now no longer spoke of as *Huei-huei,* or *Siao-chiao,* but by the more appropriate title, as they thought, *tseh.* .

Activity in the collection of old iron increased, the furnaces glowed day and night with an intenser heat, and louder rang the anvils under the blows of an army of smiths in response to the general clamor for swords, spear-points and guns. On all the main roads leading to the village *tiao-lo* were built, two-storied mud-brick towers, a gateway underneath, and a room above through the wall of which were loop-holes for guns, while a small rampart branched off on either side. The *Sin-chiao* Mohammedans living in Lusar gradually and quietly sold their property, or taking it along with their families, left for Topa, the rebel stronghold on the Hsi-ho, where there were soon 40,-000 fighting men. We little suspected that even Mohammedans who had become our friends, particularly one old man who lived almost next door to us, were so soon to take up arms against their fellow-citizens, ourselves included.

The lamas provided themselves with arms of every kind, were organized into an army under the leadership of Shertoch Fuyeh, one of the "living buddhas" of Kumbum, and met on the hills for drill, besides being as busy as bees at the construction of strong brick towers for the protection of their homes and temples. Ishinima, though an arrant coward, prepared a spear for himself, and our lessons in Tibetan became very irregular and almost useless, for our professor had utterly lost his equilibrium. The inhabitants of Lusar carried all their valuables over to Kumbum and placed them in the hands of the lamas, intending to flee to the lamasery should the rebels in strength attack the village, knowing that the lamas would die fighting for their treasures, and so the lives of the sojourners there would be comparatively safe. Refugees from isolated villages swarmed to Kumbum for safety, and soon, as a result of the overcrowding, diphtheria and smallpox were raging, while food, fodder, and everything had risen to such exhorbitant prices that beggars were added in immense crowds to the already existing number, occupying every cave and stable, in fact, every available corner they could find. Many of our friends in Lusar advised us to leave for home, or at least go to Sining, which had a good wall and an army to defend it; but we felt that we had not unprovidentially arrived in Kumbum at that especial time, and in order that we might not thwart the plans of Him whose work we were doing, we remained among the people, and made preparations to save our goods in the event of an attack, by putting them in a cave off our storeroom.

Barely had we decided to share the fears and fortunes of our Chinese and Tibetan friends, by facing with them the dreadful possibilities of a long and bloody siege, when an event of no small importance occurred, one, in fact, which to a great extent changed the current of our lives and affected the whole course of our future relations with the people. To our amazement we received from the *kanpo* an invitation to take up our abode in the lamasery during the rebellion, an offer which, needless to say, we eagerly accepted, not only because of the safety it offered us, but also because of the prestige it would give us in the eyes of those whom we were seeking to help. This apparently sudden kindness on the part of the abbot was dependent upon an amusing incident during Mr. Rijnhart's visit to Kumbum in 1892. One day he was sent for by one of the "living buddhas" of Kumbum, and, expecting to have a pleasant and profitable conversation about spiritual matters, he went immediately to the buddha's apartment, where he learned with some disappointment that he had been summoned not from any religious motive, but to be consulted about a music-box which the buddha had bought as a curiosity when on a visit to Pekin. The music-box was, to express literally what the lama had said, "sick," and had ceased to give forth music; and the lama had concluded that since it had been made by foreigners it could surely be cured by a foreigner. Mr. Rijnhart carefully examined the instrument, and finding it only needed lubricating, gave it a liberal treatment of castor-oil, the only kind available, whereupon its powers returned, and the wonderful box was, as the lama expressed it, "cured." He had therefore conceived great confidence in the skill of the foreigner, for if he could cure a sick music-box with one dose of medicine, how much more could he do for a sick man! The result of an apparently insignificant act of kindness cannot be estimated. The music-box incident, though forgotten by Mr. Rijnhart, had evidently left an impression on the lama, who had in the meantime risen to the dignity of the abbotship, for he it was who now again summoned the foreign doctor with his magic oil to come and treat the treasurer of the lamasery, who had fallen ill, although he did not know at the time that Mr. Rijnhart was the same foreigner who had "cured his sick instrument."

Following a guide, we climbed up steep, stony paths until we reached the most imposing of the buildings, the *kanpo's* residence, in a part of which the treasurer resided. Ishinima had often spoken of the *kanpo,* or *fa-tai,* the great man who presided over the spiritual welfare of the four thousand Kumbum lamas, assuring us that he could only be seen when, clad in his saffron robes, crowned with his glittering mitre, and followed by a long retinue of attendants, he descended from his lofty and sacred abode to preside over some important religious function. Ishinima's surprise may well be imagined when we told him we were going to the *kanpo's* residence to visit such an illustrious patient as Hsam-tso, the treasurer. Indignantly he repudiated the possibility of such a thing, for the entrance of foreigners into the sacred residence of the great incarnation of Buddha was unheard of. Yet to the equally great surprise of Ishinima and ourselves, we not only visited the treasurer, carefully diagnosed his case, and gave him treatment, but by special invitation were ushered into the audience chamber of the *kanpo* himself. Climbing a steep staircase, we arrived in the courtyard immediately confronting his apartments, where we saw a youthful lama with flying red garments, bare feet, and countenance wreathed in smiles, rush across the courtyard and enter a room as if to apprise his master of our approach, and when we reached the door he was there with characteristic oriental obsequiousness to usher us in. Another moment and we were standing in the presence of the greatest Buddhist dignitary of all northeastern Tibet, the man who was looked up to as spiritual guide and teacher not only by the lamas who sat under his immediate tutelage, but by thousands of laymen outside, to whom his personality was known. Sublime in the consciousness of his own greatness, he did not descend from his throne on perceiving us; in fact, his stolid countenance betrayed no sign of pleasure or surprise, for why, indeed, should the calm and monotonous flow of his feelings be disconcerted by the arrival of a couple of foreign teachers more than by the worshippers of high rank whom, from far and near, he was accustomed to receive daily? He asked us to be seated on some beautiful rugs, while his lama servant brought us tea in china basins, which were placed before us on little tables ten inches high, painted in bright colors. During the conversation the *kanpo* explained that a past experience with a foreigner had given him the desire to meet another, and great was his pleasure when he found out that Mr. Rijnhart was the identical foreigner who had "doctored" his music-box three years previous.

This brief visit was preliminary to many others that followed in quick succession, resulting in an intimate acquaintance, mutually agreeable, which soon ripened into a firm friendship. The *kanpo* was particularly interested in the fact that Mr. Rijnhart had a wife, and as more ominous reports of the progress of the rebellion reached the lamasery, he evinced a sincere anxiety about our welfare. He had indeed a greater surprise in store for us than the privilege of paying him a visit, for he told us very cordially that his own home in the lamasery was at our disposal, and bade us move our goods at once to his apartments and take up our abode there until the rebellion was over. "If the Mohammedans attack Lusar," he said gravely, "the people will take shelter in the lamasery and leave you to be killed." We could but feel that the *kanpo's* offer was providential, so, accepting it as heartily as it was given, we removed those of our valuables which were not hidden in the cave, over to his house, where we found he had prepared for our occupancy two large rooms and a kitchen.

Our life in the lamasery was a busy one. Hundreds of diphtheria cases were dealt with, and many wounded people were brought to us from the surrounding districts. In connection with medical work in the lamasery, a very interesting and pathetic incident occurred, that served to give us a clear idea of one of the fundamental beliefs of Buddhism, viz: re-incarnation. A young lama came requesting us to visit a lad who was very ill—a little *fuyeh,* or buddha, about ten years old. Following a guide into the capacious courtyard of one of Kumbum's best residences, past many rooms decorated in gay colors, with windows of lattice-work covered with bright paper and colored glass, we came to the door of a suite of apartments, where stood an old lama with white beard and hair, down whose cheeks flowed copious tears, as wringing his hands he besought us to do our best for the boy and not let him die; as if he died, he, the lama, would have seen his elder brother die a second time. Though the little *fuyeh* was that old lama's nephew by birth, he was looked upon as his elder brother; the latter had died ten years previously, and the soul, it was believed, had returned into the body of the little boy, to spend another period on its progress toward Nirvana, the state of blessedness. Hence it was that the man who now confronted us was in such great sorrow fearing that he should a second time witness his elder brother's death. We promised all the help we could give, and were ushered into a small, beautifully adorned room, where we saw reclining on the *k'ang* a sick child, a glance at whom told us that we were in the presence of a victim of a virulent type of diphtheria. Upon careful examination we felt that there was scant hope of his recovery, and informed the old man that the only chance for the patient lay in our staying with him. Whereupon the old lama told us to do what we thought best, adding that he would procure for us anything we desired, no matter what the cost would be, for, he added, "that boy has great wealth—thousands of horses, cattle and sheep and valuable property are his." We prepared the necessaries for the treatment of our little patient and settled down beside the *k'ang* to watch him.

Daylight faded into twilight, and the secular work of the lamasery was done. As the tumultuous hubbub of voices died away and even the sound of the water-carriers' footsteps had ceased, the lamasery was pervaded by a strange and melancholy quiet, indescribably peculiar, but somewhat akin to that atmosphere of silent awe that fills the galleries and crypts of some old mediæval cathedral, subduing the voice and even the thoughts of the traveler, as he stands with uncovered head before the tombs of the illustrious and saintly dead. And as that silence is sometimes broken by the strains of the choristers' song sounding soft and low from their practice-room, or by snatches of muffled harmony floating down from the organ-loft, so on that night was the stillness broken by the musical voices of the lamas chanting their prayers in the temples, or on the housetops where they lighted fires of juniper leaves, the smoke of which curled up and spent its fragrance far and wide until the very air seemed redolent with the sense of worship. In some respects the æsthetic side of Tibetan Buddhism is irresistible, and it is not surprising that it has thrown a strong fascination over the credulous Tibetans. It is, however, like the Pharisaism of old, only a whited sepulchre, having a beautiful exterior, but full of rottenness and dead men's bones within. How forcibly the wail of the white-haired old lama, with his rayless belief in the doctrine of reincarnation brought home to our hearts that night the unsatisfying emptiness, the bitter darkness of a system which offers the human spirit no brighter prospect than to be broken again and again on the "Wheel of Existence," struggling in its own strength for countless ages, with the forces of evil, with no better promise than annihilation at the end. Those who get their conceptions of existing Buddhism from Sir Edwin Arnold's "Light of Asia" would be sadly disillusioned could they see it as it is really believed and practiced by the people of Tibet.

Night-time had settled down upon us in our places beside the boy, all the lamas, even the old man, having retired. We sat reading or conversing in low whispers, our hearts awed by the strangeness of our surroundings, the dim light of the primitive lamp casting weird shadows on some objects about the room, now in this corner upon a spear and two guns ready for use, suggestive of anything but peace, then upon a yellow satin hat with wide brim and peaked crown, and a yellow jacket belonging to the boy. He was not to use them again, for from the bed came stertorous breathing, which continually reminded us that death was claiming its victim. Suddenly through the impressive stillness rang a shout, then another, some barking of dogs, then a few shots, and almost in a flash from the housetops near and far rang cries of "*Sha sa! Sha sa!*" (Eat meat! Eat meat!), the war-cry of the lamas. A lama rushed through the room where we sat, calling out, "Where's my spear? Give me my spear! The rebels have come!"—and, having obtained it, joined his comrades on the roof. Mr. Rijnhart said he would go for a moment to the house-top to see if there were really danger, and being alone with the child, I prayed that God would preserve us from falling alive into the hands of the Mohammedans. The noise soon ceased, and, to our joy, we found that it had been a false alarm caught up by the sentries around Kumbum, from those about Lusar, who had seen a large body of rebels passing in the distance to pillage another village, and had given the note of alarm, thinking that we were to be attacked. This was only one of the many times that alarms were sounded during both night and day for the following months.

Early the next morning the young *fuyeh* died, and his old uncle, to whom the little life was so precious, shortly afterwards committed suicide by taking a large dose of opium; for he said he could not bear to live in prospect of the known possibility of seeing his elder brother die a third time!

> Om mani padme hum, the Sunrise comes!
> The Dewdrop slips into the shining Sea!

So sings the poet, but for that old lama there was neither sunrise nor shining sea, but, according to his own confession, grief, despair and darkness.

CHAPTER IV

WITH THE WOUNDED

Refugees at Sining—Our Isolation at Kumbum—The Siege of Shen-Ch'un—To the Battlefield—A Ride for Life—Rout of the Mohammedans.

Preparations for meeting the rebels went on apace. Sentries were placed on the lamasery towers and on the almost contiguous hills, ready to give the alarm when danger threatened. Crowds of lamas with drawn swords surged through the streets, or assembled on the house-tops to discuss the latest reports from the field. Our co-worker, Mr. Ferguson, having important business at Shanghai, decided to leave for the coast. It was a hazardous undertaking, yet it seemed inevitable. As the road was still open we accompanied him to Sining. Anticipating perilous times during the months to come, we thought we might not live to see him again. Moreover we desired, while still possible, to visit Mr. and Mrs. Ridley before being cut off altogether from all intercourse with European friends or from the sight of a white face, and again more particularly, our presence in Sining was necessary in order to make final arrangements for Mr. Ferguson's journey. As we went along there were no signs of trouble; in many of the villages the people did not seem to appreciate the gravity of the situation, for they were engaged in their ordinary avocations; and, except a body of red-jacketed Chinese troops who crossed our path on their way to attack a rebel encampment in a town two days' journey to the north, we saw nothing to suggest the terror which had spread in other parts. Upon reaching Sining, however, we found the rebellion had been raging in earnest in the northern valley. Hundreds of homeless and wounded people seeking shelter were flocking into the already overcrowded city, where the temples were turned into temporary hospitals, to which the Chinese missionaries, Mr. and Mrs. Ridley and Mr. Hall, daily repaired, ministering with soothing ointments to the poor creatures who had been burned in the flames that had turned their homes to ashes, and bandaging the ghastly wounds made by Mohammedan bullets and swords. Some of the wounded had crawled on their hands and knees for distances as great as seventeen miles, and arrived more dead than alive. As the refugees increased in number diphtheria and smallpox were rife, and Mrs. Ridley moved among the patients stricken with these dread diseases hoping against the danger of infection to which herself and her precious little Dora, only a few months old, were subjected, yet not able to do otherwise than help to alleviate the awful suffering about her. Travel to Lancheo being still possible, though not very safe, Mr. Ferguson adhered to his purpose to press on to the coast, so we said good-bye to him and reluctantly turned back to

Kumbum, where we were soon completely isolated. Ten miles to the northwest of us the Mohammedans had massed in thousands at Topa, from which stronghold marauding bands of them scoured the country between their own position and Kumbum, rendering it unsafe for anyone to venture more than two miles north of the lamasery; while five miles on the opposite side, the village of Shen-ch'un, the Mohammedan portion of whose inhabitants joined the rebels, became a veritable seat of war. The combined rebel forces of Shen-ch'un and Iangmaoko, another village over the hills, blocked all the roads in their district and massacred the Chinese by hundreds. Thus imprisoned for nearly six months, we received no reliable information as to what was happening at Sining and in other districts, but events around Kumbum were stirring enough and quite sufficient to absorb our attention, until the road to Sining should be again open and we could learn the intervening history of the rebels' movements.

Mina Fuyeh, for that was the *kanpo's* name, gave us every day new evidences of his friendship. Side by side with the problems of defending the lamasery and superintending the great priesthood, he seemed to have placed that of our personal safety. He had devised a plan whereby we might escape should the Mohammedans in superior force attack the lamasery, and should it become evident that the lamas could not repulse them. Under cover of darkness he proposed that we should flee with him to Kuei-teh, where he had a house and where he would give us shelter, food and clothing until we could hear from the homeland. While the road to Kuei-teh was yet passable, and the reports kept coming in that the rebels were burning one village after another, the *kanpo* sent trusty men thither with boxes containing his precious treasures. Returning to Kumbum the men were fallen upon by robbers, who made off with the *kanpo's* valuable mules, eleven in number, and severely wounded two of the men. So unsafe had the road become that even the *kanpo's* sacred possessions were not free from brigandage.

The discussion of plans for our safety was apparently not premature, for every day came news of fresh victories for the Mohammedans, whose arms seemed to prevail on every hand. Every day refugees arrived at the lamasery; sick and wounded were brought in from all directions to receive our treatment, the news having spread that the foreign doctors, under the very roof and patronage of the abbot, were performing miracles of healing and were prepared to treat all who came to them.

Among the most interesting of our patients was an old man, Chinese by birth, but possessing the courage and daring of a Tibetan, who had been appointed a leader over fifty of the local troops, and had set out one morning to aid some Chinese in an adjoining village to repulse an attack by rebels. Treacherously one of his men, a carpenter, had stabbed him in the elbow, some said because the former was in the pay of the Mohammedans, who were anxious to be rid of such an able opponent as Cheo Lao-yeh, the old man, was proving himself to be. They remembered his efficient service in the former rebellion, in which, though wounded seven times, he had dealt them many a crushing defeat. The treacherous thrust had made an ugly wound in his arm, but the family being rich, and consequently able to give him every attention, while I spared no pains to aid in his recovery, each day marked improvement. His wife was a Mongol. His only child was an attractive young married woman of twenty wearing the Mongol costume, which was very becoming to her, while her pretty little baby completed the family group and added much gladness to the lonely hours the old man spent on the *k'ang*. Many were the presents and incalculable kindnesses bestowed upon us by this man, and when later he died while we were away from home, he asked his daughter to give each of us a rosary he had worn, gifts which we prized very much for we knew they were tokens of sincere gratitude and love.

Shen-ch'un was the scene of much strife, at first only between the Mohammedans and Chinese intrenched in their respective forts, and consisting of battles between small parties who would sally out to glean in the fields, or gather fuel, the successes and failures being about evenly divided between the opposing forces. By degrees the strength of the Chinese portion of the village had been reduced, the last detachment of young men having been completely cut to pieces during a sortie, so that the beleagured and helpless inhabitants, consisting now only of old men, women and children, appealed for succor to the lamas' army, and the local Chinese troops. Contrary to the abbot's wishes, the lama soldiers, having taken all their arms to a temple to be blessed, sallied out one morning to attack the rebels. Their priestly robes thrown aside for the moment, they wore the ordinary layman's red and yellow garments with multifold red turbans of raw silk wound around their heads. Armed with guns, swords, and spears, equally divided between infantry and cavalry, the latter being mounted on splendid ponies, the dark eyes of all flashing with rage and the thirst for revenge, they presented such a warlike appearance as facilitated our realization of the gallant defense our lama army would offer in case the rebels attacked the lamasery fortress. Presently the Chinese soldiers from Lusar having formed in battle array, some wearing bright scarlet military jackets, but the majority clad in the blue of everyday life, marched out to join the lamas. A few were mounted and carried bright colored flags, while the remainder on foot were furnished with swords, and a few guns. The departure of the two detachments was among the most affecting and picturesque sights I have ever witnessed. The entire population of Kumbum and Lusar was massed on the flat roofs of the lamasery buildings to see them off, while above the din that rose from the multitude could be heard the click of prayer-wheels, ardent mutterings of the mystic phrase, *om mani padme hum,* and low incantations of the remaining lamas, all of which augured success to their brothers-in-arms. The more daring mounted their horses and accompanied them to the summit of a hill which overlooked the scene of the impending battle, ourselves being among the number. The morning sun, now high in the heavens, gilded the crests of the distant hills and likewise threw his brilliant sheen upon the turbans, red, blue and yellow robes of the dusky lamas and bronzed-faced Chinamen, the many-colored banners of the mounted ensigns, the broad-bladed spears and swords, and the glittering caparisons of the fiery steeds, while every remaining dew drop amid the green sward over which they trod added its ray of splendor to the scene. Having accompanied the troops to the brow of the hill, we watched their winding course through the valley and across the little river until they came into proximity to the Mohammedan fort. On the trail at a little distance behind the army stood the *sung kuan,* with sword in hand, ready to kill the first Chinaman who should run away from the fight. It appears that the Chinese had in former crises left the lamas in the lurch, hence the effective measure to prevent a repetition of such cowardice.

The storming of the fort was soon in full swing, the lamas doing the greater share of the fighting. In an attempt to set fire to the gate they were met by such showers of stones hurled down upon them from the wall that they were obliged to retreat, not without loss. But such fighting ability did they betray that the rebels, fearing another onslaught, summoned the aid of five hundred expert Salar marksmen, and reinforced by the latter made a fresh attack on the Chinese fort opposite them. While they had been engaged with the Kumbum troops, the Chinese women and what few old men were left, had placed great piles of stones on the walls, with which they expected to beat back the Mohammedans, or at least keep them from entering the gate; but the latter, during the night, had quietly dug through the mud wall, several feet in thickness, and early next morning effected an entrance. The Chinese women fought like tigresses, and though many of them died like heroines in defense of their homes, they were of course overpowered. Almost the whole remaining population was put to the sword, except only a few, who made their escape to Kumbum. On the day of their arrival there was almost as much excitement as on the day of the departure of the troops. Again the roofs of the lamasery were crowded, as well as the streets, to see, as they passed through the gates, the sole survivors of the long siege, a few old men, some women and children, each carrying some sad memento of the sanguinary struggle, a bag of food, a basin or a brass pot, all that now remained to them in the world. What tales of woe and suffering were written in their sad faces! Fathers and brothers slain and homes destroyed! Only a sense of fear seemed to be left in their nature after so many long nights of dreadful vigil in the fort, their hearts filled with horror by the wanton cruelty and flagrant inhumanity with which the Mohammedans had treated even defenseless women and children. There were few dry eyes in Kumbum that morning. The sentiment of revenge was high, and what wonder? as tales kept pouring into the lamasery of women and children burned alive, of little shepherd boys pierced through and through while beside some stream they watched their fathers' flocks, of little infants carried about on the points of spears, while ever and anon some wound-covered victim, perhaps a

Chinese woman with her small crippled feet, would crawl into the lamasery weak from the loss of blood, and death staring from the eyes. The Buddhist lamasery of Kumbum, like the Chinese temple of the God of Literature in Sining, had become a hospital, and our hands were full. Among the patients whose sufferings most touched our hearts was a child brought to us with sixteen spear thrusts in his little body. Tenderly we cared for him, and to our great joy he got well.

Soon after the stirring episode of Shen-ch'un a body of Chinese and Tibetan soldiers, armed with foreign guns, under Commander Li, an old opium smoker, came to Kiai-ya, a well fortified Chinese village one mile from the cluster of forts that had in part been wrenched from those brave Chinese women, and we all felt that probably the day of retribution for the Mohammedans was at hand. In the morning in good order the former attacked one side of the rebel position, while the lama army simultaneously assaulted the other; bodies of Mohammedan horsemen were seen to be parrying the attacks and endeavoring to mislead the soldiers, but with great force the two opposing bodies met and the Tibetans had at dark almost won the day, when, for some mysterious reason, a retreat was ordered by Commander Li, and the whole army returned. In the morning it was expected, of course, that another attack would be made, but it was learned that so far as Li Lao-yeh was concerned, the Mohammedans might remain in peace; and it was so loudly whispered that he had "eaten Mohammedan silver," or in other words, been bribed, that he lost his prestige, and if he did not lose his head, it was only because the *peh-sing,* or common people, could not get their hands on him to carry out the sentence which all had passed on him in their minds.

Though numbers of the rebels had fallen during the day's fighting, the casualties among the Chinese and Tibetans were also serious. Early in the day a band of twenty soldiers came to the lamasery requesting Mr. Rijnhart and myself to go to the battlefield and look after their wounded companions, offering themselves as our escort to the scene of carnage. The prospect of riding to within a mile of the rebel position was not inviting, but when we thought of the sufferings of our lama soldiers, and our ability to help those who had risked their lives in defense of helpless women and children, and who might ere long be called upon to defend us at the lamasery, and remembering that we were servants of Him who "went about healing all that were oppressed," we hesitated not. Having prepared our surgical and medical supplies we rode off with our escort, each one of whom was armed to the teeth. As we traveled on among the hills, some acted as scouts to see that the road was clear, while the others surrounding us sought to make us feel safe in their keeping, at the same time expressing their gratitude to us for having come.

On our arrival at the village we found it teeming with soldiers, some of whom ushered us at once into the quarters of the wounded. We worked hard all day bandaging cuts and extracting bullets, attending to the most serious cases first, but at sunset we had not come to the end of the list. Feeling it was unwise to pass the night so near the Mohammedan position, especially as every available corner in the village was already occupied by soldiers, we decided to return to Kumbum, intending to finish treating the wounded men on the following day. Silently, accompanied by our escort, we traveled homeward under the light of the harvest moon, our scouts peering through every valley and defile, lest haply we might be fallen upon by lurking Mohammedan horsemen. On our arrival at Kumbum we found the lamasery gates closed, and as the eye of the sentry caught sight of such a large body of soldiers, he became suspicious and refused to admit us, fearing some kind of treachery or strategem. The lamas gathered on the roof, Mr. Rijnhart stepped out where he could be heard and shouted to them that he was the foreign doctor returning from a visit to the wounded, and that the soldiers were his escort. I also spoke up corroborating Mr. Rijnhart's words, whereupon the gate-keeper cautiously opened the ponderous gate and let us in.

Shortly after sunrise next day we started again for Kiai-ya. The morning air was crisp and exhilarating, and we rode with a feeling of greater repose than on the evening previous. As yet very few people were astir, here a lama carrying a water-bucket on his broad back, there an early traveler setting out for the Lusar market, or a farmer with a donkey-load of straw, or *fen-kuai-tsi, argols* pressed into brick form, to be sold to the lamas. When we reached Kiai-ya we found our wounded men doing well, and by noon we had attended to the cases left over from the preceding day. Our reputation having spread through the village we were called upon to visit a young girl of sixteen who had been accidentally shot below the left knee two months before. The wound was a ghastly sight, the leg being shattered for several inches. Native doctors could do nothing; the limb had not even been bandaged. Only after such a sight does one appreciate the blessings which the sciences of medicine and surgery lay at the feet of the sick and suffering in Christian lands. We informed the girl's friends that only the amputation of the diseased member could effect a cure, a proposal which they resolutely refused to entertain, in accordance with the Confucian teaching that a person should quit this life with an entire body. And so we had to leave her, though the whole house reeked with the stench of the wound, nor were we surprised to hear shortly afterwards that she was dead.

Our medical work being done, we were sitting in the *yamen* being entertained at luncheon by the Chinese commander, when suddenly the call to arms was beaten and the alarm given that the Mohammedans in large forces were issuing from their stronghold. While the soldiers seized their weapons and rushed into battle array, we demanded our escort and set out for home. The first part of the way led along a hollow road worn deep with the travel of ages, with sides so steep and high, that everything was concealed from view, and when we had emerged from it, on an incline overlooking the valley, we saw galloping toward us a body of rebel horsemen, who had seen us leave Kiai-ya and were endeavoring to head us off. The Tibetans spurring on our horses we rode for our lives, gaining in speed as we galloped down the hillside, at times the feet of our animals scarcely seeming to touch the ground. There was not only the danger of our being overtaken by our pursuers. Who knew but at any turn we might be met by another band ? Perhaps already they were hurrying to meet us along another road that joined the one we were traveling on, not far from the lamasery.

We were not the only ones who had taken to flight. The feeling of alarm at the rebels' sally having spread among all the villages, and even among travelers who had heard the news as they journeyed along, many were fleeing for their lives on the same road as ourselves. Not far off, galloping over the hills and valleys we saw a Koko-nor Tibetan, preferring, according to habit, the rough ground to the smooth road, presenting a doubly awkward appearance in his bulky sheepskin gown inflated by the wind, and his unwieldy matchlock shifting about with every plunge of his pony, which with shouts and various gesticulations, he urged on toward the lamasery. Safely passing the junction of the roads where we had feared to meet a second band of rebels, and having far outrun our pursuers whom the hills now hid from view, we dismissed our escort, thinking the moment opportune for them to turn about unobserved and go back to the village by another route. Then scarcely slackening our speed we rode on alone, overtaking many men and women who had been out in the fields gathering *argols* and grain, now dazed with fear and running helter-skelter toward the haven for which we also were aiming. On reaching the lamasery, we found the roofs crowded with our lama friends, who had been apprised by the sentries of the rebels' manœuvre, and had been anxious as to our fate. How welcome the sense of safety as we passed behind the huge gate that shut our enemies outside. Had our ponies stumbled or any other accident impeded our progress; had there been any difficulty at the gate as on the preceding night, any delay of five minutes would have made it forever impossible for us to tell the tale. Jambula, an old Mongol lama living in the room near ours, who had become very much attached to us, almost wept when taking my husband by the hands, he told us how concerned he had been for our safety and how glad he was to see us back alive.

There was great rejoicing when it was reported that General Ho in command of ten thousand soldiers well armed with foreign guns had pressed his way past the rebels who had been massed in great numbers in the *Siao-hsia* or "Narrow Gorge", where they had hoped to cut off the advance of the imperial troops. General Ho's army was so formidable that the rebels, on being advised to disband rather than be cut to pieces, had acted the part of discretion and left for home, thus leaving free passage to General Ho, who soon arrived at Sining and joined hands with Brigadier-General Teng, the *chen-tai,* or chief military official of the city. The *chen-tai* deserves the credit of keeping the rebels in check until the arrival of the reinforcements; and the excellent service rendered by the latter with their heavy cannon, well-manned, and firing balls strong enough to shatter the Mohammedan defence-tower, temporarily freed the city from danger and made it possible for the united imperial troops to hasten to the relief of Shen-ch'un. The announcement that the imperial army was coming to storm Shen-ch'un caused thrilling excitement and deep-felt joy throughout the villages near Kumbum and on the road to Sining. The day that the army was expected, nearly all the Lusar people went either to a hill commanding a good view of the scene of battle, or towards the forts in order to plunder as soon as an entry into Mohammedan quarters had been made by the conquering hero, Brigadier-General Teng, who was to those Chinese what Lord Roberts is to the British army and Admiral Dewey to the American, the idol of the people. A squadron of cavalry came into sight along the Nan Chuan or Southern Valley. We could see their numerous bright pennons waving in the breeze, the great cannon drawn by mules, and the *chen-tai* conspicuous by his brilliant uniform and white steed, leading the procession. Then followed the infantry, all in much better marching order than any Chinese soldiers we had previously seen. On they came amid the cheers of the people on the hills and the quaking hearts of the Mohammedans, who were no doubt watching from their loop-holes. Soon they had halted near the rebel forts where they were welcomed by the Chinese and lama leaders of the local troops that had gone forth to meet them. The cannon was brought into good position for aiming at the weakest fort, the soldiers were placed in battle order, while the Iangmaoko

Mohammedans dashed courageously down the hills to help their comrades even against such odds. A puff of smoke from the cannon, a crash, and down went part of the tower, attended by a dense cloud of dust and deafening cheers from our neighbors on the hills, while a look through our telescope told us that one end of the far from impregnable tower was gone. A few more well-aimed shots reduced the wall, and General Ho, commanding a regiment, rushed upon one of the forts, the general himself being shot in the thigh as a result. Mohammedans fled in groups up the hill, hoping to escape across to another valley, but they only fell into the hands of soldiers who had concealed themselves in a hollow road to cut off any retreat. Many a mounted fugitive we saw fall from his horse, as suddenly a crouching Chinaman leaped up and transfixed him with his spear. Those who got out of the reach of sword and spear were picked off by the unerring bullet. The entire hillside had become a battle-field, the autumnal grass being literally stained with blood. It was a terrible sight for us; but to the Chinese and Tibetans there was in it the sweetness of revenge. Unspeakable, indeed, was the retribution that now fell upon those who, when they had the upper hand, hesitated at no cruelty and stooped to every atrocity known to the darkened mind of man. Several forts were taken before dusk and as the Chinese object to fighting in the dark, they withdrew, but General Teng placed his forces so that the besieged might not escape during the night. As we saw several wounded being carried in from the field, we betook ourselves to their quarters to render them whatever service we could. We were shown into a little room, a few feet long, with only a window a foot square, from which a soldier, by vigorously using a whip, kept the heads of the curious ones from shutting out the light, while a number of orderlies amid general shouting, kept us supplied with warm and cold water, wood for splints and other necessities. When we succeeded in extracting a bullet from a soldier's limb he would ask to see it, and when it was given to him he would take it between his teeth and gnash and grind it in revenge for the pain and suffering it had caused him. Always we found that in the minds of the wounded, the main hope of recovery as well as of the cessation of pain, lay in the extraction of the bullet. Darkness overtook us before we had treated all our wounded that night, and as we wended our way through the narrow streets of the small village of twenty homes that quartered two thousand troops, we saw soldiers sleeping spear in hand, lying in corners of courtyards and along the streets all worn out with the day's fighting, yet ready on the slightest alarm to follow their trusted leader to new dangers and new victories.

Just as we were ready to retire a loud knocking at our front gate announced the arrival of visitors, who proved to be some soldiers coming to invite Mr. Rijnhart to go with them to see a corporal who had been shot in the mouth. Though conscious of the risk, he accompanied them to the village where the *chen-tai* was quartered and was ushered into the presence of his patient, who was swearing in a loud voice and abusing everyone that came within his hearing. The bullet was imbedded between the gum and the cheek and had to be probed for. During the operation the corporal swore and issued rough commands to his men whenever the instrument allowed him an opportunity to use his tongue. Mr. Rijnhart maintained that there was a mingling of the pathetic and ridiculous in the rage which his patient manifested over being obliged to carry in his mouth even for a short time a rebel's bullet.

The *chen-tai,* though such an efficient general, had not made his investment of the besieged forts complete, for during the night stealthily the Mohammedans withdrew with their families and valuables. Making their way through the ranks of the enemy, they effected their escape to Topa, and the following morning the soldiers and a swarm of *peh sing* who intended to loot and plunder, entered the deserted houses, finding bread half-baked in the fire, and other tokens of a hasty flight. The Lusar people returned after they had secured their booty, presenting an amusing scene with their prizes, which were for the most part worthless baggage, old tables, cupboards, broken pots, worn out bags with perhaps a little grain. We realized how bitter was the feeling against the rebels when we heard many express such delight at the great massacre of Mohammedans of the day before, for eight hundred had been killed.

CHAPTER V

MISSIONS AND MASSACRES

Bible School at Lusar—Mohammedan Revolt at Sining—Terrible Slaughter by Imperial Soldiers—The Fall of Topa—Peace at Last.

In the midst of these stirring times when thoughts of murder and revenge were uppermost in the people's minds, we endeavored to carry on the work of preaching and teaching as well as of healing. The abbot's invitation to reside in the lamasery we could but interpret as a divine call to a larger field of usefulness, and the influence which his patronage gave us in the eyes of the people was but another name for opportunity—a sacred trust for which we felt we should be held responsible. Priests and laymen, women and children, rallied round us, consulting us in their difficulties and giving us every evidence of their trust in us. One of the most encouraging features of our missionary work was the Bible School, which was begun soon after our removal to the lamasery, and held every Wednesday and Sunday afternoon in our house at Lusar. The children, who had become attached to us, even following us in the street, were easily gathered in and became at once interested in the colored Bible pictures that hung on our walls. The lessons embraced the salient points in Bible history and doctrine, beginning with the story of Creation and the Garden of Eden in the Old Testament and ending with the death and resurrection of Jesus in the New. We also gave them talks on the Life and Journeys of St. Paul. How delighted they were at the story of Jacob's ladder, telling us, as they gazed on the picture, that they, too, would like to climb that ladder to be among the angels. Soon not only the children but also the mothers came to the lessons. All were touched by the story of the Good Samaritan. "The priest and the Levite are just like our priests," said one woman. "They, too, pass by on the other side when anyone is in trouble." The women were particularly interested in the miracle at the gate of Nain. Our picture showed a city gate just like a Chinese one, and that made it so vivid; and then the women could enter into the mother's grief at the death of a son and share her joy when the Great Physician restored the vital spark. Other pictures and the lessons suggested by them made deep impressions, viz: The Healing of Blind Bartimeus, The Prodigal Son, The Death, Resurrection and Ascension of Jesus, Paul chained to a Roman Soldier, and Peter in Prison.

Special mention must be made of one little Tibetan boy who never forgot anything we told him; the amount of Bible knowledge he acquired was truly astonishing, and I fondly believe that his heart was good ground, and that some day the good seed sown in it will bring forth fruit. I shall never forget how heartily the children sang the hymns which with great difficulty we taught them. The Tibetans, we found, possess much better ideas of melody than the Chinese. The discords at first were shocking, but by the help of Mr. Rijnhart's concertina and my violin the tunes were carried through. On Christmas of 1895 we gave the children a feast of waffles and milk tea. Some of the women present said that if their people followed our doctrine they would be better, and added that we taught the children only what was good. Mr. Rijnhart spoke much with the lamas about religious matters, losing no opportunity of pressing the Gospel message. Ishinima declared that if the Mohammedans did not come to attack Lusar and Kumbum it would be because we were there and had prayed to the "Heavenly Ruler" to guard us, and to our certain knowledge Ishinima himself laid aside a Buddha idol which he had always taken to bed for protection, and put his trust in the "Heavenly Ruler."

The Chinese said we were carrying on our mission for the purpose of accumulating merit for ourselves, although they did not dispute that our work was good. They seemed incapable of conceiving the possibility of a single disinterested action, much less a life of altruism, and still less a mission of sacrifice and service out of love to God and man.

The fall of Shen-ch'un, described in the preceding chapter, led to the temporary opening of the road to Sining, though as yet only large bodies of men would attempt the journey, for thousands of Mohammedans roamed about the valleys on either side of the Nan Chuan sweeping everything before them. Strange as it may seem, though Sining was not twenty miles from us, we knew very little about the progress of the rebellion in its vicinity, so close had been the investment of Kumbum and the surrounding villages. At length we learned that for months after the rebellion broke out the Mohammedans in the large eastern suburb of the city had remained neutral, and had emphatically expressed their intention to take no part whatever in the struggle of their co-religionists. But the Chinese did not trust their word implicitly, and kept thousands of soldiers on the city walls, being especially vigilant on the side overlooking the Mohammedan quarter. The double gates had been barricaded and all the houses near the walls had been destroyed, lest they might be used for protection in case of an attack. On September 1, owing, no doubt, to reported successes of the rebel arms elsewhere, that which was long feared took place. The Mohammedans in the suburb began to attack the city, and their cannon played with great precision on the troops stationed on the wall. The *chen-tai's* gunners also made good practice on the rebels who swarmed on the walls of the suburb, and so courageous and determined were the latter that when the man who served the cannon was struck he was dragged away by another, who took his place, and this was repeated six times. When shortly afterwards the government troops occupied the suburb a man was found pinned to his cannon, having been killed while standing bravely at his post. For days the *Tong Kuan*, or "Eastern Suburb," provided a safe retreat for rebels from surrounding districts who were daring enough to brave the cavalry of the *chen-tai*, and approach the very wall of the city, while the thousands of courageous inhabitants of the suburb seemed to be filled with recklessness; for, devoid of all fear, they swarmed over the hills adjacent to the city, apparently unaffected by the rifles and cannon of the Chinese troops, who were straining every effort to hold the city until reinforcements arrived. Nothing incensed the Chinese more than the willful destruction of the beautiful Nan Hsi Si temples on a hill just beside the city walls, to which the Sining people resorted sometimes for worship, and sometimes to witness theatrical performances. These temples were the pride of the district and so strong was the popular feeling regarding their destruction, that as soon as the war was over, the *chen-tai* and his troops undertook the work of rebuilding them, sparing no pains to restore their former beauty and magnificence.

After ineffectual attempts to storm the city, the *Tong Kuan* Mohammedans assumed an inoffensive attitude, and finally tendered submission to the city government, an act that was never looked upon with favor on account of their great treachery in rebelling at all. When General Li with his troops arrived from Lancheo at the city gates, he was not allowed to enter because his coming had not been officially announced, but being regarded as a sympathizer with the rebels, was compelled to take up quarters in the suburb with the Mohammedans. He it was who had advised the latter to give up further resistance at the Siao Hsia, and acted as arbitrator or mediator between the belligerents, even calling a meeting of all the rebel chiefs from the Northern Valley and Topa to discuss terms of peace. Communication with Lancheo was now opened, bodies of soldiers were stationed along the roads, and reinforcements began to arrive in large numbers at Sining. We took advantage of the situation to pay a visit to the latter city. With what delight we anticipated, and how much we enjoyed, a reunion with the missionaries there, may be imagined, for six long weary months had passed away since we had seen a white face.

Soon after our return to Kumbum some of the *Tong Kuan* Mohammedans, fearing treachery on the part of the Chinese, quietly left Sining for other places, and one of them, disguised as an ordinary Chinaman, arrived at Lusar, but was recognized by some one and put to death. As his captors were cutting his throat with a very blunt knife, he told them to use a sharper one and to be quick about it. About noon that day a young farmer came to our door bringing on the end of a stick a human heart, saying that he had been told we foreigners used parts of the human body to make medicine of, and he had brought us the heart of a Mohammedan for sale, expecting a large price for it. He was disappointed and even incredulous when we said we never used any part of the human body for such a purpose. The belief of the Chinese that foreigners in this way manufacture medicines is made much of by the "Boxers" and other fanatics, and is the cause that leads up to many anti-foreign riots, in which mission houses are looted and the missionaries themselves sometimes killed.

There was considerable traffic on the Sining road and by means of messages that came up, and our repeated visits, we were thenceforth able to follow the course of events in and around the city. Toward the end of February General Wei arrived at Sining with his army of soldiers from Central China, determined to settle the Mohammedans of the *Tong Kuan* once for all. For this purpose thousands of the Emperor's soldiers were quartered in the suburb. Eighty-five of the young leaders were captured, led into the city amid the cheers of the excited and delighted populace, and beheaded in the front of the *chen-tai yamen,* the heads and bodies being thrown outside of the western gate where the dogs that had been half starved for months snapped and snarled, while they feasted on human flesh. The work of carnage then began in the suburb and thousands of men, women and children were ruthlessly massacred by the imperial soldiers, some said by Hunan men, others by Sining men, for all recognized that the slaughter of those defenseless people was a breach of honor, a disgrace to the army, and so endeavored to shift the responsibility of the deed. Many a meal of human hearts and livers was partaken of by soldiers, who were anxious to possess the courage their enemies had displayed; and believing that the qualities would be transferred from the eaten heart to the one who devoured it, they lost no opportunity of in this way possessing themselves of the admired reckless daring of the rebels.

As Topa had been the refuge of the Mohammedans from captured villages, it was also the center from which the armed rebels had sallied forth on their warlike manœuvres, and at the time General Wei had arrived at Sining, was the stronghold where it was estimated that forty thousand were prepared to make a final stand against the government troops. The *chen-tai* and his soldiers occupied Chen hai pu, a well fortified impregnable Chinese fort a mile from Topa, which latter was situated across the Hsi-ho river that protected it on one side as there was no bridge, while hills surrounded it on the other sides, providing on the whole, a strong position for defense. At the invitation of one of the commanders of the Chinese army, we went to the above mentioned fort, where we treated all the wounded and sick soldiers during the remaining time that hostilities were in operation. On our arrival, we found the place full of troops, and were it not for the influence of some leaders we would have had no room to stay in; and even then, we shared one corner of the *k'ang* where slept nearly a dozen men, women and children who had vacated every other room in the house for the Sining troops, while the Hunan army was stationed outside the fort in tents. We were not long there before we had many wounded to treat, and in the evening we mounted steps up to the wall and had a good view of the great fort of Topa and surrounding country. The suburbs of Chen hai pu had been destroyed by the Chinese themselves, temples, shops and houses having been almost razed to the ground, while every available tree had been used for fuel. The wall had heaps of stones that were intended for use in times of attack, and little mud-brick houses had been built only a few feet apart along the whole length of the wall, to be used as protection during the cold nights of the winter, while the appointed guard patrolled the walls, the citizens taking this task in turns.

As we walked on the wall we met Brigadier-General Teng, the *chen-tai* of Sining, an unassuming man dressed plainly and with such a pleasant smile as he greeted us in passing, for no one appreciated more than he the services rendered the sufferers in the rebellion by the missionaries in Sining and Kumbum. He returned to the former place with all his soldiers the following day and the task of reducing Topa fell to General Wei, half of whose troops were quartered outside Chen hai pu and half at Heh tsui tsi on the river five miles beyond, so that they held the Mohammedan stronghold between two bodies of men, who unfortunately, did not and would not work in unison during an attack; yet they both did good service, as a result of which thousands of Mohammedans were killed and wounded, and the others became demoralized. With other spectators we watched from the wall the bombardment of Topa, on more than one occasion, and noticed with what precision and order the foot soldiers, who had received foreign drill, marched onward in a black mass to the attack, while the cavalry—who were, as a rule, unaccustomed to ride over such uneven ground as the harvest fields about the forts—rode on in full tilt against the Mohammedans who endeavored to meet the attacking party and turn it outside the fort. Once the cavalry put one party of five hundred rebels to flight back toward the gates which had been closed by the frenzied people within, and only a half dozen of that party escaped, the remainder having been killed just beside their own gates. The casualties among the Chinese cavalry that day were large, but their victory was a telling one, and had its effect in bringing home to the Mohammedans the hopelessness of their struggle.

Another bombardment was planned in which the infantry and cannon attacked one side while the cavalry engaged the other. We repaired to the camps of the soldiers as the wounded had begun to arrive, carried in by their companions sometimes in a basket made from a garment hung on a spear, sometimes on a man's back, but always with tenderness. They lay in rows in the open beside the tents, while, as swiftly as we could, we gave each one in his turn the attention he needed, the patient's companions running after water and whatever was necessary; and so for hours and hours, as the battle raged outside, the men were brought in and laid down to await their treatment. The hundreds of wounded that received attention those days necessitated the use of so many bandages and dressings that the demand for suitable cloth was supplied by using our sheets and pillow cases that had been provided for use in a hospital which we had hoped to found at Lusar. The commander had put at our disposal a *puhtsi* or shop, to which the wounded who could walk came for dressings, and those who could not come were treated in their tents in the different camps. Our food was brought to us already prepared from the commander's kitchen, a great help indeed, for the immense number of soldiers made food very scarce, and, besides, we had no kitchen in our "shop." The men from Central China who had been accustomed to rice food fared very poorly in Chen hai pu, for only flour could be bought, and they did not know how to prepare *m'ien,* but put it in large lumps instead of thin strips into the water, and as a result ate indigestible pieces of tough half-cooked dough. This lack of proper food, the cold to which they were unaccustomed and for which they were inadequately clad, the deep cellars they dug under their tents to provide more room for the thirteen men quartered in each tent, where their cooking also had to be done, caused an outbreak of disease among the troops, so that we had in all a thousand or more patients. Many of the wounded men received rice, vermicelli and eggs from us, or they would certainly have succumbed to their wounds. Also, we used our influence with the commanders, inducing them to provide from their personal stores some suitable food for their men.

The practice made by the gunners of these troops was bad; hence the cannon were of very little use, and the land torpedoes that had been placed were of no avail, for the Mohammedans did not pass over the spot where they had been buried. One had in the night been put just outside one of the gates of the rebel fort, where it was discovered very early the following morning by a little group of Mohammedans who cut the wire attached to it, carried it into the fort and instead of knocking it open, as a Chinaman would have done, buried it where it could do no harm; but the torpedoes filled them with fear and superstition, for soon afterwards they proffered submission, which was accepted on condition that their leaders and all their arms should be brought to Chen hai pu. This was done and bodies of rebels guarded by troops marched past our door, with large bundles of guns and spears over their shoulders, and when they had deposited them at the *yamen* were allowed to return to their homes, the leaders alone having been retained. These latter, stripped to the waist, were marched past our door two by two to the outside of the city gate, and beheaded, each by one stroke of a soldier's knife. The bodies were buried and the heads carried in baskets back to the *yamen,* one occasionally rolling out into the dust in the road. Such scenes have a demoralizing effect on a community, and in this generation the evil effects of that rebellion with its cruelty and bloodshed, will have worn away neither from the Mohammedans nor Chinese.

Not long afterwards we were provided with a "shop" in Topa where were quartered certain detachments of imperial troops which had all left Chen hai pu, and after a little hesitation I went with my husband and a large escort of picked men well mounted into the rebel town. We found that the suburbs had been almost destroyed in the bombardment by cannon, also that the Chinese temples having been used by the Mohammedans as dwellings, were scarcely injured. There were two walls around Topa, an exterior and an interior one, the latter surrounding a closely built fort, separated from the other by many buildings. Within the outer wall had been dug deep trenches for further defence, and it was plain that had the troops succeeded in forcing an entrance into the outer fort, thousands would have fallen, for the Mohammedans were well armed with guns, swords and spears, even foreign guns being possessed in large numbers. The Mohammedan woman who owned the shop we were in, told me that even before the final bombardment, many of the young Mohammedan men had been killed, and she said that most of them were pressed into the fray by circumstances and the commands of their leaders. She and her husband, a shoe-maker by trade, had lived in the suburbs of Chen hai pu, and having been warned by the Chinese one day, had gone to Topa to sleep, not taking anything with them except the clothing they wore and a little money. That very night the Chinese had attacked the suburb, stolen what they could and destroyed every house and temple. They were then forced to remain in Topa, but her husband kept out of sight as much as possible, refusing to take any part in the fighting, until one morning he found a small piece of paper at his door with an order from the leader or *ahon* for him to join a sortie in the valley toward Sining. Having no horse, but not daring to disobey, for that would mean death, her husband took a spear and joined the party of two hundred, only eighteen of whom returned alive, he not being of the number.

The war was now practically over. A large proportion of the fighting men of Topa had been killed, some had submitted, while fully 20,000 fled toward Turkestan, spreading consternation among the nomads of the Koko-nor, as they passed through their country, plundering and devastating without mercy. Many of them perished of cold and starvation on the desolate plains.

General Wei and his troops returned to Sining, while General Teng, a military officer of still higher rank, took his place, and, saying that his predecessor had no authority to accept submission on the conditions he had made, he demanded one thousand more heads of leaders. These were reluctantly and yet speedily caught by their companions, taken down to Sining and beheaded. The remaining population of Topa were robbed by the soldiers of almost everything of value they possessed, and were then sent to the small northern valley where they were permitted to reside, their lands having been confiscated. Thus the Government of China had displayed, through the commanders of its army, such treachery and lack of honor as might easily lead to fresh trouble, and yet the Mohammedans around Sining have received such a crushing defeat as to render them unable to rebel, unless as a revenge for the atrocities in the *Tong Kuan,* those of Hocheo should sweep all before them, capture Sining, which would make an admirable stronghold, and gain possession of the whole western portion of Kansu. Tankar has no more Mohammedans, the people having at the command of the official, fallen upon the few hundred residing there, slaughtering them all. The walls of Topa have been almost leveled, the beautiful mosque has been destroyed, and the green tiles and bricks composing it have been taken to Sining at the order of the *fu-tai* to be used probably for building temples for the Chinese. The only Mohammedans to be seen for some time afterwards in the *Tong Kuan* were beggars, and those who had come to sell small wares, and I understand that the

Sining authorities are not again to permit them to reside even in a suburb, though if they adhere to their purpose, trade will not be by any means so brisk.

All the troops from Central China were disbanded in Western Kansu and as many of them had no means of livelihood, they became highwaymen, being as much a terror to the timid Chinese as had been the Mohammedans, for they attacked and killed without mercy.

As a total of 100,000 were estimated to have been slain during the war, there were in many districts no farmers left to cultivate the land, and in some places the people had great difficulty in getting enough seed to sow and implements to work with, though the officials had granted considerable relief for this purpose. When the harvest had been sown, it was in large part destroyed by rats, which, attracted probably by so many bodies that had been given improper burial, spread like another army over the fields, leaving waste and sorrowing hearts behind it. For these various reasons, there was, when even two summers had intervened after the war, great want among the laboring classes, and years will elapse before even in a slight degree the effects of the rebellion will wear away.

When peace had been declared Mr. Rijnhart, to the consternation of both Tibetans and Chinese, went to the Mohammedan quarters at Topa to treat the Mohammedan wounded. It had been understood that because we had helped the Chinese and Tibetan soldiers, therefore we shared their hatred of their enemies and could not possibly have a kind thought for them. When they saw that the missionary was just as kind and tender to the Mohammedans as to themselves, they were utterly amazed. The law of Christian kindness impelling love and mercy even for one's enemies was vividly brought to their attention, and some, as they pondered the lesson, thought again of the colored Bible picture on the wall of our house in Lusar—the picture of the Good Samaritan. There they had learned the lesson in story —the missionary had translated it into action.

CHAPTER VI

THE LAMASERY OF KUMBUM

Tibetan Lamaseries—Legend of Tsong K'aba—Origin of Kumbum—The Gold Tiled Temple and Sacred Tree—Nocturnal Devotions and Worship of the Butter God.

The lamaseries in Central Asia are, like the cathedrals in Europe, the most imposing monuments of religious life; but while the spires and domes of the latter tower above the teeming city and look down upon all the refinements and activities of civilization, these rude sanctuaries of Buddhism are frequently situated in the most secluded and sometimes even in the most inaccessible spots on the rugged Tibetan plateau. Some of them are miles away from any village or encampment, and though they cannot boast the exquisite artistic finish and massive splendor of Cologne, Strassburg or San Marco, yet they possess a sturdy picturesqueness all their own. They are built sometimes in a sheltered ravine, but more usually on the mountain side, often perched high upon some jutting mass of rock, and reached after laborious climbing by means of zig-zag stairways hewn out of the stone. The architecture is fantastic and irregular, consisting of a number of square and oblong buildings rising tier above tier against the hillside or thrown together without any apparent plan, and ornamented by rude battlements, bridges and exterior stairways, the whole crowned by an abrupt flat-roofed tower, or by several small turrets varying in shape.

These lamaseries, or *gombas,* are the abodes of the Tibetan priesthood which constitutes, it is estimated, about one-seventh of the entire population of Tibet. In the *gombas* at Lhasa there are said to be no less than 15,000 lamas, while in the province of Amdo alone, according to information gathered by W. W. Rockhill, the number of lamas is somewhere between 25,000 and 30,000, residing in twenty-four lamaseries, each accommodating from 200 to 5,000. Two-thirds of these lamas are Koko-nor Tibetans, the remaining third Koko-nor and Ts'aidam Mongols, Eastern Mongols and Tibetans.

The lamasery of Kumbum, in which we resided during the rebellion, and with which, on account of our friendship with the abbot, we had such rare opportunities to become acquainted, is, as already intimated, one of the greatest and most famous in all Central Asia. More than a half century ago, M. Huc visited it and described its site as "one of enchanting beauty." It reposes in a fertile valley, through which a stream flows, dividing it into two parts. On either side of the stream and up the opposite hillsides repose the white dwellings of the lamas, rising terrace above terrace in amphitheatrical order. The more pretentious residence of the *kanpo* situated upon the highest row up the hillside, is conspicuous by its bright red colored walls.

The ordinary lamas' dwellings are kept spotlessly white, a coat of lime-wash being periodically applied in a very novel but not the less effective manner, for instead of putting it on with a brush, the lamas stand high up on a ladder or on the roof and empty large pitcherfuls of the liquid on to the walls, letting it run down to the ground, doing its work as it goes. On the western side of the stream are the temples, well-built structures of burnt brick with gaudily painted walls surrounded by colonnades, having roofs of slanting tiles, the ends of which, projecting over the walls, are tinged with bright blue or green. There is one temple which stands out in bold and dazzling relief against all others. It is the gold-roofed temple of Tsong K'aba, which the lamas call Jo K'ang, or "Home of the Buddha." This temple is the center of interest in Kumbum and is the crowning pride of all the people of Amdo, who hold it to be particularly sacred. It is about fifty feet square; its walls are of sculptured wood and present a mosaic of many tints which led Huc to speak of them as "sparkling with a thousand brilliant colors;" it has two roofs, a lower one and an upper one, the latter resting on a row of short red lacquered pillars; the lower roof is much wider than the top one, projecting considerably beyond the main wall after the usual Chinese style. The tiles of both roofs are covered with heavy gold plate, concerning the precise thickness of which there seems to be a difference of opinion. Some of the lamas told us it was an eighth of an inch in thickness, others said half an inch.

Tsong K'aba, whose name the gold-tiled temple commemorates, was the Luther of Tibetan Buddhism and flourished in the fourteenth century. The lamasery chronicles are rich in records, half mythical and half historical, of the career of this wonderful man, the lamasery itself deriving its name from an incident in connection with his birth. The word "Kumbum" is a combination of two Tibetan words meaning "ten thousand images" and was first applied to a marvelous tree, a descendant of which still exists at the lamasery. The lamas gravely relate the story of the wonderful child, how he was born with a white beard, long flowing locks, wise countenance, fully developed mental powers and ready speech. At the age of three years he resolved to renounce the world and to devote himself to the contemplation of the Buddha's doctrine. His mother, sympathizing with the holy ambition of her son, cut off his beautiful hair and threw it into the courtyard, when lo, immediately there sprang up from it a tree, on every leaf of which was visible an image of the "Lord Buddha." The young student sat at the feet of the most illustrious lamas of his day, resided some time at Lhasa, and eventually led a reform movement which resulted in the founding of a new sect, that of the *Gelu,* or "Yellow Caps" as distinguished from the "Red Caps" or those of the conservative school. Tsong K'aba introduced radical changes in the Buddhist liturgy, and on the basis of the new worship, founded the great lamasery of Kaldan which still flourishes about nine miles from Lhasa, and is said to contain 8,000 lamas. Not only by the immense number of adherents that were won to his views during his lifetime, but also by the literary productions he left behind him, Tsong K'aba's influence has been great during the last five centuries of Tibetan history. The most important of his works are an edition of the sayings of Gautama Buddha and a religio-philosophical treatise on "The Progressive Path to Perfection." The early followers of Tsong K'aba were very zealous in propagating the Gelupa doctrines and as a result of their missionary labors, fraternities of the yellew sect were established in all parts of Tibet and in Mongolia. Even the Tibetan king was among the converts. Tsong K'aba died in 1419 and his body, the lamas assert, is still preserved in the monastery of Kaldan where it may be seen in all its freshness, by a perpetual miracle poised in the air a few feet above the ground, and to those who are far advanced on the way to buddhahood, the great man still speaks words of wisdom and encouragement, although none of the common herd can hear his voice or see his lips move!

No more interesting question offers itself to Christian scholarship than that concerning the remarkable resemblances between the ritual of the Gelupa sect and that still in vogue in the Roman Catholic and Anglican branches of Christendom. M. Huc, himself a Roman Catholic, who visited several Gelupa lamaseries, says:

"Upon the most superficial examination of the reforms and innovations introduced by Tsong K'aba into the lamanesque worship, one must be struck with their affinity to Catholicism. The cross, the miter, the delmatica, the cope, which the grand lamas wear on their journeys or when they are performing some ceremony out of the temple, the service with double choirs, the psalmody, the exorcisms, the censer, suspended from five chains, and which you can open or close at pleasure, the benedictions given by the lamas by extending the right hand over the heads of the faithful, the chaplet, ecclesiastical celibacy, spiritual retirement, the worship of the saints, the fasts, the processions, the litanies, the holy water, all these are analogies between the Buddhists and ourselves."*

What is the origin of these striking analogies? The Tibetan lamas themselves have never been great travelers, and the supposition that Tsong K'aba visited a Christian country at that early date is highly improbable. Huc conjectures that Tsong K'aba met some of the Roman Catholic missionaries who were operating in China under Jean de Monteorvin, Archbishop of Pekin, as early as the fourteenth century, and who had even trained a choir of Mongols to chant psalms, and taught them Roman Catholic ceremonies. Anent this question the Tibetan legends speak of a strange lama who came to the land of Amdo from the far western regions and resided in Tsong K'aba's tent, a man of wondrous learning and piety, having a big nose and bright flashing eyes. Tsong K'aba, it is said, sat at the feet of the great stranger and received instruction in all the doctrines of the west, until the teacher fell into a deep sleep from which he never wakened. Whence this legend of the stranger from the west? It is both possible and probable that Amdo was visited by some of the early missionaries to Asia, perhaps by

*Travels in Tartary, Thibet and China, by M. Huc, Vol. II, pp. 45-46.

the Nestorians who had missions in Western China as early as the seventh century. Again, it is known that in 1325 a Roman Catholic missionary named Friar Odoric made a journey from Northwestern China through Tibet to India, and resided some time in Lhasa; that Fathers Grüber and Dorville in 1661, and Desideri and Freyre in 1716 made missionary tours, the latter residing in Lhasa for thirteen years; that in 1719 the Capuchin friar, Francisco della Penna, with twelve co-workers of the same order, began a mission in Lhasa which flourished until 1760. Who can tell to what extent the residence and teaching of these missionaries in Tibet is responsible for the resemblances in ritual between Romanism and Tibetan Buddhism? Legend has in all probability attributed to Tsong K'aba more than his due with respect to the introduction of Christian forms. That they have been gradually incorporated into the Tibetan worship as a net result of all the early contact with westerners is a reasonable view. We found the legend of "the white lama from the west" quite fresh in the people's minds. Mina Fuyeh told us that Tsong K'aba had a large nose and looked like a European.

The importance and sacredness of Kumbum, in the eyes of Buddhists, can then be easily understood when it is remembered that the lamasery is so intimately connected with such a commanding personage as the great Buddhist reformer, for although he did not actually found the lamasery, yet to him alone it owes its origin. Pilgrims flocked to worship at the foot of the mountain where he was born; soon Buddhist priests

TIBETAN BUDDHIST LAYMAN

from Inner Tibet, China, Mongolia, and Manchuria, came to build their cells there; the emperors of China extended to it their protection, and thus it has grown to its present status.

Through Mina Fuyeh's influence we had many opportunities to visit the "Golden Tiled Temple." Around its outer court are small shrines with a row of prayer-wheels, about three feet apart. These are small cylinders containing rolls of printed prayers. To turn these prayer-wheels is, according to the Buddhist idea, to accumulate merit, and they are hardly ever still, for every one who passes by gives them a spin. In the wooden planks which form the threshold of the shrine are visible abrasions about three or four inches deep, made by the hands and foreheads of pilgrims prostrating themselves before the great altar and image inside. Even when approaching the temple afar-off worshippers may be seen *kotowing* to the very dust at every third step, gathering zeal and momentum, as it were, for the final prostration on the hard planks. By the thousands of Buddhist devotees who resort thither every year and place their hands and foreheads in the same spots as the thousands who have preceded them, these planks are looked upon as quite as sacred as are the marble steps leading to St. Peter's, by the multitudes of Roman Catholic pilgrims who flock annually to the Eternal City.

It is only once a year, on the first day of the third moon, that women are permitted to enter the temple, and when that auspicious day came I was privileged, through the influence of Mina Fuyeh, to go in with the

Mongol and Tibetan women, although it was known that I would not take part in their idolatrous worship. The first thing that greeted us on entering was a huge image of Tsong K'aba in sitting posture upon a decorated throne. The throne is about ten feet high, and the image wrought, the lamas told us, in solid gold, is perhaps six feet high. If the image is of gold it must be of fabulous worth, for it is altogether of massive proportions, and indeed, if it is only plated, as we sometimes supposed, it would still be one of the most valuable possessions of the lamasery, from a material standpoint as well as from a religious one. Immediately in front of the image was an immense oblong altar literally covered with holy water vases, and butter lamps large and small. Of the butter lamps there must have been several hundred all lighted for this special occasion. Standing before the altar and amid the blazing light of the lamps, I looked up into the face of one of the greatest idols of Tibetan Buddhism, while all around me were bowed the worshippers, muttering prayers and pouring out before it the homage of their hearts. The idol truly had never been more radiant than on that day, when the sheen of many sacred flames beat upon it and caused the golden rays to flash out like the beams of the sun. But as I looked I found no spark of intelligence darting from the pupilless eyes; there was no change of expression on the placid countenance to indicate that the ears had been touched by the heart-cries of the prostrate worshippers; no word of blessing fell from those silent lips, immobile and set as on the day when they received the last touch of the artist's hand. How appropriate the words of the poet of Israel:

> " The idols of the nations are silver and gold,
> The work of men's hands.
> They have mouths, but they speak not;
> Eyes have they, but they see not;
> They have ears, but they hear not,
> Neither is there any breath in their mouths.
> They that make them shall be like unto them;
> Yea, every one that trusteth in them." (1)

Yet there is something pathetic in this spectacle of heathen worship, and it is not, in my opinion, the part of the Christian missionary to assume an air of ridicule and contempt for the religious ideas and practices of peoples less enlightened than his own; for in every religious service, however absurd or degraded from the Christian view-point, there is some feeble acknowledgment of and groping after the one great God to whom all men and nations are alike dear; even in the worship of idols there are to him who has the willing ear and the understanding heart "painful cries of the soul, torn from its center and separated from its object." (2) The work of Christian missions is hindered by antagonizing the non-Christian peoples through dogmatic assertion of doctrines and the failure of the Christian missionary to recognize and rejoice in the great underlying truths of all religions. Only as he appreciates the light, however dim, that gleams amid the darkness and superstition of the heathen systems, can he hope to turn men's eyes to Him who is the Sun of Righteousness and the Light of the World.

1 Psalm cxxxv. 2 Vinet.

Besides the image and altar, the gold-tiled temple contains many interesting relics, chief among them being the stone on which Tsong K'aba was born. The walls are covered with Buddhist books, and *khatas*, some of them fifty feet long, hang from the ceiling. Closely connected with the sanctuary are the "reading halls," one of them large enough to accommodate 2,500 priests at one time. Before entering the reading-room each priest is obliged to remove his shoes. Sometimes there is a pile of shoes at the entrance comprising 2,000 pairs or more, thrown promiscuously together, and yet the owners seem to have no difficulty in finding each his own pair. Above the reading-rooms is the museum, containing a collection of sacred relics, musical instruments (principally big horns and conch shells), gold and silver vases, lamps and works of art. The most prized among the relics is a picture of Tsong K'aba which the saint himself is said to have sketched in his own blood. This was done in the city of Lhasa when the saint was there pursuing his studies. His mother in Amdo, desiring to know how he was faring, he drew the sketch of himself and sent it to her, instead of writing a letter, and as soon as she received it the picture spoke, assuring her that her son was in the best of health! Another remarkable thing in the museum is a mud image of a buddha named Mete Fuyeh, upon whose muddy head it is declared hair began to grow soon after he was completed. He is carefully preserved in a glass case.

Of the sacred tree from which the lamasery takes its name, and which grew up from the hairs of Tsong

K'aba, a word must be said. There are three of these trees in a yard near the Golden Tiled Temple. All pilgrims visiting the lamasery take special pains to pay reverence to the central tree, and to receive some of its leaves, on each one of which is clearly discernible to the eye of the faithful the image of Tsong K'aba. No one around Kumbum seemed to question this marvel but the two foreigners. We frequently visited the tree and had the leaves in our hands, but our eyes were holden from seeing the image or anything approaching it, a disability which the lamas coolly informed us arose from the fact that we were not true followers of the Buddha. This explanation is rather damaging to the reputation of MM. Huc and Gabet, who declare they saw on the leaves of the tree, not images of Tsong K'aba, but well-formed Tibetan characters. There is nothing in Huc's narrative so perplexing as this, and without questioning his veracity one cannot refrain from wondering to what extent he fell under the magic spell of the Tsong K'aba legends; nor is it any the less clear why the leaves which in Huc's day bore Tibetan characters, should have passed on from literature to art, producing now only images of the saint! The tree has been variously classified. Rockhill, following Kreitner, first thought it was a lilac (*Philadelphus coronarius*), but later he concluded it was a species of syringa (*syringa villosa,* Vahl). We saw the tree once when it was in bloom—the flowers are very much like lilacs, but the leaves seem to be stiffer.

Besides the worship of Tsong K'aba's image, we witnessed many other weird and interesting ceremonies during our residence in Kumbum. One of the most impressive was that of "nocturnal devotions," celebrated periodically by the lamas. At nightfall the people are called to the housetops by loud blasts on a horn made of a large shell from the Koko-nor. The women and children from Lusar carry bundles of fragrant wood, which is burned in little fire-places arranged for the purpose on the roof. As the incense of the burning wood rises as a sweet offering to the Buddha, all voices unite in the chanting of some unintelligible song or hymn. On the roof of each house some one does duty at the prayer-wheel, sitting down cross-legged and revolving it at the utmost speed, for it is believed the faster the cylinder turns the greater the merit accruing to the worshipper. Some of the lamas and women are busy passing their rosary through their fingers, while other lamas stand with bowed heads uttering the famous six-syllabled invocation, "*Om mani padme hum.*" From the first sound of the signal horn at nine o'clock, the night becomes hideous and sleep is out of the question. The beating of gongs and cymbals and the ringing of bells accompany the worship, while with these discordant sounds blend the voices of a thousand lamas until the noise seems like an echo from pandemonium. The whole scene is illuminated by thousands of red paper lanterns suspended on poles, and by incense fires that are kept fresh by constant adding of the fragrant fuel. The night slowly creeps away, but the noise does not subside. The untiring muscular energy of the devotees who beat huge gongs hour after hour, and the lung power of others who blow incessantly on the gigantic horns, is truly marvelous. The lamas hold the ceremony of "nocturnal devotions" to be one of great merit, and it is therefore participated in with the greatest of solemnity and fervor.

Another imposing ceremony, celebrated once a year on the fifteenth of the first moon, is "The Butter God Festival." For some days previous to it the roads leading to the lamasery are literally covered with travelers arriving from China, Mongolia, and all Tibetan territories. Some are mounted on horses, driving before them their heavily-burdened yaks; others, of higher rank, are borne on stately camels, with long retinues of pedestrian pilgrims following behind. There are priests with closely shaven heads and wooden knapsacks thrown over their shoulders, and laymen with long, tattered sheepskin gowns and short wild-looking hair. As the pilgrims arrive, the rooms of the lamasery are first occupied, then the black tents of the Tibetans begin to rise until the entire valley and hillside become as one vast encampment resounding with the shouts and laughter of men, women and children, the whining of camels, the neighing of horses and mules, the barking of dogs, the clattering of gongs and cymbals, the blowing of horns and the ringing of bells. On the main road to the temple are scores of white tents of Mongol and Chinese merchants who have come not only to pay their respects to the Buddha, but to dispose of their wares, consisting chiefly of cutlery, needles, cloth boots, tea, charm-boxes, idols and other articles. The people in motley processions surge toward the center of attraction in the courtyard of the Golden Tiled Temple, where in a pavillion erected as a temporary shrine stands the great butter image they have come to worship. The shrine is about forty feet high, twenty feet long and twenty feet wide, made of four wooden pillars connected at the top by large, painted beams from which are suspended strips of satin that serve as walls. The satin is beautifully worked in devices representing the different forms in which Shayka Muni appeared on the earth before his last incarnation, in which he became the Buddha. At the rear is a large table on which burn hundreds of butter-lamps, and above it rise, layer upon layer, a series of butter bas-reliefs of most exquisite workmanship. The first layer represents a famous temple in Lhasa across the doorways of which, by some clever machanism, paper guards are made to move to and fro, and a huge dragon with wide open jaws seems to crawl from side to side. On the second layer stands the giant butter image of Buddha, about twenty feet high. His features, his cap and robes are admirably rendered. He is represented as blessing his people; his hands are stretched out over them and his head slightly bowed down. By his side stand still other pieces of butter art, such as small reptiles, flowers, vegetables and different kinds of animals. Above the great image is a smaller image of Buddha, which represents him sitting in a temple receiving the homage of the people. His head moves mechanically in recognition of the homage given. Everything is beautifully executed, not only the moulding of the images, but also the painting, being artistic in the true sense of the word.

Confronting the table on which are the butter-lamps is a long, low bench covered with red cloth, prepared for the lama dignitaries who are to come to worship the image. These dignitaries are accompanied by some half dozen attendants carrying big red lanterns. On arriving in front of the butter god the attendants bow down to the ground, put their hands to their foreheads three times and utter the prayer "*Om mani padme hum,*" while their master kneels on the red covered bench, offering some sticks of incense to the greasy deity. The ordinary rank and file are not allowed to kneel on the bench in offering their devotions; they must be content with the bare ground. At a certain stage in the proceedings there is a great commotion, as the *heh-ho-shang,* or black lamas, who are the policemen of Kumbum, push through the crowd, cracking their big whips in order to clear the way for the greatest dignitary of all, who is coming to inspect the images. It is the great "god-man," the incarnation of Tsong K'aba. The *heh-ho-shang* head the procession; after them follows a lama of high rank carrying a bundle of burning incense sticks, and another with a pyramid of *tsamba* decorated with paper of many colors, inscribed with mystic characters. Another lama follows, holding in his hand a sceptre adorned with a cross and on either side of him is a lama bearing a lighted torch. Next comes the great incarnation in yellow satin robes, holding in one hand a sceptre and in the other a beautifully finished rosary of polished ivory. On his head is a high yellow miter and his feet are shod with velvet-topped Chinese boots. With stately step he moves toward the butter images, but he is too holy to offer homage to the Buddha idol. He alone remains standing while all the other dignitaries prostrate themselves. After inspecting the images the great incarnation returns slowly to his palace on the hillside overlooking the Golden Tiled Temple. His departure is the signal for loud jubilation. The multitude suddenly leap out of their religious mood and give themselves over to boisterous songs and laughter. They seem to lose all control of themselves, dancing and yelling like madmen. It is plain that the ceremony is at an end. If the people have changed so have the gods. The heat of the hundreds of lamps has had its effect on the surface of the images even though covered with paint; streams of grease are dripping from the noses and fingers of the deities, and soon nothing is left but shapeless masses. In the early morning priests appointed to the task remove the remains from the boards and throw them into the ravine where the dogs, wolves and birds devour them for breakfast.

Of the origin of this festival little can be said. The answers received from the natives, whom we asked for an explanation, gave us plainly to understand that it was not generally known. Some said that it was a feast in honor of the great Tsong K'aba; others said that it was a ceremony illustrative of the unreality and worthlessness of earthly honor in a material body. In the beginning of the eighth moon the preparations for the feast are begun. The council of the lamasery comes together and selects molders and places them under the supervision of a lama of great fame in this art. The butter is then collected, and from that time on, until late in the last moon, it is scarce and dear. The butter is brought into cool places, where it is subjected to a thorough kneading process, whereby it becomes more solid. During this time of the year it is very cold, which adds to making the butter better for the purpose for which it is to be used, but also increases the suffering of the artists because they have to put their hands constantly in cold water to lower their temperature, lest they should spoil the features, newly formed, by touching them with their warm hands. After the forming and molding are finished, the council meets again and appoints the painters. The molders then leave their work entirely in the hands of the latter. Both are bent upon one thing, that of harvesting the praise of their superiors and fellow-lamas, and thus obtain the prize, a sum of money given for the best designs. Much has been written of the heathen in other countries who worship the heavenly bodies, animals, images of clay, wood, stone and metal, but the Tibetans with their monstrous butter buddha occupy a unique place in the world's idolatry.

CHAPTER VII

A BUDDHIST SAINT

Mina Fuyeh's Abode—His Previous Incarnations—Mahatmas—Conversations on Christianity—Jambula—Behind the Scenes.

The name of the lamasery-dwelling in which we lived was "*Mina Karwa,*" that is, the palace belonging to Mina Fuyeh. Each of the Kumbum lamas of high rank has a *karwa* in which he entertains his *pesing,* or people from his district who come to visit the lamasery. During his abbotship Mina Fuyeh dwelt principally in a house bearing the name of Tsong K'aba, the reformer, and called also *la-rong,* or official residence. *Mina Karwa* was surrounded by a high wall painted red and white, through which there were two entrances. One of them, large and very imposing, was for the exclusive use of the master of the house, or some great visiting *fuyeh;* the other was for ordinary use and led through a smaller courtyard. There were two large stone-paved courtyards—the outer one was surrounded by two-storied compartments, and had communication with the inner one by means of massive doors. In the inner courtyard were the household temple, the private apartments of the buddha when at home, and the three

MINA FUYEH

living-rooms which he had placed at our disposal. All the apartments were well built, the woodwork was painted, the lattice windows, contrary to custom, had glass panes, while a liberal supply of the very best Chinese furniture gave the whole interior a comparatively luxurious appearance. On one side of the building, and at the rear, flourished a grassy lawn relieved by flower beds in full bloom, Mina Fuyeh being very fond of flowers and quite successful in cultivating them. Two or three large trees supplied shelter from the sun's rays, which, at an altitude of nine thousand feet above the sea level, are very strong, especially in summer time. Before the Mohammedan rebellion of 1861-74 the house had been much larger and more magnificent. There still remain massive stone steps leading to an elevation which Mina Fuyeh pointed out as the site of the splendid apartments he had occupied in his previous lifetime, but which had been destroyed by Mohammedan fire and not rebuilt.

Mina Fuyeh was only twenty-seven years old, yet he confidently asserted that he had lived in this palatial abode previous to the year 1861. He professed even to have vivid recollections of all that pertained to his previous incarnation, and, more than that, he could tell some things that were going to happen in the next! He took great pleasure in prophesying that Mr. Rijnhart would in his next lifetime reappear on the earth as a buddha, as a reward for the good work he was doing in the present existence. One project was dear to Mina Fuyeh's heart—it was that of restoring the former residence to its original grandeur; but as yet he had never been quite rich enough to undertake it, and during the troublous times of the second rebellion he more than once congratulated himself that he had not spent any money in rearing an edifice that might again succumb to the flames.

During our stay in the *Karwa,* Mina Fuyeh came with his secretary and treasurer to perform religious devotions in his household temple during a period of three days. Their worship consisted mainly in the chanting of prayers to the accompaniment of the jingling of bells, and the beating of little drums made of skins stretched over human skulls. When they had chanted themselves hoarse they swallowed copious quantities of tea, and then came into our apartments, seeming to enjoy the respite from the dull routine as keenly as school children enjoy recess. During such intermittent visits much time was spent in conversation on Christianity and Buddhism, subjects of which Mina Fuyeh never seemed to tire. Soon after we had made his acquaintance Mr. Rijnhart had given him copies of the Christian Gospels in the Tibetan character, among them a copy of St. John, which he prized very highly. He had a marvelous memory, and was soon almost as familiar with the text of the Gospels as we ourselves, and was able quite intelligently to discuss the various incidents of the life of Jesus, quoting passages with astonishing accuracy and appositeness. He told us that he believed thoroughly in Jesus, but that he did not see any reason why he should renounce Buddhism and become a Christian. He could not see any insurmountable difficulties in accepting both systems, for even on the great doctrine of reincarnation with respect to which Christianity and Buddhism are supposed to stand at the opposite poles, be claimed that whereas the Gospels did not explicitly teach the doctrine, yet they did not expressly deny it. He indeed went further and declared his belief that Jesus was no other than a reincarnation of Buddha, and that Tsong K'aba, the great Tibetan reformer, was a later incarnation of Jesus. At the same time Mina Fuyeh confessed himself charmed with the gospel story. He told us there were many parallels between Jesus and Tsong K'aba; that the latter had gone about healing the sick and teaching the people just like Jesus. When we spoke of the crucifixion he said that Tsong K'aba had been persecuted, too, and added that even to-day in Tibet it was not wise for a lama to be "too good." I believe that, all unconsciously perhaps, Mina Fuyeh has been the means of spreading gospel teaching among his people to an extent that has as yet been possible for no Christian missionary. With all the famous lamas and pilgrims from the far interior, even from Lhasa, as also from Mongolia, he conversed on the subject, telling them what he knew about Christian doctrines, and teaching them to pronounce for the first time the name "*Yesu Ma'shika,*" Jesus Christ.

The *kanpo* was far superior to the average lama in intelligence. He had been educated, so he told us, in his former lifetime, in Lhasa, and had enjoyed the instruction of a very wise snowy-bearded old lama at Kumbum; yet his knowledge was exceedingly limited, a fact which he cheerfully admitted. He knew practically nothing of the outside world, had traveled but little, and had an idea that Pekin, which he once visited, lay at the other end of the world. He questioned Mr. Rijnhart by the hour, carefully noting the answers, and marveling at the white teacher's wonderful range of knowledge. When Mr. Rijnhart demonstrated to him in a series of object lessons with globe and candle the rotundity of the earth, his interest and pleasure knew no bounds, for he had always believed it to be flat. He studied geography with all the aptness of a school-boy, learning from an old atlas given him by Mr. Rijnhart the names of many western countries and seas. Frequently he expressed an ardent longing to accompany us to America or to Europe if we should ever go home, in order that he might see for himself and learn something of the world beyond, so full of mystery. Of the occult knowledge of the hidden things of nature, attributed by Theosophists to the Tibetan priests Mina Fuyeh, although abbot of one of the greatest lamaseries in all Tibet and occupying a position of spiritual and intellectual eminence surpassed only by the "Dalai Lama" at Lhasa, knew nothing. He had never seen a mahatma, and was much surprised when we told him that western people believed such to exist in Tibet. On the question of mahatmas we made very careful and minute inquiries of many lamas, all of whom confessed their ignorance of any such beings. There was no record or even legend of any having ever visited Kumbum, and one of the oldest priests in the lamasery, who had spent years in Lhasa, told us he never heard of a mahatma, even in that

"City of Spirits." There are, it is true, some lamas who profess to have magical powers by which they are able to control the rains and turn paper horses into real ones, to be carried by the winds to the help of travelers overtaken by the mountain storms; in fact, Ishinima, our Tibetan teacher, once brought to Mr. Rijnhart the wood-cut from which these *long-ta*, or "wind horses," are printed, and allowed him to make as many copies as he wished to send home to friends. But nothing could be further from the truth than the belief entertained by many occidentals that the lamas are superior beings endowed with transcendent physical and intellectual gifts. On the contrary, they are mere children in knowledge, swayed by the emotions that play on the very surface of being. During all our four years' sojourn among Tibetans of various tribes and districts, we did not meet a single lama who was conversant with even the simple facts of nature. Mina Fuyeh was far above the average, for the great mass of them we found to be ignorant, superstitious and intellectually atrophied like all other priesthoods that have never come into contact with the enlightening and uplifting influence of Christian education. They are living in the dark ages, and are themselves so blind that they are not aware of the darkness. Ten centuries of Buddhism have brought them to their present state of moral and mental stagnation, and it is difficult to believe that any force less than the Gospel of Christ can give them life and progress in the true sense.

Tibetan lamas would as soon doubt their present existence as question the truth of the doctrine of reincarnation. With them it is more than a speculation—it is a fact, the basic postulate of their entire philosophy of life. Mina Fuyeh spoke with the utmost assurance not only of his lifetime immediately preceding the present one, but of a score of incarnations through which he had passed since he attained sainthood, and concerning each of which his memory stood him good service. He was not so far advanced, however, as Sakya Muni, the founder of Buddhism, who, he assured us, was incarnated 551 times and could remember the 510 incarnations that preceded his attainment of sainthood as well as the forty that followed! The way in which the Tibetans keep track of the line of successive incarnations is interesting, and is well illustrated by an incident from Mina Fuyeh's own experience. When a mere child, before he was sent to the lamasery to be trained as a priest, it had been ascertained of course what ego or individuality had reappeared in his body. A number of articles belonging to various deceased lamas were placed before him, and he was required to select those he had used in a former lifetime. Among the articles from which the selection was to be made were a number of rosaries, and as the young child chose the rosary and other things that had belonged to a former lama named Mina Fuyeh, his identity was ungainsayably established, and he not only inherited the name but also the property and rank which had been his in the previous incarnation. Speaking of his choice of rosary he said, "Why should I not recognize it among all others, the one I had used for years?" When Mr. Rijnhart laughed good-naturedly at the *kanpo's* credulity, he adduced what in the minds of all who had witnessed the proceedings, had been the most convincing proof of his former individuality, as well as of his marvelous insight. When a number of horses, some of them young, dashing and well-nourished animals, and others lean and decrepit, were brought before him, he chose as the one belonging to his former life the most dilapidated of them all. An ordinary child, it was held, would certainly have selected the most attractive looking pony. In conversation with many lamas we were given repeated descriptions of this ceremony of identification, and although MM. Huc and Gabet were inclined to believe it is often carried on in good faith, and that the mysterious results accompanying it are to be accounted for only on the supposition of the agency of Satan, we had reason to believe it is a piece of purely human deception in which the deceivers, it is true, are largely self-deceived. There are not a few of the more intelligent laymen who are sufficiently unorthodox to suspect, and with reason, that the young child before choosing the article has been prompted by his parents or by influential lamas who, for a consideration, become specially interested in his career!

Although Mina Fuyeh was woefully ignorant of natural science, we found him an accomplished linguist, conversant with Tibetan both classical and colloquial, Chinese and Mongolian. So proficient was he in the latter tongue that he once made a tour among the Eastern Mongols somewhat after the fashion of a mendicant friar, reading the Buddhist sacred books from village to village, and from tent to tent, and receiving therefor whatever the people were pleased to bestow. Chinese he had spoken at Pekin, where he had also for the first time seen "foreigners." Among the curios he had brought back from the Chinese capital was a collection of photographs which he had taken to be representations of Buddha, but which turned out to be mostly photos of French and American actresses arrayed in costume. When we told Mina Fuyeh this he was quite ashamed, and handed the same over to us to be disposed of, begging us not to say anything about it, as no lama is supposed to have pictures of women in his possession. Mina Fuyeh was quite conscientious in this matter, and willingly sacrificed the entire collection with the sole exception of a photo of Alexander of Russia.

So intimate did the friendship between the *kanpo* and Mr. Rijnhart become that the former freely discussed in our presence not only his personal affairs, but also all matters pertaining to the lamasery. Very few days passed, especially during the rebellion, without an interview, the *kanpo* sometimes coming to see us, and just as often Mr. Rijnhart being summoned to the official residence. On such visits I, as a rule, accompanied my husband. One day we were sent for in a great hurry by Hsam-tso, the *kanpo's* treasurer, and on our arrival we found that official's countenance badly disfigured by blows from the hand of his master, who had fallen into a fit of distemper and lost control of himself. The news of the *kanpo's* illness spread through the lamasery and everyone seemed to fear lest something serious should happen him. In our diagnosis of the case we found him in a peculiar condition, like one demented, though docile as a child. His illness had been caused, we discovered, by the inordinate quantity of fruits sent from Kuei-teh, which he had eaten that morning. Some powerful sedatives and a large dose of calomel, a drug we found particularly useful among orientals, relieved him completely, so that he was quite himself the next day, and very grateful for his recovery.

Shortly after this incident I was stricken with an attack of diphtheria which well nigh proved fatal, and when I was barely convalescent K'ai-i-tan, our young servant, contracted the same disease. We entreated him to remain with us, offering him every attention, but of no avail. Sick as he was, he insisted on going home because his father had summoned him to perform certain religious duties on hearing that the boy had recently slaughtered a sheep. To a really devout Buddhist the taking of life is a sin which is not easily atoned for. K'ai-i-tan left for home, and within four days the carpenters were manufacturing a coffin under the roof of his father's house. Death had deprived the father of a dutiful son and us of a faithful servant, to fill whose place we secured no one for a long time.

Jambula, a Mongol priest, of whom mention has already been made, had first come to our notice by being one of five or six strong lamas, who were beating a little acolyte for letting fall a water bucket which lay smashed in pieces at their feet. Mr. Rijnhart interfered, standing ready to defend the little child from their cruelty by more than words if need be; and, on account of this act, even though directed against himself, Jambula had conceived a great liking for my husband. When we were without a servant he undertook to help us in every way he could, making our tea in the morning, sweeping our rooms and finally helping us to move when we returned to Lusar. Sometimes he would drink tea with us, and when he had finished with his basin, he would lick it out with his tongue in order to save further washing. Needless to say, we kept our eye on Jambula's basin, and saw that it got a thorough scouring, but at the same time we would not, on account of æsthetic sentiment, betray any word of disgust to wound his large and loyal heart.

The little boy whom Mr. Rijnhart had rescued was a Mongol lama who lived with his teacher in the house that we occupied, and we often had occasion to pity him, for the teacher treated him with great cruelty, sometimes beating him severely and never giving him even a pleasant glance. In common with other acolytes of the same age, he was only too eager to combine play and mischief with his various tasks. Sometimes, indeed, these boys were transformed into veritable little scamps, the terror of all whenever their particular teachers were out of sight. The spirit of mischief is not confined to the very young lamas, but takes on a more serious aspect when the older ones lay aside their religious duties and turn their attention to other things, for even fighting is not eschewed by some. One day a young lama came to invite us to accompany him to his home, where a companion lay ill, and as he seemed anxious to have no delay, and Mr. Rijnhart could not at the time go with him, I went, on his promising to bring me home again. On my arrival I found that my patient was a Mongol lama, who had been fighting in the night with some of his companions, and had several large gashes on his head. After binding up his wounds I left for home, mounted on my mule, which was led by my Tibetan boy, while the lama walked near us. Suddenly we heard excited cries, but not understanding the language well enough I did not know what was meant, so paid no heed, when unexpectedly a stone thrown by a priest from across the ravine flew past me, just missing my head. My boy, frightened beyond control, rushed into the temple to say his prayers; my guide was nowhere to be seen, but the mule took me safely home, for there he was accustomed to be fed. The abbot explained afterwards, when Mr. Rijnhart indignantly protested against such treatment, that no one is allowed to ride through the monastery, and I had broken that important rule; but the lama, the abbot admitted, had displayed poor manners to thus try to injure me when I was innocent, and especially when I had been trying to relieve suffering.

The matter of discipline in the lamasery is a serious one. Mina Fuyeh, not having learned the virtue of self-control, found it no easy task to rule the four thousand lamas under his charge. On festive occasions a large company of specially appointed lamas arrive with huge black whips and try to keep order. Peevishness and turbulency leading to acts of insubordination are distinguishing characteristics of the priests. The atmosphere of holy meditation and blissful calm with which some from afar would fill the Tibetan lamasery, with its sublime mahatmas, too exalted and pure to live among ordinary men, is only the atmosphere of an uninformed and rose-colored imagination. Distance lends enchantment, but at the first contact the mirage disappears.

CHAPTER VIII

OUR REMOVAL TO TANKAR

Tankar and Surroundings—A New Opportunity—Ani and Doma—The Lhasa Officials—Drunken Lamas—Visit of Capt. Wellby.

Situated on the Hsi-ho River, about twenty-four miles northwest of Kumbum and twenty miles east of Topa, the Mohammedan stronghold, is Tankar (or Donkyr), a town of considerable commercial importance, being a sort of distributing depot for Chinese merchandise going into the interior. Hither come the caravans of the Dalai Lama from Lhasa, that dignitary driving no small trade with the Chinese; and, there being a direct route from Tankar to Lhasa, a large caravan leaves for the "sacred city" annually in the fourth moon. The town is one also of political and strategical importance. Here the Sining Amban halts on his way to worship the Koko-nor, or "Blue Lake;" here he also receives the Mongol princes once a year and distributes presents in the name of the Emperor. Ten miles to the east passes a part of the great wall in which is a gate called *Kuan men,* now in ruins, but at which a guard of soldiers was previously stationed. The town was once within Tibetan territory, but gradually the Chinese have encroached for agricultural purposes upon the district in which it stands.

Along the Hsi-ho are narrow gorges which make the entrance to the Tankar valley very difficult, and of which during the rebellion, the Chinese took advantage to keep the Mohammedans in check. The approach from the east is made charming by a mill and some trees outside the east gate, with beautiful temples on the hills in the rear. There is one principal long street lined on either side by stores in which are to be found Chinese wares, goods for bartering with the Si-fan from the Lake district, grain, bread and foodstuffs of the Chinese. The yamens opening out into this street, a small lamasery, several wool depots, houses of citizens and of Tibetans from Lhasa, and more Chinese temples, fill up the remainder of the space within the wall of the town. Through the latter are two gates, the eastern and western, outside of which are suburbs, that without the eastern gate being for the most part ruins, with the exception of some inns and shops. Previous to the Mohammedan rebellion of 1861-74 ten thousand, mostly Mohammedans, was the estimated population of this suburb. Without the western gate, every day are to be found Chinese merchants squatted for some distance along both sides of the road, with their small stock of goods spread underneath an awning—thread, beads, bracelets, bread and other things. These petty merchants are patronized by the poorer classes of people whom they fleece in every way possible. In this respect they are especially severe on the Tibetans. In the space between the outer and inner gates carpenters and toolmakers are at work.

During the recent rebellion, as already stated, a large proportion of the Mohammedan population left their homes and joined the rebel forces, while the remaining part, estimated at four hundred, were peaceably following their callings, having presented themselves before the Chinese official saying they were loyal to China. Their professions of loyalty were accepted and peace might have prevailed were it not for a quarrel that arose between a Chinaman and his Mohammedan wife. The woman stated that some night the Topa Mohammedans would come to attack Tankar, and would give the signal by setting fire to the beautiful temples on the hills just outside the town, upon which their co-religionists inside were to rise up and open the gates. The husband carried his information to the official, and early the next morning the streets were running with blood, the Chinese having fallen upon and murdered every Mohammedan man, woman and child, except a few girls who were wanted as wives for Chinese sons.

The Hsi-ho itself is too broad and tumultuous to work the quaint mills, but small streams deflected on either bank serve that purpose. The banks are lined by willows and poplars in profusion, and altogether the river is a great boon to the people. Many of the rich merchants from the city resort to it in the spring and summer, camping in sheltered spots, enjoying the freedom of the country with its shady copses, rolling hills, and its verdant fields far-stretching and spangled with flowers. The region literally teems with game of all kinds, and in the river fish abound. The Chinese being clever sportsmen, and impeded by no religious scruples, avail themselves to the full of the opportunity of stocking their larders with pheasants, hare, trout and other delicacies; but the Tibetan Buddhists, believing that in every living animal is a soul on its way to sainthood and Nirvana, hesitate to kill the game, nor can they be induced to taste any of it until after they have mingled for some time with the Chinese on the border. It may be observed, in passing, that the Tibetans are grossly inconsistent in the matter of taking life, for while they, as a rule, refrain from killing game, and have the most indulgent compassion on a louse, yet they slaughter sheep, expose their children and helpless aged, and even commit murder. Winter at Tankar is not so enjoyable as summer, the thermometer registering occasionally 12 degrees below zero, and continuing at that temperature a considerable time, except in the middle of the day, when, owing to the latitude and altitude, the sun's rays are strong. After a fall of snow the natives swarm upon the roofs to clear it off to avoid leakage, throwing it over into the street below, where it remains until it melts away. But even with the mercury below zero when the sun is bright, sitting out of doors in the sunshine upon warm rugs is preferable to being indoors.

The inhabitants are a motley crowd, ten thousand in number, consisting of Chinese, Mongols with their characteristic face, genial and good-natured, the women with their headdress of velvet embroidered with colored silks and set with silver and beads worn in front instead of at the back, the dress being otherwise the same as that of the Tibetans; then there are gorgeously-arrayed Tibetans from Lhasa and the Si-fan Tibetans from the Lake district, smart and neat looking in comparison with many other tribes, their women having the heavy, cumbersome headdress at the back with shells, bright beads and pieces of cloth.

For various reasons it occurred to us that it would be advantageous to open a mission station at Tankar. Lusar, it is true, had served us well as a starting point, and at Kumbum we had so thoroughly won the confidence of the people that we felt perfectly at home in our work. Indeed, the temptation was to settle down in Kumbum and Lusar for a life mission. Had we not under the providence of God overcome all the preliminary difficulties of establishing a foothold? Were we not preaching the gospel to those who had never heard it, and might we not reasonably expect that, continuing in our present field, we should in due time see results? Besides, other ties bound us: we had really come to love the people; our tears had flowed together, and we had now many interests in common. Throughout the months of terror, disease and slaughter we had known the fellowship of their sufferings, we had gone down into the valley with them, passed under the cloud with them—yes, we had literally been baptized with their baptism of blood, and it was only when the thought of our leaving them began to stir in our hearts that we realized how close and tender were the ties that bound us to them. Then there was the yearning to see them all won to the Saviour and rejoicing, as we were, in the freedom of the gospel of God's love, and, had we acted merely upon our own feelings in the matter, we would have remained at the great lamasery, instructing the dear children of the Bible School, conversing with the lamas concerning the Christ, and amid our medical ministrations preaching the gospel to the poor.

But how often there comes to the Christian the "stirring of the eagle's nest!" Abraham, going forth to the Promised Land, yet "not knowing whither he went," cannot remain at Haran; Elijah is summoned to stern duty from the quiet home at Zarapeth; the Apostle Paul, preaching the gospel in Asia Minor and leaving behind him thousands who heeded not the message, sees visions of larger regions beyond; and even the Master must leave the brooks and sunlit slopes of Judean hills setting his face toward Gethsemane with all its dark, unspeakable agony, and the awful immolation on the cross. As I have already said, we had from the beginning felt called especially for itinerating work, the work of looking out new fields and preparing the way for other laborers, the work of preparing the soil in uncultivated regions, that by twos and threes, and in greater numbers when God's time arrived, the sowers of the Word might come to dark Tibet to scatter the seed unto a glorious harvest. The door was standing wide open at Tankar, and as we were now alone, Mr. Ferguson having taken up other work in China, we felt we must go in. After the rebellion we received invitations from many of its influential inhabitants to come up and open a medical dispensary, and we knew that meant an opportunity to preach the gospel to many who had never heard the name of Christ. The people of Tankar would not be so completely under the influence of the lamas as were those of Lusar, and thus we should perhaps more quickly have visible results. Again, the town lay on the great caravan route, travelers were continually leaving for and arriving from Lhasa, and who knew whether by moving up there and making new friends we might not be permitted to accompany some expedition to the interior and thus learn more about the people to whose uplifting we had devoted ourselves, and find out how far beyond the border and at what points missionaries might reside? Having fully decided, we bade good-bye, very reluctantly, to Mina Fuyeh, the abbot, Ishinima, our teacher, and the many friends who had become so dear to us at Kumbum, and set out for Tankar.

The matter of securing suitable quarters was expedited by the aid extended to us by the officials and wealthy merchants of the place, who knew us well by the reputation we had acquired during the rebellion. The house which we rented for the modest sum of $13 per year, exclusive of many repairs, was less pretentious than the one we had had at Lusar, but it suited us admirably, especially as it was situated near the western gate of the town. At first we found it impossible to secure any domestic help, for owing to the late war having taken for service so many of the good young men, and the wool depots at Tankar giving employment and high wages to many others, our call for a boy was answered only by thieves and opium smokers for many months, though we succeeded in securing the help of two women who were of inestimable value to us. One of these was the young wife of a gambler and opium smoker who had seen better days; consequently her feet were very small, and I had an opportunity of carefully examining them. The four smaller toes were bent and bound under the foot, the heel was pressed forward and turned partly underneath, making the instep protrude unnaturally, yards and yards of bandages about two inches in width being used to bind them with. When her feet, which had open sores at the heels, would become painful from use, she would remove the bandages and try the soothing effects of warm water, replacing the cloth wet, wearing shoes and all both night and day. During the time of binding the feet in, when the girls are three or four years of age, the pain is excruciating, and for two years the little things suffer extremely, but after the feet have been bound and compressed the removal of the bandages causes great pain, and has to be gradually done, allowing the feet to expand slowly. There is a movement in China to do away with this barbarous custom, but though some influential natives give it their support, many a year will elapse before natural feet are the fashion in the Celestial Empire.

The other woman, by far the more valued of the two, was an old Mongolian widow, called Ani, whose husband had been a Lhasa Tibetan, and whose only child was a girl of fourteen years of age, by name Doma. These two became my faithful friends, doing their utmost to serve me in every way. For nearly two years Ani brought us water on her donkey, a wooden bucketful on each side of the saddle, while Doma for over a year acted as "housemaid." Their home was in a respectable-looking courtyard just a few doors from ours, and consisted of a kitchen and two rooms, in the inner one of which was a *k'ang* with cupboards and a little altar with its idols, butter lamps, small shallow brass basins and innumerable *khatas*. On the *k'ang* was a *hopen,* in which there was invariably fire, while a pot of tea well seasoned with milk and salt always stood ready on the iron tripod standing in the fire. There was also a little square brightly painted box with a sliding lid that held *tsamba*. Whenever I visited Ani's home bread and butter were ready waiting for me (she had learned of my aversion to *tsamba*), clean rugs were spread on the *k'ang,* and the tea had no salt in it. Ani always made profuse apologies for not having anything to offer me, but the hospitality was genuine, and received as heartily as it was given.

Tibetan and Mongolian women are great wine-drinkers, whenever they have company, or are visiting, and Ani was no exception to the rule. When under the influence of liquor she was very loquacious, beating and abusing Doma in barbarous fashion. The latter rather liked wine, too, for when she had the chance she would imbibe freely, but after a while they both abstained because I objected to it. Repeatedly, and with final success, I coaxed Ani to keep Doma away from drinking companies and allow her to follow the natural girlish instinct of purity I felt she possessed. To my exhortations Ani would reply in great sincerity,

"What a pity it is that poor women in our land are not respected as in yours; here they are not expected by parents or any one else to lead what you call moral lives." Alas, poor Ani's words tell only too truly the sad story of Tibetan women's lives. So far as we were able to observe, morality among them was an accident rather than a rule, this statement applying to all classes, married or single. Though at times there is affection between husband and wife, fidelity is not at all deemed an essential quality of womanhood, and when a man goes away from home he is just as liable to bring another wife home with him as not. This occurred in a house not far from us, where a man and his wife had lived comfortably and agreeably together for years. Suddenly, on his return from Sining, he brought another very young wife with him. The first wife was angry, and treated the poor young woman with such cruelty that the latter committed suicide by taking a large dose of opium. Her parents then demanded indemnity from the husband for the loss of their child, and the home became one of misery. The entire social system, and especially the domestic relationship of the Tibetans, needs purifying.

Doma was a very bright girl, speaking fluently Mongolian, Chinese and Lhasa Tibetan, and as she gave us lessons in Mongolian, we found that she possessed great latent ability, having a good memory and sharp insight. Every small particle of cloth and any of our cast-off clothes were greatly appreciated by her, and afterwards when we had our Tibetan servant Rahim, who came in for a share, she was quite jealous, proving how easily spoiled the natives are. Had we stayed long in Tankar and Rahim remained with us, he and Doma would probably have been married, for it had been discussed by him and Ani, and I often think that he may yet some day from his far-away home in Ladak find his way again north of the Kuenluns and settle down at Tankar as the old woman's son-in-law, for Doma possessed great charms for him. But these are dreams, idle dreams.

A visit with Ani to the home of a Mongol woman married to a wealthy Lhasa Tibetan was quite an event to me, for she was the most respected native woman in Tankar with the exception of the wife of the highest Chinese official. Her little daughter, thirteen years old, was engaged to be married to a young boy aged eleven, son of the Mongol Prince of the Koko-nor, and this boy was living in his betrothed's home where he and the little girl studied the Chinese character, played, ate and slept together, the girl always obeyed and respected by the boy, conspicuous wherever he went in his yellow silk clothing. The rooms in this home were luxuriously furnished with carved and highly polished cupboards, tables and chairs of Chinese make, beautiful rugs, many brightly shining brass fixtures, fresh white and colored paper on the lattice windows, all indicating wealth and a certain degree of cleanliness and æsthetic taste. Her husband, politely called Tsun bo, was a large, well-built and well-dressed man, who looked as if he partook too freely of *chang,* an alcoholic beverage which he made in his home and sold in large quantities to the Tibetans. As the appointments in this house were of the highest order, the refreshments that were offered to guests were of good quality, notably the tea, which was the real churned tea, the kind most favored by all Tibetans from the interior. It is made from brick tea, boiled for five minutes or longer in salted water; the liquid is then strained into a churn in which butter and *tsamba* have been put, and the whole churned up together by some peculiar twists of the churndash. It looks like chocolate, but it does not taste in the slightest degree the same, especially when the butter is tainted, as it very frequently is.

Among the most interesting personages we met at Tankar were the four *kushok,* or representatives of the Dalai Lama. These are lamas specially sent from Lhasa to look after the commercial interests of the great potentate, and at the same time they are empowered to act in a semi-official capacity in all matters pertaining to the commerce of the *kopas,* or Lhasa Tibetans, many of whom trade at Tankar. Every year the large trade caravans sent by the Dalai Lama to Pekin pass through Tankar and are superintended by the *kushok*. Dr. Sven Hedin has fallen into the error of confounding these trade caravans with the tribute-mission which the Dalai Lama sends the Chinese Emperor once every three years. The tribute-mission formerly traveled over the Ts'aidam-Tankar road, but ever since the Mohammedan rebellion of 1861-74, by order of the Emperor, it has gone by way of Ta-chien-lu, although the Tibetans have frequently petitioned to be allowed to send it by the former route because it is much easier to travel on, though now not so safe, owing to the unsettled state of the country. By way of Ta-chien-lu come also the trade caravans of the great Trashil'unpo Lama, who dwells in the monastery at Shigatsze near Lhasa, and who is reverenced by many Tibetan tribes and some Mongols to a greater degree even than the Dalai Lama. Though both the spiritual lords of Tibet engage in mundane traffic, they do it with mutual respect, and with no thought of competition, the one not infringing on the territory of the other.

The four *kushok* have large establishments in Tankar, houses gorgeously painted and beautifully furnished, where they sometimes spend many months on their way from Lhasa to Pekin. Having experienced the difficulties of travel between Lhasa and Tankar, they are not anxious to repeat that portion of the journey, and so, frequently, on returning from the Chinese capital, they send the proceeds of their enterprise on to Lhasa in the care of trusty stewards and await the return of the latter with a fresh caravan of trade supplies. Thus every year one caravan departs for, and another arrives from, both Pekin and Lhasa. The principal one of these four agents was Shar-je-ja-ba, while the fourth in rank was *Karpon* Losang Kindum, *karpon* being a title given to responsible agents who have complete control of all their master's merchandise. We knew both of them well. The former was a large, corpulent lama with a round, fat face, a small tumor on his forehead, while across his head was a scar several inches in length, the result of a wound dealt him by robbers some years previous. He was dressed in yellow and red brocaded silk garments, with a small circular hat that looked like a cap of gold, so bright it was. Two of his front teeth were missing, and so much anxiety did he display to have them replaced that at his earnest solicitation Mr. Rijnhart, by means of a steel file, made him two from the ivory handle of a tooth brush, and fastened them in place by a silver wire attached to them through holes, and then bound around the other teeth. No one in this land of scientific dentistry could be better pleased with the most perfect crown tooth than was that Tibetan *kushok* with his two crudely-wrought ones, which were, it must be confessed, more ornamental than useful.

Losang Kindum, dressed mostly in red silks and satins, was of slight build, tall and straight, with a good-natured, though cynical expression on his face. He, too, had had experience with robbers, for the year we arrived in Kumbum he had lost a whole caravan, and, knowing the people who had attacked him, he was endeavoring to obtain restitution through the Amban.

Both Shar-je-ja-ba and Losang Kindum were exceedingly friendly, inviting us frequently to their sumptuous quarters and visiting us just as often in our own home. Once when our old friend Mina Fuyeh, now no longer abbot of Kumbum, had come up to spend a few days with us, Shar-je-ja-ba invited the latter and Mr. Rijnhart, together with a number of noted officials, to a feast. The occasion was so great as to receive the official recognition of the Amban, who sent tablets of honorary inscriptions in gold letters to be placed over the door of the courtyard. When all the ordinary lamas and *kopas* were seated on rugs under awnings in the courtyard, and the guests of honor were on the *k'angs* in the rooms, wine and tea were served in profusion, with viands that would be most relished according as the guests were Chinese or Tibetan in their appetites. Mina Fuyeh, another living buddha, Mr. Rijnhart, a wealthy Chinaman, and Losang Kindum sat on one *k'ang* and had a very enjoyable time together which almost became unpleasant through a joke, which only the latter enjoyed. Though he was a lama, he was an inordinate wine-drinker, while his three guest-companions on the *k'ang* limited themselves to tea, and probably from a sense of impropriety of his so freely imbibing, or a wish to be jovial and hospitable, he asked Mr. Rijnhart to have some. Not receiving the expected acquiescence, when the little basin covered with a silver lid, from which my husband drank his tea, was sent to be refilled, Losang Kindum whispered something to the servant. When the cup was returned Mr. Rijnhart found that it contained wine, whereupon Mina Fuyeh was greatly incensed and informed Shar-je-ja-ba of the trick. The only compensation the genial host could offer was to give the poor servant a beating for lack of civility, when really Losang Kindum was to blame. When asked for a reason for the indignity he had heaped upon Mr. Rijnhart, Losang Kindum replied that he had simply supposed Mr. Rijnhart to be like the ordinary Tibetan lama, who refuses to drink only until the first drop has passed his lips as a result of persuasion, and is then ready to do his share. The drunken habits of some lamas are shocking. No fair or festival takes place without fights and disorderly conduct caused by alcoholic beverages. I do not say that all lamas drink, but to say that the majority of them are not only addicted to drink but also to gluttony is not at all wide of the truth, and this despite the teachings of Buddha on temperance and self-control. The ethereal, abstemious, vegetarian Buddhist lama is a pure figment. I have seen a lama devour several pounds of meat at one sitting.

Entertainment is carried on in a sumptuous manner by these wealthy Tibetans, and at times no expense is spared for their own pleasure or that of their friends. They have at various seasons of the year what may be called theatricals for the want of a better name, and invitations are issued to special friends, while any others who wish to see may take up positions on the roof from which they can look into the courtyard below. We had the privilege of attending one of these performances, which we found interesting for the time that we remained. The performers were all men, some of whom, however, personated women, and were dressed in cloth gowns with richly embroidered jackets, having their hair ornamented by corals and green stones, and square cloth veils over their faces. The play consisted of the representation of a reception by a great potentate of embassies from different nations. The potentate was some holy man, a great lama seated on a throne. The first to be presented is the Chinese embassy, headed by a gorgeously arrayed mandarin with feather and button, and followed by a retinue of minor officials. He presents his *khata* to the potentate with elaborate ceremony, but to the apparently great chagrin of the Chinamen and to the amusement of the spectators, the *khata* is returned and the great mandarin fails to win favor. Then appear *K'a-ches,* men with long white beards, dressed in white plaited skirts and turbans, one of them with bent form personating an elephant with a white sheet thrown over him. Next follow Hindustani Mohammedans in their dark red gowns and turbans, calling aloud as they enter in an attitude of worship "Allah! Allah!" The Mohammedan embassies share the same fate as the Chinese one, all their *khatas* being rejected; but the climax is complete when a well-dressed young prince of a royal Tibetan house presents his *khata* and is graciously received by the big man amid much rejoicing. The entire representation was accompanied by much singing and dancing, the latter consisting now of a slow, dignified step, now of a vigorous swinging of the body until the rope ends attached to the girdle stood out perpendicular to the waist and had the appearance of a rapidly revolving wheel. A drum beaten at intervals controlled the players, who at times danced forward to drink wine from a basin on the rim of which were three little pyramids of butter. With the other guests we were served refreshments, such as tea, delicious bread, and Tibetan soup, made of finely chopped meat, onions and rice reduced to pulp, a very appetizing and digestible food. Though the entertainment was not by any means ended, we did not feel that after the first little while our time would be well spent, so left the natives to the full enjoyment of their play.

The visit of Mina Fuyeh to our home in Tankar was full of interest. How many hours we spent talking over the harrowing experience through which we all had passed during the rebellion. We also reviewed the happy days we had passed together in Kumbum and renewed our discussions about Christianity and Buddhism. There was no mistaking the fact that, though Mina Fuyeh had been much touched by the gospel story, and though he had long ago come to the point of expressing his admiration for Christ and Christian teaching, he showed no signs of willingness to openly renounce his ancestral faith; he was still a Buddhist by profession. We had done our best to enlighten him. We had taught him with the most diligent and conscientious care; we had prayed over him, and sought by the example of our daily walk to open his eyes to the beauty and joyousness of the Christian life, and therefore strange thoughts passed through our minds as, during that visit, we saw the people come to him with *khatas* and gifts, prostrate themselves before him, worship him as a god and wait to receive his blessing. To the missionary who works only for visible results there are certainly many disappointments on the foreign field, and during the long pioneer days, the days of waiting and of sowing seed, only the consciousness that one is doing his duty and obeying the great Lord of the Harvest can keep the heart full of peace and full of faith as to the ultimate results.

How difficult it was to realize that our visitor with whom we sat and conversed was a man of such influence, purity and power in the eyes of the people as to be adored like a god, for, according to our standard, he was ignorant and materialistic to a degree.

Mina Fuyeh was accompanied by his little disciple, a boy of about ten years of age, whom we had known at Kumbum. He was lively as a cricket, and many a prank did he play upon us and his exalted master. Thinking his appearance might be improved by a good wash, I provided him with the essentials and gave him full instructions; whereupon he very carefully gave his hands, arms, face and neck a scrubbing with plenty of hot water and soap, and there was such a transformation that he was really good-looking. Having gone across the courtyard to another room for a time, I was amazed on my return to see him at the kitchen door, his face shining with something more oily than smiles, and, upon questioning him, found that, feeling uncomfortable, he had smeared the washed parts with butter, a cosmetic that every Tibetan uses freely.

In connection with our regular medical and preaching work at Tankar, we sometimes went on short journeys into the surrounding districts—the beginnings of more extensive pioneer work to which we were looking forward. In October of 1896, on our return from a trip to the grass country, we were met at the gate by a messenger who informed us that a foreigner had arrived in the suburbs and was staying at an inn. Mr. Rijnhart at once rode off to inquire who the unexpected stranger might be, and, as a visit from European or

American travelers is so rare in this distant frontier town, he had decided beforehand to invite him to our home. I therefore made all haste to get the house in order, and had not finished when Mr. Rijnhart returned, followed into the courtyard by an English gentleman dressed in a tweed suit with sheepskin epaulettes, bearing the marks of exposure. What a thrill of delight when we exchanged greetings in good old Anglo-Saxon! The stranger proved to be Capt. M. S. Wellby, of the 18th Hussars, who had made a journey from India, through Ladak and Northern Tibet.

He had been traveling for nearly seven months, and had encountered many difficulties. It had been his intention to penetrate into Inner Tibet from Ladak through Rudok, but arriving at the latter place was prevented from proceeding further by a large body of Tibetan soldiers stationed there to guard the Lhasa road. He was then obliged to turn northeastward in a sort of zig-zag course and spend many weeks in barren, uninhabited country. His provisions had given out, many of his animals died, and his men mutinied and deserted him, so that all that remained of the caravan when it reached Tankar was Captain Wellby himself, Lieutenant Malcolm and Duffadar Shahzad Mir, his *compagnons de voyage,* his muleteer and two body-servants with one load of effects. The journey across Northern Tibet, though disastrous in many respects, had not been fruitless. Valuable observations had been made on the way, and geographical science enriched by the discovery of the source of the Chumar river. We shall let Captain Wellby in his own words describe Mr.

Rijnhart's arrival in the inn and what followed: "I could hardly make up my mind whether he was a European or a Chinaman, and when he addressed me in a mixture of French and Chinese I was still more mystified, so to simplify matters I replied, 'I'm an Englishman,' and held my hand out to him. He eagerly seized it, and gave me the heartiest shake I had received for many a long day, and I felt thankful that we had found a European and a friend anxious to help us in this out of the way place. Mr. Rijnhart, for that was his name, was a Dutch missionary, and had only taken up his abode in Tankar within the last three months. * * * In another moment we were trotting through the street in single file, chatting all the while, when, suddenly turning to the left, we very shortly afterwards drew up at Rijnhart's little house. One step up out of the narrow lane landed us in an open courtyard, where his kind-hearted wife, Dr. Rijnhart, was waiting to welcome us, as well as Mr. Hall, of the China Inland Mission, who had come over to Tankar from Sining and had only just returned with the Rijnharts from making a trip to the Koko-nor. Great honor was shown to me in the eyes of the Chinese by allotting to my use the room that faced the entrance. The Rijnharts, when by themselves, lived in Chinese fashion, and were on the most friendly terms with all the Chinese and Tibetan officials in the town, and we ourselves were treated with courtesy and civility."*

Captain Wellby's visit was of short duration, lasting

* Through Unknown Tibet, by Capt. M. S. Wellby, pp. 261-2.

only one day. In the afternoon we had a call from the princess of the Koko-nor, which served to add interest to the occasion. Next day, accompanied by Mr. Rijnhart, the party set out for a visit to the Kumbum lamasery,† and thence to Sining and Lancheo. Meanwhile, at the earnest solicitation of the travelers, and further because some arrangements about our mails and other business at the coast required adjusting previous to the great journey we were contemplating to the interior, Mr. Rijnhart agreed to accompany them to Pekin, acting as interpreter, a service of which Captain Wellby has made the most courteous and copious acknowledgment.‡

---

† "Very lucky we are to be able to pay this visit under the guidance of Mr. Rijnhart, for not only has he a more intimate knowledge of the monastery than any other living man, but having made his home for two years in Lusar, ten months of which were spent in the monastery itself, he has made friends with a very large number of its inmates, more especially with Mina Fuyeh, one of the greatest incarnate saints in the place." Op. Cit. p. 270.

‡ Op. Cit. pp. 267–411.

N. B.—I have since learned with great regret of the death of Capt. Wellby from wounds received in the late South African war.

CHAPTER IX

DISTINGUISHED VISITORS.

Mr. Rijnhart's Absence—Our House is Robbed—Visit of Dr. Sven Hedin—Tsanga Fuyeh—Medical Work Among Nomads—Birth of Our Little Son.

Mr. Rijnhart conducted Captain Wellby's party to Pekin, from there went overland to Hankow with a German traveler, made new arrangements for our mails and supplies, and returned to Tankar with all possible speed. During his absence the natives bestowed on me the greatest kindnesses, and I felt perfectly safe with them. The women especially did all in their power to entertain me, inviting me to their houses and bringing me gifts, thus enabling me to get acquainted with them in the most intimate way. They seemed to feel they had me under their protection, and vied with each other in bestowing upon me the most considerate attention of which they were capable. Here, too, was a golden chance to speak to them of Christ and of all that His religion had done for women in other lands, and of what it could do for them. During these memorable weeks I learned to understand and sympathize with the heathen women as never before. Besides, I was kept busy with my medical work, and the constant arrival of visitors from far and near who had heard of the foreign teachers and came to see for themselves, compensated largely for any feelings of loneliness I may have had, and made monotony and ennui impossible.

Christmastime I spent with Mrs. Ridley at Sining, and while I was away poor Ani, whom I had left in charge of the house, had a trying experience. A thief, knowing probably that we were away, broke into our house and made off with our stock of money and many others of our valuable possessions, besides destroying photographic plates by exposing them to the light, and emptying many vials of precious chemicals upon the ground. By the aid of the dog Ani located the culprit crouching in a room off the stable, and upon demanding an explanation of his presence, found herself suddenly engaged in a hand-to-hand struggle, at the end of which she was left lying in a pit near the stable, while her adversary made his escape. Undaunted, the faithful Ani gathered herself up as soon as possible and ran through the streets crying "stop thief!" But no one would stop him, or tell her who he was, although it transpired that nearly everyone knew him; but Tibetan politeness forbids anyone to give information that would convict another of theft. As soon as I returned from Sining I immediately notified the *yamen* of the outrage. Some underlings came around to tell Ani that if they did not catch the thief she would be held responsible and be dragged before the *yamen,* as it was her fault that the *iang-ta-ren,* "foreign gentleman's," house had been robbed. Many a weary week was spent before Ani's character was cleared by the catching of the real thief. I shall not forget the kindness of the official and his wife at this time when I had to visit the *yamen,* for they admitted me to their own room, where, contrary to the general custom in China, they dined alone together. Mina Fuyeh, hearing that we had been robbed, sent his treasurer over from Kumbum with a *khata* to offer me any amount of money I might need, and to invite me to return to the lamasery to live, where I would be among "friends." Losang Kindum (one of the Dalai Lama's *kushok*) also sent me several strings of cash, and offered me as many more as I wanted, saying that Chinese officials were not always to be depended upon, but that the Tibetans were big-hearted and meant what they said. Having full confidence, however, in my friends at Tankar, I did not yield to Mina Fuyeh's persuasion.

After the visit of Captain Wellby we had concluded it would be a long time ere we would again be visited by a European traveler, but this rare treat was in store for us sooner than we expected. One calm, bright November Monday the sun shone warmly upon Ani and myself as we sat on our rugs in the courtyard enjoying some *pien-shi,* for I had invited her to come and have dinner with me. A knock at the entrance was answered by the old woman, who at once called me, and I found upon my arrival that the doorway was full of men, some of whom were Mongols and some, *yamen* people. One of the latter, acting as spokesman, told me that a foreigner was just outside the west gate, and was coming to our home to be entertained. Upon questioning him closely I elicited the information that the foreigner was on his way out of Tibet; that he had sent word to the *yamen* to find lodging, fodder and firewood for him and his caravan, and that knowing we had entertained Captain Wellby and Lieutenant Malcolm, the official had directed the foreign men to proceed to our home, all of which was said with the mannerisms peculiar to messengers from the *yamen*. It did not seem possible that another explorer could have so quickly come after Captain Wellby, and I feared it was the men whom the latter had left in Tibet; and feeling thus, I replied that the official must provide entertainment for them himself, that Mr. Rijnhart was away from home. The Mongols had in the meantime been telling Ani what a great man the approaching foreigner was, an *amban* they said, and had so enlisted her sympathies that she prevailed upon me to reconsider my decision, so I said, "Surely, if this is an *amban* who is coming he must have passports and other papers," whereupon the Mongols said he had sent them with one of his men, who was forthwith called. He had been standing aside in the street and now came forward, a large man with a long black beard and a very foreign look, who, I at once concluded, was a Mohammedan from India or Kashgar; had he presented the papers at the beginning, such a long consultation would have been avoided. I looked at the papers he handed me and read in French the fact that Sven Hedin, Ph.D., was on a tour of scientific exploration in Central Asia, or something to that effect, and at once told the men that he was to be guided to our home, and added we would look after his entertainment.

In a very short time the caravan of the great Swedish traveler arrived at the door, and in the absence of Mr. Rijnhart I went at once to welcome and extend to him the hospitality of our little home. Knowing that he was a Swede I felt I must learn at once in what language we were to converse, so I asked him if he spoke English, and upon his reply in the affirmative, we were not at a loss to find topics that interested us both. Ani was delighted that he could speak Mongolian, and called him *amban* and personally welcomed him to Tankar. He had a large number of men in his caravan, some of whom took up quarters in our drug room, while the remainder with the horses went to an inn. Dr. Hedin had heard of us before his arrival. At Bayinhoshum, not far beyond the Khara Kottel, or Black Pass, a Tangut chief had told him there was a solitary Oruss or "Russian" lady at Tankar. "Russian" is the only name by which all Europeans are known in Northern Tibet. In his great work "Through Asia" Dr. Hedin has given the following account of his reception and visit at our humble home.

"Earlier in the day I had sent Parpi Bai on in advance to take my pass to the governor of the town. That dignitary now met us at the gate, bringing us a letter from the 'Russian lady' with a hearty invitation to share her hospitality. I felt it was rather presumptuous to quarter myself altogether upon a solitary lady. Nevertheless I decided, perhaps it was curiosity drove me, at any rate to go and pay her a visit. When

I reached the house indicated, a good Chinese house with an oblong courtyard, I was met by a bareheaded young lady wearing spectacles and dressed after the Chinese manner. She asked me in a friendly tone, 'Do you speak English?' I told her yes, I thought so, and very soon our tongues were going at express speed. She introduced herself as Mrs. Rheinhard (Rijnhart) an American doctor of medicine. Her husband was the Dutch missionary, Mr. Rheinhard, who fully a month earlier had started for Peking with Capt. Wellby, who was on his way home from his journey across Tibet. Mrs. Rheinhard was the personification of hospitality and amiability. It was quite a pleasure to talk to somebody whose interests ranged beyond grass and pastures, dangerous passes, wild yaks, cattle and sheep. Her husband's courage in venturing to leave her behind alone among the rabble of Tankar truly astonished me. But there was not so much danger, perhaps, after all; for through her medical knowledge and skill Mrs. Rheinhard had won several friends among the native population."*

The Chinese officials in Eastern Turkestan had shown him marked courtesy, and he had expected the same from those in the towns of Western China, but found it altogether lacking, I believe, because the Mongols who announced his arrival had called him *amban,* while his passport was almost the same as a missionary's; the official was quick to appreciate the fact that Capt. Wellby had a much better passport than

* "Through Asia," by Sven Hedin, 2 Vols., Harper & Bros., Vol. II., pp. 1156-7.

Dr. Hedin, though the latter was entitled to one of higher rank, seeing that King Oscar was personally interested in the expedition. Instead of coming to call on the traveler, the official ignored his presence in Tankar and Dr. Hedin went himself to call on the *ting*, but there were no big guns fired in his honor as there had been in Turkestan.

The *Kopas* were anxious to learn how near he had been to Lhasa, so Losang Kindum came around with his prayer-wheel in one hand, to ask particulars, and as a result Dr. Hedin visited him in the evening, to buy some curios, cloth, boots, etc., of which the *kushoks* have such large quantities, selling them as they do for the Dalai Lama. In Dr. Hedin's book "Through Asia" he speaks of this transaction as his buying some of the goods intended for tribute, and that the Emperor would that time receive less than had been intended for him. The goods did belong perhaps to the Dalai Lama, but were for trade, not for presentation to the Emperor as tribute, and it is possible that those particular articles belonged to Losang Kindum himself, for even a servant coming from Lhasa does on his own account a little trade, and the profits of that deal were boasted of by the *kushok* for a long time afterwards.

Having a desire to see Kumbum, Dr. Hedin stayed only a short time in Tankar and upon his departure I sent my servant with him, with instructions to visit Mina Fuyeh, present him a *khata* and say that Dr. Hedin wished to visit the temples, and that any kindness he showed him would be appreciated. Just before his departure two runners from the *yamen* came and offered their services, but Dr. Hedin was indignant and sent word through them to their official that he had a good revolver which he had intended to give him, but he would not do so, and he would moreover report to Pekin his lack of courtesy to him, a stranger in Tankar. The men *kotowed,* went away, but soon returned. As the caravan was leaving our gate, Dr. Hedin told his treasurer to give Ani four hundred cash. The old woman was delighted; it is certain she will never forget the great white *amban,* and if her wishes for prosperity and peace were of any avail surely he must have had a charmed life ever since. If on his return to the Ts'aidam last year he passed through Tankar, as he most probably would, Ani, if she heard of his coming, did not fail, I am sure, to give him a hearty welcome.

My next visitor, quite as distinguished in his way, was a lama, 73 years of age, a "living buddha" named Tsanga Fuyeh. Having read the Gospels of Mark and John which we had given a young friend of his, he desired, he said, to see the people from whom the books had come. He was, as far as we could afterwards learn, a pure living man, and he looked it. Inviting him with great ceremony to take his place upon the *k'ang* in the guest-room, I gave him tea, bread, *tsamba* and butter. He had evidently made up his mind that we foreign teachers were different from ordinary beings, for he was as much surprised as delighted when he found we would eat Tibetan meat and butter, and made us a present of a leg of mutton and some pears, accompanied by a *khata,* promising to supplement these gifts by some sheep's butter when he returned to his people, and he kept his promise. The old buddha was much interested in our medical skill, asked for some eye medicine for himself, and inquired about our ability to help a relative who had a tumor. A month or so later when Mr. Rijnhart had returned, the "relative," a rather young woman, came in, accompanied by her husband. Instead of a tumor, we found the patient suffering from abdominal dropsy, and were able to relieve her immediately by tapping. She and her husband rented a room, the only one they could procure, about eight feet square, with no window; and the woman lay on the *k'ang,* with a pack saddle for a pillow, as contented as possible. Her husband was one of those cheery, good natured men one does not often see the like of. He brought us presents, imitated our English, made friends with Topsy, the door-keeper, to such an extent that she would let him out without any remarks of disapproval, but he could not induce her to let him in without some member of the household restraining her. On the whole, he enjoyed us just as much as we did him and perhaps a little more, seeing that we were a trifle cleaner than he was. Among these Tibetans there is a peculiar custom we only learned after close contact with them. When anyone is ill one of the members of the family goes to a lama, gives him a *khata,* tells him about the sick one, and asks him what *mamba* is to be consulted. The lama accepts the *khata,* throws dice, to indicate a certain page in a sacred book which is turned up, whereupon the name of the *mamba* is announced. Tsanga Fuyeh was the lama to whom they went for this knowledge, and after his relative was cured by tapping, he would send every one to us for treatment. We had never suspected that our names were recorded in the sacred books of Buddhism !

The news of this woman's cure spread far westward among the Koko-nor Tibetans, and Tsanga Fuyeh did not cease to sound our praises. As a result people came in from distances requiring twenty days on horseback. This much was amusing: anyone who had a pain of any kind in the region of the stomach wanted to be "tapped," for the Tibetans reason that what is good for one sick person is equally good for another ! I had also to be specially careful to give explicit directions about taking medicine, as another of their maxims was "if a little medicine is good, a large quantity must be so much better," and they would swallow a whole bottle of liquid or box of pills at a single dose. Frequently also they ate the papers in which the powders were wrapped, thinking that if the medicine inside the papers was good, there certainly also must be some virtue in the paper. The visit of Tsanga Fuyeh and the notoriety it gave us among the nomads of the grass country prepared the way, as will be seen, for further trips into the grass country, and later into the great beyond.

Mr. Rijnhart's return from the journey to Pekin was hailed by the natives with delight, especially by the *kopas,* who came to bid him welcome home, bringing a *khata* and large pieces of meat, sometimes as much as half a sheep. Shortly after his return the question of servants was settled, for we secured the services of Mohammed Rahim, the third of Capt. Wellby's men that had reached Tankar in safety. He had been away in the grass country herding flocks and cattle, so that when Dr. Sven Hedin appeared, he missed being taken on with his men and so found himself alone in Tankar. He came to us and a very valuable servant he proved to be, with the fault of a hasty temper which occasionally would get him into trouble.

We had in the center of our courtyard a square flower garden, where we coaxed some native flowers resembling yellow poppies, marigolds and asters to bloom with our own violets, nasturtiums and sweet peas, which gave our home a delightful whiff of old-fashioned far away gardens in the homeland; many a time we would sit on the little stone fence about the flowers, and, looking down into the depths of the blossoms, see pictured there faces of loved ones far away, made happier by sunny, bright letters from the Tibetan border. The blooming of each new flower was for us a visitor, each bringing its quota of interest and cheer. When the first dark velvety nasturtium bloomed there came to our home another blossom, who brought with him a budget of love and a stock of sunshine which will remain always, but now only in memory—dear little Charles Carson Rijnhart, who came to us on June 30th, 1897. Ani had anticipated the event with a large amount of talk and wonderment at the preparations I was making. She told me that among the nomads the mother's only bed is one made of the powdered excreta of sheep, and that when the weather is warm the little one is pasted with butter and put out to bask in the sun. If medical science is needed, none is to be had, nature alone is to be depended upon; and yet everyone is satisfied, as no one has learned that in other countries things are different. When the tub of warm water was brought in daily for the bath and baby was put into it, Ani and Doma looked upon it all as an act of almost certain insanity, though Mrs. Ridley, who was of such inestimable help to us, had been doing the same thing for her two dear little children and no harm had resulted. The natives do not allow a stranger to approach the mother until forty days after the birth of a child, owing to some superstition; and the mother goes out one hundred days after it, so that everyone was amazed to see us about the middle of August, going horseback on a journey to the south of the Koko-nor.

Mohammed Rahim, henceforth to be known as Rahim, was baby's delight, and Doma was not at all pleased that she was not looked on with as much favor as the dark-faced boy, who would walk up and down the courtyard carrying the precious burden, singing weird Hindustani and Ladaki airs, and even the British bugle call which he had learned in India. There is such a difference between Tibetan and white children, the former having apparently scarcely any nerve tissue and showing so little interest and vivacity, and though baby was only an ordinary child, he was in the eyes of the natives a great curiosity; they considered him exceeding smart to "notice things," and in comparison to theirs he certainly was. The twenty days among the nomads in August, to be described in the next chapter, were very enjoyable and will never be forgotten by those natives who came into contact with us. They would come in on tiptoe with their tongues protruding, to stand and gaze upon Charles asleep in his hammock swinging between the tent poles, and hold up both thumbs and put the tongue out still further if possible, as a token of approbation. When his bath time came and the tent door was closed on account of the draught, the women and men too would run to our tent, pick up the flap around the bottom and the whole aperture would be filled with dark faces and laughing black eyes, while they watched the performance interesting to them and enjoyable to Charles. Such remarks as the following were common: "White child," "See her put him into the water," "He will die," and "Why does she not paste him with butter and put him out in the sun?" Tibetan children living in the tents are experts at riding, jumping on the backs of horses and even cows and running down hill at full speed. They are in sunny warm weather to be seen playing about the tents with only a string of something that serves as a charm around the neck, with perhaps a tiny bell, added to the covering nature herself gave them. Their lives are destitute of pleasures, for they have no playthings, no candy, fruit, or cake, which children in this land and even in China have in such abundance. They are not loved and cuddled the way children are in the homeland, and oftentimes the calves and fawns tied to the post in the tent receive more attention than the bairnies.

Shortly after we were settled in Tankar Mr. Rijnhart went down to Sining and had his bicycle brought up the mountainous road. As riding from Sining to Tankar was impossible, it was necessary for a man to carry it on his back. This wonderful "one man cart" (the literal translation of the name the natives gave it) will never be forgotten by the people, and though very much interested in its mechanism not one of them could ever be induced to mount. As far as real use in traveling was concerned it was nil, but Tibetans came in large numbers wanting to see it, and we were glad to have such a powerful magnet attracting the people to us almost daily, thus enlarging the circle of our acquaintance and usefulness. To satisfy them Mr. Rijnhart gave exhibitions. Crowds of people came to witness the "foreign teacher" ride on "the one man cart." The great difficulty was to keep the men and boys from following too closely, as if any accident should happen, the rider was in danger of being tramped upon by the multitude behind. Outside the east gate was a decline, and they never ceased commenting upon the speed with which the bicycle would "run" down that hill "faster than the best horse." My sewing machine also attracted its share of attention and was called the "iron tailor," one woman even going so far as to come to inquire if it were true that when I finished sewing I carried him to the kitchen, put him on the table and he made food for us? Poor Tibetan women and often men would give me a small piece of cloth and ask me to make it into a bag, that they might take it home to show their mothers what wonderful sewing it did. By degrees we had won as many friends in Tankar as in Kumbum and Lusar, besides we had gathered a fund of information about the nomads of the grass country. Our name and work were known among them many days' journey west and south, and the Scriptures we had given away to visitors were being read in districts to which we never yet had gone.

CHAPTER X

AMONG THE TANGUTS OF THE KOKO-NOR

Tangut Customs—Journey to the Koko-nor—Nomadic Tent-Life—A Glimpse of the Blue Lake—Robbers—Distributing Gospels.

Never since our memorable attempt to reach the Koko-nor under the guidance of Ishinima, had we given up the project of visiting that wondrous lake, not merely because of the pleasure we anticipated at gazing again on an extensive body af water, but rather to spy out the country, get better acquainted with the nomads in their temporary settlements, distribute copies of the Gospels, preach the doctrine, and ascertain the prospects and possibilities of future missionary work among them. These nomads, called Tanguts, or Koko-nor Tibetans, who frequently visited us at Tankar, talked about the lake continually and supplied us with minute information as to the nature of the country through which we should pass. We had become so well acquainted with the Tanguts that, although we knew most of them were robbers, we lost all fear of them. Their costume consists of the ordinary sheepskin gown worn with the woolly side next the body, high top-boots and sometimes a hat with a peaked crown surmounted by a red tassel, and the brim lined with white lambskin. The men have hanging from their girdles their flint and tinder, knife-case, powder-horn, and, stuck through the girdle from right to left is a sword encased in a sheath made sometimes of wood, but often of metal inlaid with silver and stones. When they are traveling they seldom take their hand off the hilt of the sword. Many of them carry also guns and spears. All the smaller baggage, such as the drinking-bowl, snuff-box, money, weighing-scales, etc., is carried inside the blouse. The women could scarcely be distinguished from the men except for the headdress. The hair, thoroughly greased, is braided into fifty or more small plaits which are bound together at the back with wide strips of cloth covered with shells and beads, the whole weighing several pounds, extending below the waist and dangling at every step. The fashion of dressing the hair among the men varies in different localities. Some have the Chinese queue, others have the front hair trimmed into butter-smeared fringes and bangs, while that from the back of the head flies in the wind; others have the hair, augmented by silk or cotton coils, wound round the head and adorned with rings, corals and other stones; still others have their heads utterly unkempt. The women's gowns, like the men's, are held by girdles from which hang knives, needle-cases and other appendages. Both men and women wear a charm-box around the neck, containing a small idol, pieces of old cloth and small parcels of medicine. The women always wear large earrings in both ears, and as many rings on their fingers as they can procure. The men wear an earring generally in the left ear only.

As the fur garments are worn by the Tanguts for years and bathing is unknown, the odor of their bodies is decidedly disagreeable; in my medical capacity I have had to come into such close contact with the Tibetan women as to feel positively nauseated by the smell, and the liberal supply of vermin that sometimes would be on my wrist after feeling a patient's pulse. They seem to suffer no discomfort on account of the vermin. They have no desire to exterminate them; to kill a louse, in fact, is regarded as a sin against the teachings of Buddha, and they rarely do kill them except to eat them. That I have seen them do, picking them not only from their own bodies but from others'.

A visit from a party of these Tangut Tibetans at Tankar we always regarded of great moment, taking the time of every one in the household, some to talk to them, others to doctor the sick ones, as invariably some of them wanted medicine; and nearly always we gave them some of their much-relished brick tea. A call of *aro* at the door, a rush to hold the doorkeeper, our dog Topsy, a quick entrance of several people with their rustling leather gowns, heavy boots, clanging swords, knives and women's headdress announce their coming. Then there are holding out of hands, the profuse salutations with cries of *dimo-dimo-ing,* the presentation of the *khata,* or perhaps a sheep's stomach full of sweet milk, or a piece of butter drawn from the depth of a dirty skin bag, with hands that leave black marks wherever they touch, and some *churma,* all given with liberality and genuine good feeling, and accepted with the greatest grace and thankfulness, because we knew that it was the best they could give, and their hearts came with the gifts. The boy in the meantime is busy in the kitchen preparing a huge pot of tea, and some basins are filled, and much smacking of lips and chitter-chatter shows the genuine enjoyment with which it is partaken of. If there is a man of any social standing among them he is invited into the best room, the one farthest from the entrance, and entertained there. If they are ordinary people they are entertained in the courtyard with rugs spread on the floor, or in the drug-room.

The particular journey into the Tangut country of which I now write was one we made at the invitation of a *panaka,* who requested us to go and operate on the eyes of his aged father afflicted with cataract. The *panaka* provided us with animals to carry our supplies, which consisted of a tent, rugs for bedding, two iron pots, and a wooden basin for each of us, a pair of goat-skin bellows, besides drugs and copies of the Gospels for distribution. For food we took plenty of dried doughstrings, a bag of roasted barley meal, butter, *churma,* a half brick of tea, and some hard baked bread. Bread taken on a journey in this compact form has the advantage of being always very palatable, and of remaining good for months if made well.

Although little Charles was only forty-two days old it was decided that I should accompany the expedition, and the 12th of August, a lucky day in the estimation of the natives, was fixed for our departure. Early in the morning the *panaka* came to our gate with two fine yak and it was not long until we joined the caravan, which consisted altogether of nine yak and one horse, laden with stores, and five ponies with their riders, our *panaka,* a medical lama, and his Chinese bookkeeper, Rahim our Ladaki servant, Mr. Rijnhart and myself. Mr. Rijnhart carried baby, while Topsy with wagging tail ran between the horses' feet as excited as if she too had visions of the Blue Lake.

About five miles west of Tankar, we forded the Hsi-ho (Western River) and turning south-west entered the Ra-la valley, in which we passed a small lamasery of the same name, containing about two hundred priests. At about 5 p. m. we reached the limit of cultivated fields and having met some caravans of merchants on their way to Tankar with wool and barley, camped with them for the night, continuing our journey on the following morning into the western wilderness, leaving every trace of the work of man's hand behind. We had not gone far when one of the yak fell down ill, and, as the Tibetans would not think of leaving the animal in its sad condition, the whole caravan was obliged to pitch tents and wait until he either recovered or died. While we prepared a fire and boiled some tea, the lama doctor, seeing an opportunity to prove his skill, undertook to restore the animal to its wonted vigor. While murmuring low incantations he drew his sword and kept patting the animal's back and sides with it, all the while marching round it and from time to time offering prayers. Now and then he threw a handful of road dust on its head and back. Suddenly the incantations ceased, and the *panaka* was directed to secure a dry herb, twist it into two pyramids and setting fire to them, put one up each of the yak's nostrils. This done, the incantations were resumed until finally the yak gave a vigorous kick and the holy man came to join us at our fire, having concluded that his work was done, or that there was no use continuing any longer. As we thought of the night coming on, we fervently wished the animal would take a sudden change one way or the other. Looking about for a suitable place to pitch our tent, and trying to get reconciled to the idea of passing the night in that robber-infested district, Mr. Rijnhart cast another look at the animal and found he had ceased to breathe, so that we were now able to proceed. The lama had given us reason to believe that this district full of gullies and crevices, favorite hiding-places for thieves, was particularly dangerous, and we were all glad to leave it. At 3 p. m. we crossed the Ra-la, a very high mountain pass, from which we got sight of the Koko-nor, blue indeed and glittering in the bright sun. The Ra-la mountains are rich in iron and there is every indication of the presence of more precious metal. That night we encamped with another caravan of Tibetans, keeping watch during the night, as much for fear of them as of the attacks of brigands. These *panaka* dwelling south of the lake have all more or less the appearance of thieves and robbers, and considering this, it is amusing to witness one of their customs. As soon as a caravan stops, two or three of the men boil the tea, while others unload the yak. When the tea is boiling, all are called around the fire. One of them throws a small lump of butter into the tea, takes the ladle, dips it out, and throws it with a little tea towards the sky. Then all take off their hats and join the man who sprinkled the tea in a kind of prayer, while the latter twice again dips out tea and throws it up. The tea is offered to a god, and the prayer invites him to come and drink it, asking him to keep them from sickness, to give them peace on the road, and to let them meet with only good, honest people. After the tea is finished the same prayer is said again while one man turns out the remaining tea and all the leaves by the side of the camp fire.

Early the following morning we crossed the sand hills by which the lake is lined, after which we followed the shore, over a mile from the water's edge. Here was most beautiful pasture ground, gradually ascending from the water and towering some three to five miles off into lofty mountains, covered with the finest grass. Until noon we saw no tents and then only far out of our way. We stopped at Tso-nitag ("The Lake's Neck") where we were visited by some Tibetans, to whom we talked while tea was being prepared; in the distance we saw a large caravan, recognized as belonging to the Kambas, a wild tribe of Tibetans living farther in, the same barbarians by whom the French travelers, Dutreuil de Rhins and Grenard, were attacked, and the former killed, about four years previous. But they stayed far from us, continuing their march. On the slopes of the mountains we saw herds of antelopes, here and there a stray wolf, and a number of white-headed eagles; also a large species of hawk. The lakeside was literally covered with ducks, geese, sheldrakes and bustards. Our servant shot a goose, but as it tasted so much like sea-water, it was uneatable. In some parts the ground was full of holes, in which live lizards, a small, white bird, and a species of lagomys, all very plentiful. During the night there fell in the valley copious rains, which the chill air of the high altitudes turned into snow, so that with the coming day we saw the mountains covered with their glistening white mantle. It was the 16th of August when we reached the *panaka's* camp, two hundred yards from the water's edge. It included six tents situated close together, while many others were visible further down the shore. As we approached the tents a pack of about twenty of the fiercest dogs imaginable surrounded us, and with hideous yelping sought to drag us from our ponies, being prevented from accomplishing their object only by the arrival of some of the tent people who subdued them with stout clubs. After dismounting we were led to a tent and asked to sit down on some rugs beside a rude furnace made of mud and stones. A handful of *churma* and barley meal was put into a basin, tea poured upon it and a large lump of butter added, the whole being stirred up and handed to us with a polite request that we refresh ourselves with a drink, while our own tent was being erected.

The tents are made of woolen stuff, manufactured by the inhabitants. Inside are four, or sometimes five, poles over which the ropes run that hold up the tent, while outside there are also poles to hold the same ropes tight. The tents which, when viewed from the outside, resemble huge spiders, are invariably black, the inhabitants therefore often being called "Black Tibetans." In the center of the cloth of the tent a narrow strip is left open as an exit for the smoke ascending from the temporary furnace below it, which divides the tent into two parts. To the right of this furnace is the place of honor; in it guests are received, and at night the men sleep there. The left-hand side is occupied by the women, children, and in this case some little goats and young deer. The first night while we were asleep in our tent, a huge dog entered and carried away our candlestick and candle (a home-made one of mutton fat), Mr. Rijnhart's hat as well as all the meat he could get. The candlestick we did not find for days afterwards and the meat not at all, though the hat was not far away, but the incident induced Rahim to hang up nearly everything to the crossbeam of the tent during the remainder of our stay.

The South Koko-nor Tibetans are on the whole jovial, and roars of laughter and merry song are not uncommon in their encampments. Musical instruments are, however, not found among them except the drum and cymbals. Their needs are few, and apparently they are contented, each having his one or two garments, a matchlock, sword, flint and steel, a wooden basin, knife and chopsticks (the latter less needful, the fingers serving). Each family has a tent, some horses, cows and sheep, the number being now depleted, now augmented by the constant robberies practised first by one, then by another marauding tribe. The *panaka* whose guests we were owned about twenty horses, twelve cows and eight hundred sheep, and was regarded as well-to-do. In their primitive way of living they are rather clever, manufacturing themselves the things they need, with few exceptions. We found them much more stingy and dirty than Tibetans from any other part. The women were so filthy that close contact with them inside the tents was as usual nauseating to me, so I spent as much time as possible outside, where they congregated round me and evinced the deepest interest in the white baby. Even the fresh lake breezes, the limpid azure sky above and the crystal clearness of the little stream near by could not drive away the odor of their gowns, or make us unconscious of the abandoned filthiness of their persons. Multitudinous vermin and the accumulated grease of years have made them proof against any further adhesion of dirt. While the men go to the hills, always heavily armed, to guard the flocks and herds, the women remain at home making the butter and cheese, and collecting *argols* to be dried in the sun and used for fuel. Without the slightest scruple they would pass from the manipulation of the *argols* to the mixture of butter, the milking of the cows, or the making of tea, without washing their hands, but simply wiping them off on the grass!

One strange feature about this part of the country was the conspicuous absence of prayer-flags, prayer-wheels or prayer-stones so abundant in every other place inhabited by Tibetans. We saw only one prayer-wheel, and it belonged to a priest, who had come for contributions. Mendicant priests abound even among these nomads and their solicitations are nearly always liberally responded to by gifts of butter, sheep and even cows, horses, or anything else the cause may require. The liberality of these people for religious purposes is proverbial, while they are most niggardly in every other way.

The cattle found among the Koko-nor Tibetans for the most part are the long-haired black ones of the same breed as the yak (*Bos Grunniens*) which flourishes best at high altitudes. They originated from wild cattle and are yet not by any means so tame as cows in the homeland. They grunt instead of bawling and thus remind one of pigs rather than cattle. They are pastured on the hills and in the valleys wherever there is grass. The calves are always driven in a different direction from the cows; both sheep and cattle are rounded up with the help of a sling, made of a piece of flat rope about twenty inches in length on each side of the pouch, all woven of wool. The natives are experts at using these slings and the animals know the sound of them, for often have we seen the girls go through the motion of throwing a stone from them though they had none to throw, when the snap of the sling would be enough to make the animals run. The cattle are driven in at night and tethered, some to either side of long ropes fastened to the ground with pegs, and when milking time arrives the calves have to be mothered by the cows or no milk will be forthcoming. When we read in M. Huc's book, his account of the "stuffed calf" we were incredulous, deciding that it was only a creation of the author's imagination, and we had also affirmed our intention to educate the Tibetan cows that are as primitive as the people, but it was of no avail and we had the mortification of acknowledging ourselves beaten by our own cows. The little calf belonging to one of the latter took sick and died, though, in order to save it, a native woman burned pyramids of edelweiss on its spine, and carried it three times across a fire to prevent the demon from remaining with it. The mother was disconsolate, and refused to give any milk, so we resorted to deception and stuffed the hide of the calf with straw. When milking time arrived the woman carried the calf from the straw room, and the cow complacently licked her stuffed baby while she willingly allowed us to milk her.

The milk is not strained but is scalded, part of it used for tea and to make butter; the other part is mixed with a very little junket left for the purpose from the day before, poured into vessels and allowed to remain; in the morning it is "set" into junket, though not so sweet, and becomes the *sho* so highly esteemed by the Tibetans. The cream removed from the scalded milk is placed in a not scrupulously clean wooden churn and is churned with a dash as our old fashioned churns have; the butter is squeezed by the hands, thereby removing the milk, and pressed into small flat round pieces, or into a skin sometimes with part of the fur in it, or into a sheep's stomach. The butter is very often full of hairs from the animals, and other kinds of dirt, and often streaked with green, but is prized highly as an article of diet. Among some tribes I have heard the older the butter the better it is liked, but wherever we have been, the fresher it is the higher price it commands. The butter-milk is curded and the curds are dried, sometimes in the sun, becoming *churma,* which is eaten with barley meal and tea or with barley meal and butter when there is no opportunity to boil tea, the whole mixed up with the fingers and eaten in lumps.

The meat used by the Tibetans is as a rule mutton, and though the lamas consume large quantities of the meat, they avoid killing it if possible. The natives are exceedingly skilful in catching the very sheep they want out of a flock of several hundred by means of a lasso, and the Tibetans we knew best, unless we expressly desired it otherwise, slaughtered the animals by tying a rope tightly about the nose, thereby cutting off the supply of air. Immediately afterwards the throat was cut, all being accomplished amidst the mumbling of the prayer *Om mani padme hum.* The hide is removed carefully and cured in a primitive manner, becoming the material of which the gowns are made, or perhaps it is shipped to China. Almost every particle of the animal is eaten, the entrails are turned inside out, imperfectly washed and filled with chopped up liver, lights, heart, and kidney, seasoned with salt and mixed with *tsamba,* not unlike haggis when properly prepared. I have seen Tibetans when traveling, cut up the hearts and kidneys, mix some blood with it, put all in a pot, and just bring it to a boil and eat it with great relish. Often they put pieces of meat right on the fire, notwithstanding the kind of fuel they use, and broil it. As a rule the meat is boiled and eaten in large quantities, the fattest being considered the choicest; hence the tail is given to guests as a mark of respect or honor. The bones are picked very clean and then cracked on a stone, or by a sharp blow from a knife, and the marrow removed and eaten. The scapula, or shoulder bone, is put into the fire very often and used to tell fortunes with, according to the cracks made by the heat. Some prayers are usually written on them and they are then hung up near water prayer wheels on strings across a road or near a tent.

The tea is the most important item in Tibetan culinary art, and any one who can make it to suit the fastidious is indeed clever. The tea used is the brick tea, made of the coarse leaves and small twigs of the tea plant in China, pressed into bricks bound around by basket work, and sent up to the Tibetan border on the backs of coolies, and then into the interior of Tibet on the backs of oxen. There are three principal grades and the best grade goes in very large quantities to Lhasa. The brass pot in which the tea is to be made is thoroughly cleaned with some dried *argols* if nothing else is at hand, and, the correct amount of water having been poured in, is placed upon a good fire; the leaves are then in large quantities put into the water, and a little salt and sometimes soda, if they have it, is added, and the whole is thoroughly boiled. The tea is then strained into a churn containing butter and *tsamba* and the whole is churned up into a mixture looking not unlike chocolate, but with a very different taste. The leaves are often used a second time or are fed to the horses. Should the harder brick tea be the kind used, a piece is put in a wooden mortar and with a stone pestle is powdered up and then added to the water. Tea poured into a basin on a piece of butter is drunk in very large quantities, composing the only breakfast partaken of before 10 o'clock. Every one carries along with him in the blouse of his gown his own drinking bowl made of wood, among the better class lined with silver or white metal. The butter sinks into the wood and as it is often rancid, the basin soon takes on a peculiar, not at all inviting odor, especially as the only dishcloth the natives possess is their tongue, the bowl being thoroughly licked out after use. When partaking of Tibetan hospitality, tea drinking is sometimes more of a bore than a pleasure, the pressure brought upon you to drink more, your basin being filled up whenever set down, being so hard to resist, and yet if the butter is not fresh the tea acts almost like an emetic. There is no more genuine hospitality than that to be found among these nomadic people and not to accept it with the grace with which it is proffered, at once raises a barrier between you and them. Frequently we have seen travelers insist upon perfect strangers eating their butter and *tsamba;* and almost invariably the latter would do so, and upon finishing, leave as much of their own in the place of what they had eaten. Delightful, pleasant intercourse with these tent-dwellers living so simple and so natural a life!

In some families the *tsamba* is ground fresh every morning. A half basin of tea with a liberal supply of butter is heaped up with *tsamba* from a skin bag, and without spilling a particle of the meal, the natives skilfully knead the whole into a mass and eat it from the hand in pieces, as we eat bread. It is remarkable that the natives prize the *tsamba* so highly as an article of diet, and yet except in certain places none of the land is cultivated, the people preferring to lead nomadic lives and go sometimes a month's journey for their *tsamba* to doing agricultural work even on a small scale. The barley is used to make *chang,* an alcoholic drink of which the natives imbibe very large quantities. It is made by soaking the barley at a moderate heat for some days and then crushing and straining it. Chinese wine is freely used along the border and even long distances into Tibetan territory. Both men and women drink freely, becoming jovial, and often, if away from home, avaricious and quarrelsome, and pity the poor travelers falling unprotected into the hands of drunken Tibetans.

Among the Koko-nor Tibetans the women are vested with all authority in household affairs. We wanted to barter a knife for another pair of bellows, and the man with whom we bargained said, "I must first go to the tent and ask my wife if I may do so."

As soon as our own tent was erected we repaired to it and were immediately visited by our *panaka* bearing a present of dried meat which we graciously acknowledged. We also had visits from many priests and others with whom we conversed on Christianity, and presented each one with a copy of the Gospels in their own tongue. Our tent was pitched in a charming situation whence we had a splendid view of the lake and its environs. To the south and west stretched ranges of mountains covered with fine grass, their summits burned to crimson by the setting sun. On the other side, like a gigantic jewel of the desert, lay the lake, while faintly visible in the distance beyond its northern and eastern shores other mountain ranges blended their bluey outlines with the sky. The lake is not large, being, according to Rockhill, about 230 miles in circumference.* The same author calculates the altitude as 10,900 feet, while Dr. Sven Hedin places it at 9,975 feet. The lake is, so the natives informed us, fed by seventy-two streams; of these we had already crossed thirty-one, none of them large enough to merit the appellation of river, but they supply man and beast with fresh water, a mission which the Koko-nor with all its beauty cannot fulfill, since its waters are salty. On the side where we were camped there was no beach, the grass continuing right to the water's edge.

In the lake are three distinct islands a considerable distance apart; the western one, a low strip of land, is uninhabited, and is named Tso-ri-wa-ri; the middle one, called Sam-me-che-kur, lying near the southern shore, is a mass of white rock (probably granite, which abounds in all the mountain ranges of the district) rising perpendicular out of the water; the third one, first mentioned by Huc and later by Rockhill and Prjevalski, is called Tso-ri-niah. Projecting high above the surface of the water, it is at once an island and a truncated hill. The natives attribute to it a legendary origin which is as follows: The waters that have formed the Blue Lake flowed into the basin which they now fill through a long subterranean passage leading from Lhasa, the holy city. A god having compassion on the country lest it should be completely inundated,

* Prjevalski's measurement is 266 Kilometers.

placed the Tso-ri-niah mountain rock at the mouth of the passage and caused the flow to cease. Huc has given a most elaborate version of this legend in the second volume of his work. It is only one of the many that have grown up around the lake and islands. As Dr. Hedin passed through the Koko-nor country he heard the following: "In the grey far off days of old, a great lama dug a vast hole in the ground. Then he took a white root and a black root of some plant, and, holding them over the chasm, cut the black root into two halves, out of which the water gushed fòrth in streams until it filled the lake. If he had cut the white root, the hole would have been filled with milk. It was fortunate he cut the root out of which the water flowed, for otherwise the people who lived in those parts would not have been able to keep sheep and so would have had nothing to do. After that the lama went up into a high mountain close by, and broke out of it an enormous piece of rock and cast it into the middle of the lake, and that was how the island was made."*

On the Tso-ri-niah is a small lamasery containing twelve hermit lamas and two incarnations of "living buddhas" one of whom belongs to Gomba Soma. These recluses spend most of their time on the island in prayer and meditation, coming into contact with the "world" only in winter time when they cross on the ice to the mainland to collect contributions of butter, tea, barley-meal, and other provisions necèssary for their subsistence. They are not supposed to eat any meat, but they keep goats on the island to supply them with milk. No

* "Through Asia," by Sven Hedin, Vol. II, p. 1143.

sign of a boat is to be seen along the shore, so that no communication can be had with the mainland in the summer months.

On the day after arrival we expressed our readiness to operate on our patient's eye, but, as the time for moving to their winter quarters had come, we decided at the request of the *panaka's* people to wait two days until they should have moved their camp to the adjoining mountains, to a place which marked the first of three stages to the winter camping-grounds. We distributed Gospels and talked to some priests; had a bath in the lake and saw large quantities of fish. Two days later we moved, making the ascent of a lofty mountain from which in the distance the lake appeared like a sheet of glass. The operation was duly performed and as far as we could ascertain, was very successful. The following day we gave copies of the Gospels to many Tanguts, among others to thirteen priests, who were returning to Tankar from gathering contributions, and were passing our encampment. Two days later the report reached us that they had been attacked and robbed of everything—our books likely having been carried off too. The report of the robbing of the thirteen priests, as well as the losing of their horses, struck fear into the hearts of two lamas who wanted to return, as well as into the hearts of our priest and book-keeper: so they decided to await our return and travel safely under the protection of our fire-arms. On the 2nd of the eighth moon we prepared for the journey. Standing on the mountain height as the rising sun peeped over the eastern ridges and mirrored his glowing face

TANGUT ROBBERS

on the glassy surface of the lake, we inhaled once more the exhilarating breezes that swept across it, and felt in our hearts as we gazed on its placid waters how delightful it would be ever to abide by its shores. But dangers were pressing and duty called us back to Tankar. We must turn away from those beautiful shores and from the watery oasis, so bright and pure, like the lakes that wash the shores of Ontario, my native province. Thou blue inland sea, in silence lifting thy unsullied waters to the pure heavens, reflecting in thy limpid depths the pageantry of the rolling clouds; thou fountain of legends that well up from thy mysterious depths and allure to thy shores the dark faced sons of the desert to worship the Great Spirit whose voice is heard in thy silence; thou sapphire of the wilderness, safely guarded in the embrace of encircling hills, and mirroring the radiances of the sunsets of ages, Aegean in thy grandeur with thy rocky Patmos, we bid thee farewell, but from our souls the apocalypse of thy beauty will never be effaced!

Having some Gospels left we decided to distribute them among the encampments we might meet along the road, and it was not long before we had an opportunity. The priests and people received the books gladly. Mr. Rijnhart estimated that on the trip at least two thousand Tibetans were reached with some knowledge of the gospel. As far as possible we tried to put a book into each tent and since in each is a lama who can read, it is safe to conclude that ten people would hear some reading from each book. On the whole we were much encouraged by this itinerating work, and decided it was a most effective way of preparing these rude, but interesting nomads for the reception of Christian teaching.

CHAPTER XI

TOWARD THE TIBETAN CAPITAL

Lhasa, the Home of the Dalai Lama—Need of Pioneer Work in Inner Tibet—Our Preparations for the Journey.

In the far interior of Tibet, about one hundred miles north of the Himalayan range, sheltered by sacred mountains on every side, is Lhasa, the capital, the only city in the world which is absolutely inaccessible to Westerners. To set foot within its walls has been the ambition of many travelers of the present century; one expedition after another, even after crossing the formidable passes that lead through the natural barriers enclosing the country on the south and west, has been obliged to retreat without a sight of the coveted goal. For the scant information regarding the city we are indebted to Huc and Gabet, probably the last Europeans to visit it (that was in 1846), and to the Indian Pandit A. K., who resided there for some time. The attempts of Prjevalski, Bonvalot, Rockhill, Landor and others to penetrate to the forbidden capital have been in vain, every one of them being obliged by officials to turn back, or, being unable to proceed on account of the hardships they have been compelled to endure. To-day the eyes of the traveler and scientist as well as those of the missionary, are eagerly watching for the development of events that will lead to the downfall of the barriers that too long have kept a people in darkness, and bid defiance to the march of Christian civilization.

During our residence of three years at Kumbum and Tankar, Lhasa had become a subject of almost daily conversation. The four *kushok,* and especially Shar-je-ja-ba had told us much about the city and its surroundings—its great temples, revered priests and the exalted Dalai Lama. Mina Fuyeh had spoken of the sacred college there, and of the many lamas who resort to it from all parts of Tibet to study the profound doctrine of Sakya Muni, and of the multitudes of pilgrims who feel themselves amply rewarded for months of perilous traveling by worshipping in the Dalai Lama's temple with its five golden cupolas, and receiving his blessing by touching his magic scepter. City of mystery and wisdom, what wonder that every lama's supreme ambition is to go there to study or to worship? Many of those who are not able to go in state walk all the distance, often begging as they go, so that they will be no temptation to robbers. Mina Fuyeh often told us that it would cost him a fortune to go, for, being of such high rank himself, he would be expected to give very handsome offerings to the Dalai Lama and the temples in Lhasa, otherwise he would not receive the consideration due him. The necessity of keeping up appearances —the demands that rank entails upon human beings, are the same everywhere, whether in the wilds of Tibet, or in the cultured cities of the west. Mina Fuyeh very conveniently excused himself from undertaking a journey to Lhasa, for he declared that, having paid homage to the potentate in his previous life-time, he did not intend to visit Lhasa again until his next life-time! Not long ago I received news that the former abbot had undertaken a journey to Pekin and Eastern Mongolia, a journey which will bring him a handsome income, as Tibetan lamas in those regions are greatly revered, receiving in exchange for their services the most munificent offerings. I have often thought he was more concerned in accumulating wealth for himself and increasing his own influence than in contributing to the exchequer of the Dalai Lama.

In common with all other missionaries and travelers interested in Tibet, we had thought, read, and dreamed much about Lhasa even before we reached the border, and indeed our hope and faith led us to look forward to the time when the gospel could be preached there, as well as in every nomadic encampment on the Tibetan plateau. We knew moreover that if ever the gospel were proclaimed in Lhasa, some one would have to be the first to undertake the journey, to meet the difficulties, to preach the first sermon and perhaps never return to tell the tale—who knew? Pioneer work in mission fields has from the days of the apostles down to the present entailed its martyrdoms as well as yielded its glorious results. If the opening of Africa meant the sacrifice of a Livingstone, if the Christianization of the South Sea Islands meant the cruel death of John Williams, if the triumphs of the Cross in Uganda were wrought over the body of the murdered Hannington, and if Burmah must be trod by the bleeding feet of Judson and his wife, before the great harvest of five hundred churches can be reaped, could it be possible that all Tibet should be Christianized, that witness of the Christ should be borne in the very stronghold of Buddhism without some suffering, some persecution, nay without tears and blood?

As I have already stated, we felt from the very beginning that we were specially called to do pioneer work; and now that it had been permitted us to travel among the Tanguts of the Koko-nor, preaching, teaching, doctoring, and distributing the Scriptures for many days into the grass country, we were willing to be thrust into other unknown and more distant fields. Not a single missionary was laboring in the Lhasa district, and yet there was the Master's command: "Preach the gospel to every creature." Having prayed that God would open our way to the interior, we had quietly awaited events. We asked that we might be divinely guided at every step and that the means might be provided for the journey. Our prayers were answered and, although we knew not what the results would be, we rejoiced exceedingly that we were counted worthy to traverse for the first time in the name of Christ whole districts in which His name had never been heard. Whether we should ever reach Lhasa or not, we did not know: our desire was to approach as near to it as possible, settle down for a year's work in the far interior, gain the confidence of the people as we had done on the border and then eventually—in God's time

—enter the capital. On the way too, we would take note of all points where missions might be established, conversing with the different tribes and ascertaining their attitude in the matter. Besides this, we had ordered a large supply of Scriptures which we would distribute as we journeyed, and thus our pioneer work would be sanctified by the Word of God, which cannot return unto its Author void. Let it be clearly understood that the purpose of our journey was purely missionary; it was not a mere adventure or expedition prompted by curiosity or desire for discovery, but a desire to approach our fellow men with the uplifting message of Truth and to share with them blessings that God had ordained for all mankind—and we knew that even if our mission apparently failed, the path at least would have been beaten, and that in due time other laborers would be sent forth to carry on the work.

From a human standpoint there was absolutely nothing inviting in such an undertaking. On the frontier the minds of Chinese and Tibetans alike are filled with fear of the great difficulties of the journey to Lhasa, through robber districts, over very high mountain passes, and across large rivers, and to a certain extent we had shared their apprehensions; but after the thrilling experiences of the Mohammedan rebellion, and after coming into such close contact with the people through our residence in the house of the abbot, and especially after our itinerating journeys among the nomads of the Koko-nor, every vestige of fear was gradually removed. Frequent and intimate conversations with merchants, lamas and others, including many women, who had been backwards and forwards from Lhasa several times, took away the terror of passes, rivers, arid wastes, and death-dealing winds, of which we had heard so much, and Inner Tibet did not seem so far away, so impossible to reach, as we had at first been led to believe.

Shar-je-ja-ba and many others from the sacred city had told us that we might go as far into the country as we chose, even to within one day's journey of the capital, and stay as long as we wished, provided we did not try to go to their city of worship, as contact with Europeans would defile their high priest. Knowing that a passport from the Sining Amban or Tartar General would give us the good-will of the people beyond the districts where we ourselves were so well known, Mr. Rijnhart applied for one, though other travelers going in from China, scrupulously avoid allowing this official to know they are going into Tibet, as he would not permit them to proceed, did he know their intentions. However, our aid to the soldiers and other wounded during the rebellion, was so much appreciated, that we felt if any one could procure a passport from this man we were in a good position to do so. He was very friendly indeed, but said much as he would like to help us he had not the power to give us a passport, because our Chinese ones were only for the Sze Chuan and Kansu provinces, and advised us that the next passport we applied for at Shanghai or Pekin should be made out for Kansu and the Tsing-hai or Koko-nor, and upon it he could then give us one in Tibetan which would enable us to travel in safety. Mr. Rijnhart then asked him to give us a letter saying to those who read it that we were on a peaceful mission, and that the people had nothing to fear from us; whereupon he replied that he would gladly do so, but that he could not affix his official seal, so we refused the letter, knowing that did we show to the Tibetans a letter purporting to be from the Amban, and they looked for his seal which was not there, they would think a lama had written it and at once conclude we were dishonest, so it would do more harm than good. However, he said that though he could not give us a passport or an escort, he had no power to prevent our going, and added that we might go where we chose, and stay as long as we wished.

When it became known among the natives that we intended to make a journey into the interior, our friends, though they tried to dissuade us, did all in their power to help us make our preparations. Without this help we would not have known just how to arrange, for in a country like Tibet, the natives know how to manage transport animals, pack-saddles, hobbles, food, etc., better than foreigners do. At this time Rahim was of inestimable value to us, and forwarded our going as no other servant could have done, for our journey would take him in the direction of his home in Ladak, and he was anxious to see his mother and friends who were in all probability mourning him as dead. We first decided how many men we would take with us, and then calculated how much food we would need, and so how many animals we would have to purchase. We already knew the danger of having too little food, and Rahim did not allow us to forget that either, having narrowly escaped dying from hunger in the far unpopulated interior. We did not wish to be at the mercy of petty chiefs, who might choose to dictate, saying that if we did not accede to their wishes they would not permit the people to sell us any food, a calamity that had already befallen travelers among these exclusive nomads. To avoid being boycotted in the above mentioned way, we decided to take with us food enough to last us two years, hoping we would be beyond the border for that length of time. There were two reasons why we did not take a large caravan. One was our belief that a small caravan would excite less suspicion and covetousness, and another was the fact that a small caravan would be more easily managed, requiring fewer servants to look after it. We would also have less trouble in looking after them, and further we would not require such large quantities of supplies. We decided to take only two men besides Rahim, and would therefore need five riding animals and twelve pack-animals. Besides this we sent some camel-loads ahead to the Ts'aidam, a Mongol settlement about a month's journey from Tankar.

Every year a large caravan of *kopas,* who have been trading on the border and at Pekin, leaves Tankar for home, and as the roads over the mountains are impassable in winter time, the beginning of the fourth moon is fixed as the date for starting. In the spring of 1898, this time fell about the middle of May, so all our plans were laid for leaving at the same time as this caravan, many of whom we knew very well. Tankar was a busy place indeed amid all the preparations for the departure of such an immense caravan, providing

animals, food and other things requisite for a journey of nearly three months. Though the *kopas* come out of Tibet with yak, they usually sell these animals on the border and buy mules for the return journey, the latter commanding a high price in the interior. Seeing that we expected to stay some time in the Ts'aidam we did not deem it wise to take mules, since they do not winter as well there as horses. Besides, we did not purpose to burden ourselves with grain to feed our animals, and with mules, grain is indispensable. Until we had bought the required number of horses, our courtyard presented oftentimes a peculiar aspect, and it was laughable to see some of the animals brought to us for sale by those who thought foreigners did not know very much about ordinary everyday life and its requirements; there were horses large and small, fat and lean, diseased and lame, and some with beautiful saddles under which were deep sores. On the borders of Tibet all bargaining between two persons is done through a middleman, up whose sleeve the seller puts his hand, and by the way he grasps the different fingers of the former's hand, makes known his price; whereupon the buyer is notified in the same silent and unseen manner. He then tells the middleman how much he is willing to give, and so backwards and forwards in the sleeves the price is arranged. As the business becomes brisk, however, the silence is broken, and often gives way to general confusion. There were pack saddles to be provided for our transport horses, and one must be careful not to be induced to buy yak saddles, instead of mule or horse saddles, for they are entirely

unsuitable. Pack saddles are made of wood consisting of two horizontal pieces for sides, joined to each other over the back of the horse by two rounded pieces, one in front and one behind, padding, straps and ropes completing the outfit. Blacksmiths were busy making iron hobbles—chains with cuffs which are fastened on the forefeet of one or more horses, and locked, the owner keeping the key. These are used to prevent the animals being stolen at night, and are a native invention, while others woven of wool and yak-hair are used to keep them from straying too far away when grazing, and to make the catching of them when wanted an easy matter. While horses, saddles, ropes, etc., were being got ready, we had tailors and women making for us all the Tibetan clothing we might need, and though Chinese tailors are nuisance enough when sewing for you, they bear no comparison to Mongolians and Tibetans. Never had we dreamed of the difficulties of getting garments made, so many different kinds of workmen were required; the one who cut could not sew and *vice versa,* so a lama made our good cloth gowns, a *kopa* made up the *pulu,* while a Mongol woman made the under-jackets and collars, putting silk stitching on them.

Little Charlie was well supplied with clothing made in English style, having, besides a little fur *ja-ja,* or sleeveless jacket, a fur cape and shoes, and for ceremonial occasions, a Tibetan gown and sash. No one enjoyed the busy time as well as he, for he was carried around in Rahim's arms during shopping, bargaining, etc., raising his voice in approbation as the natives be-

came excited over a transaction, and taking a general delight in the entire proceedings.

On April 5 we had an interesting visit from the Kor-luk *pei-si,* who is, so the Mongols informed us, the biggest prince in the Wu Ts'aidam, his dominions lying four days north from Barong, the place through which caravans go to Lhasa. He was a tall, rather well built man with the true Mongolian type of face, well dressed, with a turban of raw dark-red silk wound in yards around his head. He had about fifty Mongols with him, including many women, among whom was the *Achi* of the prince, but whether she was his wife or not, we could not clearly find out. The women were tall, two or three of them young and very good looking, and all were dressed in new sheepskin with borders of red cloth around the bottom and up the side. The right arms hung free from the gowns, displaying under-jackets of white, with green cloth trimming stitched in many-colored bright silk thread, while strings of beads from one earring to the other fell down to the bosom. A beaten silver wine bottle with screw top, and amulets hung in front of the gown. The hands were bedecked with rings set in coral and stones, the head was crowned with a small hat with white lamb on the brim, and a red tassel surmounting the peaked crown, giving a coquettish, graceful air to their persons. They all enjoyed their visit very much, the peals of laughter at Charlie, the sewing machine, and some little dolls, adding to the enjoyment of all. The chief was so anxious to have a pair of *kutsi* sewed on the machine, that he sent a man to the street to bring the cloth, but on his return no one could cut them out, so we gave him a pair of Mr. Rijnhart's in return for the cloth and he presented us with a piece of *pulu* (a piece is usually ten lengths from the finger tips of one outstretched arm to those of the other), and a lump of sugar from India by way of Lhasa. This chief hired for us two camels to carry loads as far as the Ts'aidam, to be left with the Dzassak of Barong, each one to carry 240 catties, the two to cost ten taels, worth at that time seven dollars. That night we worked until midnight, sewing bags for grain, and packing two boxes which contained, among other things, over four hundred Tibetan Gospels, and three hundred of Mrs. Grimke's text cards. In the morning early, the Mongols came for the loads. As usual, there was the regular grumbling at the weight, a pretence at giving back the money because the Mongols' scales were lighter than ours, before finally the camels were gently made to kneel, their burdens were tied on, and off went the first of our goods into the, for us, unknown.

As we appreciated the quiet that settled down upon our courtyard after the bustle of that departure was over, our hearts had a thankful yet strange feeling, as we spoke of the kindness the native chiefs had invariably shown us, and of the future with its new friends and surroundings; while Ani, good old soul, congratulated us on the great saving these camels would be to our horses as far as the Ts'aidam. Nothing was too much trouble for her to do in the way of helping us, and oftentimes tears would bedim her eyes as she looked at me and baby, who always laughed at her; perhaps thinking of her loneliness after we were gone, perhaps of the possibility of our not returning to Tankar, and even of the uncertainty of life in the far interior. My heart sometimes overflows as I think of the love and tenderness of these dark-faced women, and wish it were within my power to do more for them, to bring them out of the condition in which they live into the liberty which the gospel brings to woman wherever it is known. But we had to hurry with more preparations, and by May 20, we were ready to leave our home, where the greatest gladness had been ours, where our mail had come to us regularly, where bright, long-loved blossoms had added joy and sweetness to our labor of love among the people, and launch out into new places away from friends and associations, as well as the possibility of getting letters and papers from the homeland. We had deemed it wise to give up our house, over whose ownership there had been a lawsuit, the result of which made it unsafe for us to retain it during our absence; and we rented three rooms in another courtyard where we stored our sewing machine, some books, and other things we did not want to take with us, the landlord promising that we could have the whole house upon our return. This made it necessary for us to move the things to be left, at the same time that we were doing the packing of what we wanted to take, thereby increasing our work.

Our greatest difficulty was the securing of two men to accompany us on the journey, and for a long time it seemed as if no one suitable would offer for service, everyone having a sincere fear of perils in the interior, which had been much augmented by the tales told the year before by the men of Captain Wellby's expedition. However, through real friends we secured two men who could speak Tibetan, Mongolian and Chinese. The older, named Ja-si, was very dark, tall, neat in his attire, an earring in his left ear, and a great swagger in his walk; while he knew everything about everybody and every place, and had no fear of going wherever the foreign teacher wished him to. The younger, named Ga-chuen-tsi, was a relative of an old Mongol friend of ours, and was a short, fat-faced, laughing boy of twenty-two, always happy, except when Ja-si, of whom he stood in awe, influenced him. Of the three we liked him best, his disposition was so bright. Rahim, who was a sort of overseer, was an adept at dealing with Tibetans from the interior, Ja-si had had a Fan-tsi wife, and so was perfect in his manner towards them, while Ga-chuen-tsi was more at ease with the Mongols, which probably accounted for his cheerful, smooth manner. We provided them all with clothing and bedding, as usual, giving the relatives of the two men we had just hired a portion of their wages, which were to be four taels a month with the understanding that if we sent them back, we were to give them each a horse to ride and food, with a gun if they served us well, all of which was duly put into an agreement signed by *pao-ren*, "security."

Our supply of food was mostly native and consisted of the following:

616	catties	Tsamba (barley meal).
490	"	Wheat flour.
150	"	Kua mien (vermicelli).
300	"	Rice.
140	"	Barley.
40	"	Butter.
40	"	Brick Tea.
20	"	Sugar.

Besides these native supplies we had some stores intended mainly for Charlie, such as milk, sago, tapioca, cornstarch, arrowroot, oatmeal, etc., with some meat extract and soups. The grain, flour, and rice were put into bags made of white drilling, inside coarse native woolen sacks, just the size to constitute one half a load. The *kua mien,* stores and goods for bartering, were put into boxes, the latter consisting of buttons, needles, silk, silver and gold thread, cloth, *khatas,* otter fur and boots. Our drugs, clothing, bedding, instruments, books and sundries constituted the remainder of the loads, except the tents, of which we had two, one small, very warm white one, and one large dark blue one, with iron tent-pegs for each. Such was our equipment when the last bale was put up and we were on the eve of leaving the gates of Tankar.

CHAPTER XII

FAREWELL TO TANKAR

Leaving Faithful Friends—Our Caravan Moves Off—Through the Grass Country to the Desert—Two Mongol Guides.

With the help of our two men, our preparations were nearly all complete at daybreak on the twentieth of May. There remained yet one horse to buy, and for that of course, we had to pay double price, as everybody knew we were in a hurry. After breakfast the last remains of our housekeeping at Tankar, the big pots, were removed from our clay range and taken over to the storehouse which we had rented for two years. Mr. Rijnhart and Mr. Uang, a Chinese merchant from the eastern gate, proceeded, as a final precaution against thieves, to seal up the doors and windows. Mr. and Mrs. Uang were both profuse in their demonstrations of kindness and solicitude for our welfare, the latter, just before our departure, bringing us a delicious, refreshing dish of home-made *m'ien.* Other friends followed with gifts of various kinds, principally food stuffs to be used on the road. Ani and Doma, their eyes moist with tears, attentive to the very last and unwilling to yield to any in the matter of bestowing mementos, brought us a set of artistically woven straps with which to fasten the chopsticks to our girdles. One by one the horses were saddled and led out into the street where many willing hands were waiting to adjust the loads. All along the street the gateways were filled with women and children who had come out to watch the unusual scene. No greater interest could have been manifested if we had been high officials or great Buddhist dignitaries leaving on an important mission or pilgrimage to some distant shrine.

As soon as all the animals were loaded the caravan began to move slowly toward the western gate, and within a few moments seventeen of our ponies and our three men disappeared from view. Mr. Rijnhart and I remained behind, knowing that we could easily overtake them, while dear old faithful Ani brought us one more pot of hot tea, of which we partook with full hearts. Then we visited once more each room of the home to which we had become so attached, as if we had a sort of half unconscious presentiment that we would for a long time, and perhaps never, enter it again. As the term for which our rent was paid had not yet expired, we locked the door with a key the landlord had given us, much to the chagrin of his opponent in the lawsuit, who stood ready to rush in the moment we were gone, and claim the house on the principle that "possession is nine-tenths of the law." Then taking an affectionate farewell of our Chinese friends, many of whom we had learned to love sincerely, and followed by the more demonstrative Tibetans and Mongols, men, women and children, we sadly marched toward the great gate which all the time we were dreading, as we realized more vividly at every step how many devoted friends it would shut away from us. One man carried baby, and all remarked how white the little hands looked around his dark neck. Doma rushed away crying, the last good-byes were said at the city gate and we sped to overtake our caravan. Such a heart wrench! We scarcely realized the bond there was between us and the natives until we came to part, and then how the tears flowed! The future was veiled, or we might have hesitated—it would have been but human—and stayed indefinitely in dear old Tankar.

Never had the country around about seemed so beautiful. Vegetable gardens and harvest fields were green; the hills presented a different shade of the same refreshing color, and the river was bright and shimmering in the distance. A blue haze hung over the mountain tops which beckoned us on, holding out to us hopes of brightness in the new fields of labor we would reach in the regions beyond, which would, in a measure, compensate for the sorrowful partings of the day. Suddenly our thoughts were snatched from the future to the present by our coming in sight of one of our horses which, violently objecting to his load, finally succeeded in kicking it off, and smashing the saddle. This horse afterwards became Ja-si's, as he would never allow a load to be put on his back, but was as docile as a child when ridden. The experience of that day was that of every caravan on the first day of its march; there was the usual trouble with the horses and almost endless readjusting of baggage and saddles.

Skirting the Hsi-ho we passed the Tsa-ta-si, where lived the lama who had made some of our clothing, and reached at 5:30 the village of Pa-uen-chuan-tsi, on the opposite side of the river, approached by a cantilever bridge. Here we pitched our tents which Ga-chuen-tsĭ endeavored to make look as gorgeous as possible, as his people lived in the village and he wished to present a good appearance. We had a time of feasting and another series of good-byes accompanied with presents of potatoes, cakes, bread and milk, with peas and straw for our horses. This is the very last cultivated land, all the country beyond being *tsao-ti* or grass country.

As we were to spend Sunday at Gomba Soba* with friends, we started next morning and in a short time reached the lamasery, the same one we sneaked past on our proposed visit to the lake with Ishinima in 1895. I may say in passing that the lamasery is rightly located by Mr. W. W. Rockhill in his "Land of the Lamas" and that Capt. Wellby is quite wrong in his attempt to correct him. Here was the home of Tsanga-Fuyeh, the biggest "living buddha" in the lamasery, who had been so instrumental in securing friends for us through recommending us as doctors, and the dear old man came to our tent to visit us accompanied by his young lama acolyte, bringing a parcel of sultanas and a *khata*. He warned us about robbers and passes, and exhorted us to hurry back to Tankar before he died, that he might see us again in this life. He also gave us a beautiful *tsamba* basin, and a horse already saddled. In appre-

* This lamasery is also known as Gomba Soma. "Soma," and in some districts "Soba" is the word for "new" and "Gomba" means "lamasery."

ciation of his courtesy we gave him a feather pillow, which he thought was a most wonderful invention. For a while he seemed utterly to lose himself in the delight of shaking it up and down till it swelled to its utmost limit, then sitting on it and reducing it again. Pei-Fuyeh, a "living buddha" of the same rank, had his treasurer living at Gomba Soba, and this man, who had long been a friend of ours, brought us a large lump of loaf sugar, a parcel of dates and a little enamel pitcher for Charlie. Sunday evening a party of travelers camped beside us, consisting of the wife and young son of a Wang-yeh of the Mongols, another Mongol woman with her little girl, and three men. They had nineteen mules and horses and invited us to travel with them. The two children were about twelve years of age, dressed in cloth, the boy's clothing having a predominance of yellow indicating his rank. They were betrothed, and were being taken to Lhasa to worship and be blessed by the Dalai Lama before entering life together. It was refreshing to see them enjoy play, and rather pitiful to see them tied by their feet to the stirrups when about to ford rivers, for fear of a dizziness overcoming them, causing them to fall off. The boy's mother was intelligent, well dressed and very clean, even washing her teeth, though her finger was her only brush.

The *kopas* broke camp before daylight, traveling a few hours and then allowing their animals the whole day to graze. Although we did not start with them each morning, yet we always overtook them and were camped alongside them every day. The Mongol women would invite me and Charlie into their tent to rest and drink tea, while their men would help us to unload our animals and pitch our tents. Natives are adepts at selecting beautiful camping spots, and when we would see the encampments of the *kopas* in the distance, the white tents of various size and shape with hundreds of horses and mules grazing about, the luxuriant grass and low rolling hills, the poetry of it all struck responsive chords in our hearts. Late in the afternoon the men from the various tents went out and drove in their mules and horses, to receive their apportionment of split peas. How tame some of the mules were, going up to the tent doors and sniffing about, and asking in as plain a manner as possible for food. By and by they were tethered and saddled ready for the morning, then the men gathered about drinking their tea, and, as dusk settled down near us all, their voices were heard from near and far chanting prayers, accompanied by the ringing of bells. Then quiet reigned and everyone slept well.

The average march the first days was twelve miles, our road going through a wide valley, then along the Hsi-ho for ten miles, crossing a tributary and on for thirty miles, where we camped on the northwest corner of a little lake, really a bay, cut off from the Koko-nor by drifting sand, and called Baga-nor. The country was on the whole grassy and well watered, affording the nomads good pasturage. Many Mongol tents were dotted on either side of the road in the sheltered places and wherever the green fodder was most plentiful. Some Tibetans were also camped near the streams that flowed into the Koko-nor. Crossing the Balema gol, we camped again on the shores of the Koko-nor, next day crossed the Iki Olan, probably the same as is called Ulen Muren by Rockhill, though the latter name the natives do not seem to know at all. On Sunday, much to our regret, we were obliged to part with the *kopas,* they going on at their usual early hour, and we remaining behind to rest for the day. The people from the tents of the nomads in the neighborhood came about us freely, and we did some doctoring, for which we got a fat sheep. We also gave away some Tibetan Scriptures and text-cards. No missionary had ever been in this locality before. The next stage of our journey led us through one of the supposed robber districts, and we did not feel any too comfortable when we saw that we were being spied by four men; suddenly they disappeared over a hill, and after a little while reappeared over another hill near the road, heavily armed. On seeing our men ready with their rifles to defend our stuff, they rode up, asked a few simple questions and passed on. Shortly afterward we met the chief of the Wortug Tibetans who had a large caravan, and he said the four men were robbers. We crossed the bed of the Buha gol, the most important river in the district, although we found it nearly dry, and camped on one of its tributaries. Here we saw large herds of kiang or wild mules, called by the Chinese *ie mah* or wild horses. They are not more than fourteen hands in height, and are beautifully colored, light brown on the back, gradually fading into white on the belly. They have long ears and tails like an ordinary mule, are always found in herds and families, and, when trotting or galloping, go in single file. The animals were exceedingly bold, coming quite near our tents and mingling with our horses. They are ornamental rather than useful, the Tibetans in vain having tried to tame them for domestic use.

In this spot where the grass was so good we halted for a rest, and Rahim provided us with a most refreshing repast in the shape of twelve fishes which he had caught with his hands in the stream. A Tibetan came two days' journey offering us a large piece of green denim in exchange for medicine. He had heard from other Tibetans that some wonderful doctors were passing through, and did not want to miss an opportunity of consulting us.

The next part of the road took us through a part of the country with poor grass, and over a pass, at the top of which was a large *obo,* a heap of stones, with prayer-flags flying from the top. On nearly all the passes these *obos* are to be found. In all probability they were originally intended simply as landmarks to point out the road, as smaller mud ones are still in use for that purpose; but the mountain *obos* have long since taken on a religious significance. Whenever the natives reach the *obo* at the top of a difficult pass they all dismount, each throws a stone on the heap, and passing to the right of it, all join in chanting their gratitude to the god of the mountain for helping them to ascend. We have frequently seen our men observe this somewhat romantic ceremony, and they were much perplexed that we did not follow their example. All that day we searched in vain for water, and, when emerging from a valley, rejoiced to behold a sparkling lake, but it turned out to be the Tala-dabesun-nor, a salt lake, nearly dry. Deviating from our direct southwesterly route, we found good grass and fresh water about eight miles north of the lake, and learned that the apparent drought was caused by the natives having drained off all the water for the purpose of irrigation. This district would be wealthy but for an inroad of southern Tibetans probably from across the Yellow River, who drove off 50,000 head of cattle and sheep at one sweep, reducing the entire settlement to poverty. Knowing that we were nearing a marsh and that our trail was not any too distinct, we hired two Mongols, and, as is the custom in this part, paid their wages in advance to a middleman, a native doctor, who stood as guarantee for the good conduct and fidelity of the men. They were to take us to Barong. We learned that the Tala-dabesun-nor is called thus to distinguish it from Serkin Dabesun-nor; the former belongs to Tsing hai Wang's district, the latter to the Korluk Bei-si district.

The two Mongols were types, one of them an old man, thin, sharp featured, and very talkative and agreeable, the other a lama who had a wife whom he had stolen from another man near Barong. Therefore he was anxious not to pass through her native settlement. He was young, round-faced, with shaven head, and kept to himself, counting beads, and burning scapulæ to see what fortune had in store. Whenever he saw people, he disappeared so as not to be seen by them for fear, we presumed, of being recognized. Our Mongols

A TIBETAN TRAVELER

at first insisted upon going a southern road to Barong, saying it was shorter and there was not so much danger of being lost in the marsh; but fearing the sudden appearance of marauding bands of Tibetans from south of the Yellow River, we decided upon the northern road. This road led up towards a pass named Shara Kuto, and when about ten miles from the top we stopped where there was good grass, and water flowed in a small stream intermittently; one moment there was water and the next moment there was none. The people there were well-to-do, the women wearing their sheepskins in the early morning, and when the sun grew warmer putting on their *pulu* gowns. I felt sorry for one poor young woman who had the Mongol headdress, and upon asking her how that came, she replied that she was a Mongol whom a Tibetan had secured for a wife. The morality of the people just here was at a lower ebb than in many other places, the women especially acting, even in our presence, in an unseemly manner. Next day we were much refreshed by seeing evergreen trees, the first trees of any kind we had seen since the day we left home, and we were also rejoiced to camp on level ground on the southern bank of the Dulan gol, in sight of the Dulan Si on the opposite side of the river, while to the northeast was the Tsahan-nor, a small lake hidden from sight in its sheltered spot enclosed by three hills. Dulan Kao is a very small cluster of houses, composed mostly of lamas' homes and the residence of the prince of the Tsing hai, all built of mud brick surrounded by walls. The trail on the north bank of the river is covered with stones, but Mr.

Rijnhart and Rahim pursued that road while our caravan stayed on the south, crossing later and camping on the north bank, where there was good grass, and plenty of the most bloodthirsty mosquitoes. Dulan Kao as well as being the capital of the *wang-yeh's* dominions seemed also to be just inside the boundary of the mosquito district, for the Mongols had told us blood-curdling tales of those pests when we passed the village, and we found them only too true.

We were now facing the famous marsh, where travel was impossible unless along narrow trails, which were often not to be found except by the help of the guides. The northeast part of the plain was cultivated, watered by irrigation ditches; the southern was the marsh which we found quite dry along the trail, and only had difficulty once crossing a small stream, although our Mongols assured us that had it not been dry weather we might have found it impassable. There were two lakes in this large plain, between which our road lay; the larger one was Serkin Dabesun-nor, the western half of which was dry salt and saltpetre. It receives its water supply from the Katsa gol flowing from Dulan-nor, and another stream from the west. The Dulan nor is fed by the Dulan gol which flows past Dulan Kao. After passing the marsh we halted about a mile north of the Timurté mountains and south of the Dabesun-nor, where we came across a camp recently occupied by the *kopas*. Here we found only brackish water. Our route continued in a south southwest direction, mountain ranges on either side of us, at first of dolerite, then pudding stone, changing finally into sand-hills, some of them very high.

The sand-hills marked the beginning of the desert of Koko beileh, too barren to support any population, but roamed over by herds of kiang and antelopes. When we came within sight of the bed of the Tsa-tsan gol which was then dry, the load fell off one of our horses, and the animal exulting in the unexpected freedom, scampered away in the direction of home. As we sat by the roadside waiting until Rahim should bring him back, the guides told us there was water around the corner of the last hill to the right directly away from the road. When the pony was caught and his load re-adjusted we crossed the river bed where the road was not recognizable, and reached Talin Turgen, where we found a basin of bad water on the side of a hill, but abundance of grass and mosquitoes. While we were striking camp the next morning six deer suddenly darted from the underbrush near us, followed shortly afterwards by a bear. We were all mounted, so no attention was paid to the deer, but Rahim asked permission to have a shot at bruin, which being granted he started in pursuit, followed by such remarks from the older Mongol as "No good will come of it. Those animals are not to be touched." We saw the boy in the distance dismount and tie his horse to some brush, when the bear returned, as we afterwards saw, for her cub, whereupon the Mongol jumped off his horse, got his gun ready for firing, saying, "He is coming, he is coming; we will all be killed," and then told us a story of eight men who had been killed by a bear because one of them had attacked him. Just as Mr. Rijnhart was starting to Rahim's rescue, the two bears turned and made off with rapid strides towards the hills. Rahim's horse had run away and he came towards us, his eyes full of fear, and told us how the "wild man" (the Chinese and some Mongols call bears *ie-ren,* wild men) had stood up and looked at him, and how having fired all his cartridges he took his sword in his hand and crept away. He never wanted to shoot a bear afterwards. The old Mongol carried a scar as a result of the episode, for in dismounting quickly, his gun had struck his head and made a deep gash. He took some of the tinder (scorched edelweiss, a fluffy vegetable) and put it in the wound to stop the bleeding.

We were glad to find a pleasant camping ground to the right of the road on the banks of the Sulim gol in which was the best water we had for days and along whose banks our horses found good green grass. Here our lama-guide deserted us, taking off with him the pot and food the two of them expected to use on their return journey. Ergetsu, the next camp, was an oasis in the desert, there being good water and grass, but the march the day following was through wearisome sand dunes until we passed the Shara gol, where our second guide deserted us. Happily we found good water, but were again nearly eaten up by mosquitoes. From this pest a piece of fine netting saved baby and me, while Mr. Rijnhart kept a smoky fire all the time in the other tent; while traveling we wore *khatas* sewed into veils. After passing the Tso gol springs we lost our way and went on and on through a very wide dry river bed, in the bottom of which there had recently been running water, but which was now covered only with red earth. Towards dusk a small party of Mongols, who had been farming over the hills and who were moving their encampment to Barong, stopped beside us. They told us that the dry river bed was that of the Bayan gol, in crossing which Rockhill had experienced such difficulty owing to the mud. At their kind invitation we followed the Mongols to their camp along a road which led through a brushwood thicket in which bloomed an abundance of flowers resembling spirea, except that they were pink. How gladly we plucked them, for we had not seen a flower since leaving Tankar. The Mongol women decked their hair with them, and seemed to rejoice with us that the desert and all its barrenness was past and we were again in the midst of flowing water, green grass and fresh food.

CHAPTER XIII

IN THE TS'AIDAM.

The Ts'aidam and its People—Polyandry and Cruelty to the Aged—The Dzassak of Barong—Celebration of Baby's Birthday—Missionary Prospects.

We had now arrived in the Ts'aidam, a large plain some six hundred miles from east to west lying north of the Kuenlun Mountains. It is called Wu Ts'aidam by the Chinese (Wu means five) because it is divided into five states, Taichiner, Korluk, Koko, Dsun and Barong. The small district of Shang east of Barong is also usually included in the Ts'aidam, although politically it is distinct. It was given by the Mongol princes to the Dalai Lama and is governed by a representative from Trashil'unpo who is changed every five years. The other states are governed under the authority of the Sining Amban by Mongol princes, each of whom receives annually a government grant of from one hundred taels and four pieces of satin, to twelve hundred taels and eight pieces of satin. The satin is called *mangtuan,* being of a special design ornamented with yellow dragons and used exclusively by the chiefs, and to adorn temples. It is worth from twelve to twenty taels a piece, according to the quality. The population of the five states is estimated at from 8,000 to 16,000, for the most part Western Mongols, but among them are found many Eastern Mongol lamas who are here allowed to have wives, a privilege which is denied them in Inner Tibet or Mongolia. The Ts'aidam Mongols, as far as we were able to ascertain, practise polyandry, and marriages are often arranged for a limited length of time. It is not uncommon for traders, Chinese, Mongolian or Tibetan, to secure wives for a certain period of time, perhaps six months, a year or two years, and when they go to their own homes again, the children are left with the so-called wife. As a rule the Chinese look down upon the very loose marriage laws prevailing among these nomads, but in Tankar a respectable Chinese woman told me that Chinamen often rented or leased their wives to other men for a time varying from one day to several years. Though this may be done in that locality I have no idea that it is a usual occurrence in China, and is probably a custom born of contact with the nomads. There is another thing which stamps the inhabitants of the Ts'aidam very low in the scale of civilization and humanity, and reveals their need of the socially uplifting influence of Christianity, and that is their treatment of the aged. In many cases the old people as soon as they are no longer able to work are ejected from the house or tent, and compelled to eke out their remaining days in a cave or on a dunghill, where they soon succumb from exposure or lack of nourishment. For most cases of such treatment the daughter-in-law is responsible. Almost immediately upon entering the home she assumes a tyrannical authority over her husband's parents, making it exceedingly uncomfortable for them, denying them the necessities of life, and never ceasing until in exasperation her husband is goaded on to the cruel deed. Many of the natives speaking with us on this matter, said how much better it was to have daughters than sons, for the parents who had daughters only, would not run the same risk of being cast off in their helplessness at the instigation of a daughter-in-law. In strong contrast to the treatment of the aged by the Ts'aidam Mongols is the filial piety of the Chinese, which is occasionally carried to excess, the old people being allowed the role of tyrant, sometimes beating their grown-up sons and daughters severely with no resentment or retaliation from the latter.

The Mongols are exceedingly polite in their way. When two strangers meet they hold out both hands with the palms turned upward, and make a graceful bow uttering the salutation *Amur sambina.* A present is acknowledged simply by holding it up to the forehead; they have no words to express thanks. Their religion is as conspicuous as their politeness. While attending to their daily duties, whether drawing water, tending the flocks, gathering *argols,* churning butter, or whatever it may be, they never cease to mumble prayers. Besides this, each settlement supports a number of lamas who are engaged to chant for them, and thus assist them in the accumulation of merit. These Mongols seemed quite averse to accepting the copies of the Gospels in Tibetan which we offered them, but the *kopas,* who were then trading in the district through which we passed, took them with great eagerness and apparent pleasure. Most of the Mongols here are nomads, although they do some farming, raising all the barley they require. Whether they engage in agriculture or are pure nomads they must pay a certain tithe of their income in taxes to their chief. They dwell in tents; the houses which compose the villages are of a very inferior order and are used mostly as storerooms. The village of Barong, the home of the *dzassak*, or chief, is composed of a few mud-brick dwellings and is situated about eight miles from the foot of the Kuenlun mountains. The food of the Mongols here is the same as that of the Tibetans, and like the latter they make wine, and also a sort of koumiss from mare's milk.

They are good-natured, simple, cowardly enough to be afraid of the Tibetans, and proverbially honest, though from experience we found it best not to trust them implicitly. The spot where we were encamped was rather low ground, and in the center of a large encampment of Mongols, very near to some of their tents. The grass was excellent as was also the water, and considerable underbrush stretched about us. When it rained the place was turned into a veritable mudhole, the ground being of a sort of clay formation, and various ditches had to be dug to keep the water from our tents and fire. Our camel loads of goods sent on from Tankar in advance had arrived safely, and were in the hands of the Barong *dzassak*, but being in need of rest for both ourselves and our animals, we stayed in our first camping place for a few days, employing our time in bartering and chatting with the natives, and in writing letters. We feasted on fresh meat, milk and butter, but had to be careful that we did not unintentionally buy butter made of camel's milk, which the natives offered for sale. Cattle were very scarce in this locality, owing partly to the plague which had carried off thousands of them, and partly to the inroads of the Goloks, the mortal enemies of the Mongols, and of whom the latter are desperately afraid. Young girls and women came to see me frequently, bringing butter to barter for silk and gold thread. They were dressed for the most part in long *pulu* garments with little jackets underneath, their hair done either in many plaits fastened with cloth at the back or divided into two larger plaits, one on each side, enveloped in a broad band of black cloth or velvet, embroidered with thread or beads, going down underneath the girdle to almost the bottom of the gown. The married women had the latter custom. A profusion of beads of different colors adorned their persons, which were very dirty indeed, and it took our utmost care to keep the population of our tents from increasing to an alarming degree.

Our horses were already weary from their long march, and to spare them we decided to hire camels to transport our goods to the *dzassak's* camp, a half day's journey distant. One needs a liberal supply of patience to deal with Mongols, who are sharp, calculating and so changeable that it is difficult to keep them to a bargain after it has been made. Two of them having inspected our loads and having received the required number of *khatas* in prepayment for their services, returned next morning with an insufficient number of camels, and one of those they did bring could not carry a heavy load. They also failed to bring any ropes or pads to go underneath the loads. A lively time ensued and finally Mr. Rijnhart told them plainly our horses would not carry one atom of our stuff, that the camels had been paid for in order that our animals might have a rest. Our men then counted our ropes and watched the loads, and amidst much grumbling from the Mongols, packing and loading was finished and off we went. The aspect of the country was bleak, almost like a desert, at last settling down into a very level plain, upon which in the distance we saw hundreds of tents. The two boys drove our horses on happy without any loads, while Rahim rode alongside of us. Baby and all thoroughly enjoyed the air and sunshine. We chose a pretty camping ground near a stream of water, in the midst of blue iris, about one hundred yards from the tents of the *dzassak* of Barong, from whose tent two men immediately came to help us pitch ours. Taking Rahim and baby with us, for we never considered it wise to leave the little fellow with the servants when we were both away, we went to give the *dzassak* the presents and find out from him about the loads which the Korluk Bei-si had left in his care for us. From what Rockhill had said in his "Land of the Lamas" we expected to find this man both polite and kind, especially as our presents, which were very valuable, were made to him and to his wife, the Mongols of Tankar having advised us to seek the latter's influence. On reaching the door of the tent we were welcomed only by inferiors, and saw sitting upon some rugs a man of about thirty-seven years of age, dressed in a dark blue cloth gown, and a little circular Chinese hat, his face very fat, having by no means an attractive expression. He had not risen to receive us, thereby committing an almost unpardonable breach of politeness, one to which we were unaccustomed, but which we knew was calculated to give us an exalted opinion of his dignity. We bowed and seated ourselves upon rugs provided for us, while the women gave us tea in china basins into which a piece of butter and some *tsamba* had previously been put; we were also served some bread fried in fat, and *hong-tsao-er,* a dried Chinese fruit. The tent was a large round one made of felt with lattice work on the sides and a hole in the center to emit the smoke from the fire immediately beneath in a round clay fireplace, with the pot resting on an iron tripod. Rugs covered the floor around the sides, and boxes were piled high, giving an air of affluence not found in ordinary tents. The chief had a little wooden bed six inches high that he used in order to avoid getting rheumatism, which disease, according to Chinese doctors, comes from the earth. On either side of him sat a lama, one of them apparently engrossed in praying, but really hearing and seeing everything that was going on. The chief's wife and little daughter sat in the opposite side of the tent from us, and though we had expected to see the former clean and well dressed, she was neither, being quite indistinguishable from other Mongol women as far as her attire was concerned. Women of various ages crowded the tent, several men were sitting near the door, which was itself filled with heads. There is no such dignity found among these nomad chiefs as among Chinese mandarins, for the poorest man can go into the chief's tent and be given tea, while a bargain or a business transaction is being discussed. The chief told us our goods had come, and that he would go over to the village on the morrow with Mr. Rijnhart to get them. As we were about to leave he arose and accompanied us to the door, bowing there and watching us depart; an old woman held a big, ferocious dog until we were beyond danger and we sauntered slowly to our tent, glad to be once more in the sweet sunshine out of doors. He came over next day and brought us several pounds of fresh, moderately clean yellow butter, some *churma,* and a big fat sheep. We were not in need of any favors or kindness from him, but he had evidenty decided that we were people to be cultivated, or perhaps he concluded that as we expected to stay for some time it would pay him to be agreeable. The weather during the stay was delightful; the grassy plains stretched on all sides where were tents innumerable with flocks and herds; towards the south we could see the Nomoran and Burh'an Bota passes in the Kuenlun mountains, beyond which lay our goal. Near our tent a ground bird had her nest of five eggs hidden among the iris. How we enjoyed her, for birds, with the exception of hawks and ravens, had been very scarce.

Our boys had had turns at being cook, and while one of them would do his best with the viands, the second would look after Charlie, and the third would serve as a body servant and tend the horses in the morning and evening. The chief supplied us with fuel to make bread, and had his men bring firewood from some distance away, which was mostly roots dug out of the sand. Bread-making was an event of great importance. We had a beaten brass pot ten inches in diameter, over which a lid fitted closely lapping down an inch. Into this our bread was put and the pot was then buried in the fire of dried cow-dung, care being taken that it was not too hot. Fruitcake can be made in these pots, and many other very palatable kinds of cake and buns, provided always the ingredients are at hand, and plenty of fuel, which we sometimes found difficult to get. About our sojourn of three weeks in the Ts'aidam cluster sweet memories, for there our little family had the last quiet time together in sunny weather, without one cloud of worry or unrest to dampen the thorough enjoyment. The outstanding event was the celebration on the 30th of June of baby's birthday. In preparation for the day a birthday cake was made of flour, sugar, butter and sultanas, and the chief was invited to come over to help eat "foreign cake." In the morning the Mongols were surprised to hear the guns which were fired in honor of our little son, while each of our servants was still more surprised when called and presented with a gift. How thoroughly baby enjoyed those days, when he made the tents ring with joyousness from his musical laughter, his shouts and the beating of our Russian brass wash-basin which he used as a drum. Then from sheer weariness he would fall asleep, leaving the camp

pervaded by a stillness, made sweet by the fact that he was still there.

The chief came to our tent very often, and we did some trading with him. We had some rice that we wished to barter for sheep and he was anxious to have it, so of course no one else dared to make an offer, for he always has the pre-eminence in matters of trade, and frequently must have his share of the profits of a good bargain made by members of his tribe. We found him contemptibly mean, wanting to use small weight scales, cheat us on the price, always begging us to "add a little," the common request of a Chinese purchaser, when anything is being weighed or measured out to him. We would not have been so surprised at this man's character had we previously seen W. W. Rockhill's account of his second journey, upon which he and his old friend, the *dzassak,* had about a similar experience to that which we had had. Poor Dowe, Rockhill's guide in 1889, came to grief through his highly prized revolver, for he was exiled in Shang, his flocks and herds having been confiscated by the chief and he himself disgraced. While he was on his way to Tankar, he had some trouble with a young servant, during which he threatened to shoot the latter, and drawing the revolver fired it, though some of the Mongols said it was unintentional. However, he killed the man and the family of the deceased demanded the payment of indemnity and the *dzassak* left Dowe a poor man, though he himself no doubt profited by his steward's misfortune. When we were there Dowe was almost blind and living in Shang, but had managed to collect

a few sheep and cattle together. An old trader from Tankar who was in the Ts'aidam during the summer was a frequent visitor at our tent. He had accompanied the Chinese official who had been sent to investigate the murder of Dutrueil de Rhins, the French traveler who had been killed by the K'amba in 1894. He was near us there in connection with the wool trade, and would be returning to Tankar in August. To him we gave our letters, addressed to our friends at home, and he said he would either send them with some one reliable who would be going before him, or he would take them himself to Mr. Uang, the merchant at the east gate, who had frequently carried or sent letters to Sining for us. These letters with good news, did not reach Canada until after the letters from me announcing the great calamity that befel us later on our journey. While in the Ts'aidam we provided ourselves with fifty catties of butter and eleven sheep for use on the road south, expecting not to see people again for a month. This bartering made us thankful that we were not dependent upon these Mongols for our *tsamba,* as the price demanded was very large and it took a long time to come to terms with them at all, they are so changeable. They are also great cowards, and succeeded in infusing into the minds of our two men fears of the journey beyond, dilating on the passes and rivers, especially the robbers who would be sure to prey upon us.

Having ascertained that a party of Eastern Mongols were passing through the Ts'aidam on their way to Lhasa and Trashil'unpo, we proposed to leave two days after them, because we knew there was a possibility of

our missing the trail in the places where it was not distinct. A young lama camped in a small white tent beside the *dzassak's* was going to Lhasa with the Mongols, and through him we learned when the caravan would leave, and made our preparations accordingly.

One of our reasons for staying so long in the Ts'aidam was to acquaint ourselves with the possibilities of missionary work among the nomads, and after looking over the ground we came to the following conclusion: A mission could be successfully carried on in the Ts'aidam during the summertime, the workers returning to Tankar for the winter. To inspire confidence it would be wise for those engaged in mission work to do a little trading, otherwise the natives would suppose they got their living by magic. There is no doubt that with suitable men a good work in the distribution of Gospels could also be done, and the fact that so many travelers from Lhasa pass through the district would give the mission a wide influence.

CHAPTER XIV.

UNPOPULATED DISTRICTS.

Crossing the Kuenlun Mountains—"Buddha's Cauldron"—Marshes and Sand-hills—Dead Yak Strew the Trail—Ford of the Shuga Gol—Our Guides Desert Us—Snow Storm on the Koko-Shilis—We Meet a Caravan—The Beginning of Sorrows.

The Kuenlun mountain range stretches across Tibet from west to east at about thirty-six degrees latitude, and practically forms the northern limit of the unexplored Tibetan territory lying west of ninety-three degrees longitude. The range is also the southern boundary of the Ts'aidam, and the natives furthermore look upon it as the line of demarcation between comfortable and dangerous traveling from Tankar to Nagch'uk'a. Once the traveler gets south of the Kuenluns, they say, he is certain to encounter dangers formidable in the shape of passes, rivers and brigands. Rockhill states that this mountain range south of the Ts'aidam has no name, and Prjevalski calls it Burh'an Bota (Buddha's Cauldron), but in this the latter is mistaken, for that is the name, not of the range, but of one of the passes. Like every other caravan on its way to Inner Tibet, we had rested long in the Ts'aidam and gathered strength for the ascent and crossing of Burh'an Bota, and other high passes on the road, which on account of the scarcity of pasture, and the great altitude, tax to the utmost the traveling capacity of both man and beast. We learned from the lama previously mentioned that travelers often congregate on the very edge of the Ts'aidam plains because there is grass, and the animals are allowed to have a good feed; for immediately at the foot of the pass, where another halt is always made before the ascent is attempted, the grass is very poor. The morning after our lama's tent was missing from its position beside the *dzassak's*, we left the latter's proximity and made our way to the last halting place north of the mountains.

I have always thought of sheep as such docile animals, following quietly and meekly their shepherd, but when I look back on that day in the Ts'aidam with its treacherous marshes interspersed with grassy plains, the sheep banish everything else from my thoughts, and I again see them as they were that day jumping and running in every direction except that in which they were wanted to go: first to join the *dzassak's* flocks, and, when separated from them, off directly opposite to another flock, a particularly ambitious one always leading. Poor Ja-si and Ga-chuen-tsi were out seeking them away into the night. We set up our tent poles as a tripod upon which to place our brass wash-basin, and burned in it a great fire to serve as a beacon, for we feared they might be lost in the marsh. Not far from us there was a tent in which lived an old couple, and from them we received fresh milk which we carried along in bottles the next morning on our journey. O the bleak barrenness of that marshy district! Sand-hills, gravel and scrub! Not a sign of life in any place, not a drop of running water, only here and there in a little hollow in the bed of what had been apparently an irrigation stream, hidden in the shade of a bush, we would find a little, but not enough to refresh us and the horses. When it was nearly dark Mr. Rijnhart went ahead and found a camping-place among brushwood on the bank of a large stream of good water flowing towards Dsun, in a deep gully right at the foot of the mountain which towered in front of us. It seemed cruel to tether the horses, but there was not a blade of grass, and when such is the case animals will stray miles away in search of food unless prevented; so we gave them some barley, and all prepared for the ascent of the Burh'an Bota the following day. We started shortly after daybreak, beginning to ascend at once along a dry watercourse, where not an atom of green was to be seen, but strewn here and there were dead yak, many of them reduced to skeletons and others more recently dead. Of the latter we counted forty-two, and the sight made us pause to reflect on the name of the pass and wonder whether the explanation of its name, "Buddha's Cauldron," is not found in the fact that it claims so many sacrifices of these poor animals; or was the name suggested by the vapors that hang over it, which the natives call poisonous from the depressing effect they produce on travelers? Huc described the discomfort and pain endured in the ascent of this pass, which half of his caravan crossed in one stretch while the other half stayed part way up, intending to cross the day following. We camped some distance from the summit, where there were indications of the *kopas* having stopped, and where there were food, water and fairly good grass. Our camp was in a beautiful recess in the hills which, with their varied shapes and hues, towered cloudward in front of us. So great was the elevation to which we had attained that the country we had just traversed seemed, as we looked back upon it, to belong to another world far beneath us. Though the natives assured us that it always rained whenever anyone crossed this pass, probably from the great altitude and the clouds hanging about the summit, we had fine weather; but no one enjoyed it very much, as all except Rahim had a headache. Ga-chuen-tsï was very ill, and little Charlie was perfectly willing to lie down with me and keep quiet, for we found that we felt much better when still and in a prostrate position. On the top of the pass was a large *obo* and our native companions cast a stone upon the already large heap, chanting in loud and joyful voices their thanks to the spirits for help in climbing successfully to the top, a task of no small magnitude. Caravans coming out from the interior pay heavily in that locality by the yak and horses lost during the crossing of this pass, the severe toil and the great stretches of country without any fodder coming at the end of a long journey causing large numbers to succumb. How delightful it was after descending along rugged paths to camp in luxuriant grass, and among brushwood which provided us with plenty of firewood.

Such was our next camping-place on the bank of a pretty stream, which next day we followed down its course, to branch off from it along the caravan road which led us up another stream, showing us we were ascending again. In fact the whole month's journey might be said to be a series of ups and downs in more senses than one—the road continually ascending or descending, the grass and firewood being one day abundant, the next absolutely wanting.

As we were in uninhabited country, and expected to be for a month or more, the appearance of four men and some camels was a welcome sight and the occasion of marked politeness on both sides, Mr. Rijnhart presenting them with some bread, and Rahim exchanging tobacco with them. They were part of a large caravan on its way from Lhasa to Tankar, but the oxen were several days behind them, having to come so slowly. The mere sight of them gave us a feeling of companionship that was pleasant after the isolation of the mountains, and we proceeded with the anticipation of meeting at any moment perhaps another small party who were aiming to push on to the Ts'aidam. Well do I remember the beauty of the camping ground the following day, situated on the bank of a copious stream coming apparently from springs in some exceedingly lofty mountains a few miles up a beautiful valley at the head of which stood, as if it were a sentinel on guard, a solitary summit towering high in its magnificence above all surrounding peaks. Our tents were pitched among beds of dainty pink primulas which studded the grassy carpet. But all was not to be sunshine, for that night the rain fell in torrents, traveling was impossible the next morning, and the men found it necessary to go about ten miles for firewood. We deemed it wise to move our camp to the hills, for if the rain continued as it showed every indication of doing, we might have been in danger from the previously quiet mountain stream, now muddy and rising rapidly, though eventually it proved a needless fear. We had seen these quiet streams suddenly changed into raging torrents, in their mad course carrying everything with them, hence our determination to move to higher ground, and to avoid flowery carpets in the future, if they were on the banks of a stream liable to overflow suddenly. Wild mules, antelopes, bears and wild yak were plentiful in these regions, but owing to the wet weather fuel was hard to get, and at times yak horns cut into fine splinters, together with roots of small weeds, were all we could find; these were scarcely sufficient to more than warm water for tea, though we always had enough dry kindling wood that we carried in part of one load to make baby's food.

Now our road lay in a west southwesterly direction, following streams for the most part, these seeming to form openings in the mountains. Then we ascended a pass on which there was a small *obo*. After following a rivulet, crossing and recrossing it several times, we forded the Shuga gol, which, being greatly swollen with the recent rains, and having a sinking sand and gravel bottom, was almost unfordable, and it was with considerable anxiety that we saw some of our loaded horses almost swept away in the seething current, or sink in pitfalls. The tedious march through miry ground and red clay along the river in search of a camp with good grass and spring water, must have discouraged our two boys, Ja-si and Ga-chuen-tsï, for we noticed that they were not so amiable and happy as before. One morning when we arose we found that they had decamped in the night, taking with them their own belongings, a pot and food enough for the return journey. The discovery caused some surprise, and Mr. Rijnhart, with Rahim, mounted our best horses to go back and if possible bring the truants to camp again, leaving Charlie and myself with Topsy to await their return. Our camp was high in a sheltered nook in the hills on the river bank, with bright green grass and pretty moss along little bubbling springs, the mountains towering in the distance, the snow-capped summits of the loftier ones looking down in their calm superiority, giving one the impression that they were conscious of their own height. There is no solitude like that of the mountains, perhaps because their majesty impresses one so, and makes nature too far away to be friendly.

That day alone in the hills with no trees, birds or flowers near, made me realize the sweetness provided by the companionship of a little child and a dog, who both seemed to feel the loneliness, and endeavored to be bright and companionable, while occasionally a chill would pierce my heart as the thought came: "What if any accident should prevent their return?" Was it a foreboding of the future, a whispering of what was to be? The thought was not harbored, but a little garment that was being knitted for baby grew very rapidly under my fingers that day, and great was the rejoicing when late in the afternoon the jaded horses bore their riders home, even though they came without the two boys. We trust the latter reached the Ts'aidam in safety, for they had plenty of food, and the trail was good, but it rained next day and the rivers must have been very high, making their crossing on foot dangerous.

The desertion of these men left us in a quandary, but we rearranged our loads that they might be easily handled by two, fed some of the extra food to our horses, and continued our journey after a rest of four days. Storms seemed to be the rule, for it snowed and hailed at about twelve o'clock every day; but we pushed our way on past a lake called Uyan-khar, across a plain where the trail was scarcely visible and where quicksands were numerous, to a camp by the side of springs with plenty of wild onions, which were a great treat. Rahim had had a gruesome experience here on his way out of Tibet in 1896. He and two companions were the only survivors of the six who followed in Capt. Wellby's footsteps, keeping out of sight two days' march behind the latter, until they discovered signs of a large caravan with yak which had crossed the Chumar river just before them. They had no food except a blue flower of the labiatæ family and wild onions, and here on our camping ground they saw a tame yak, probably one that had been over-fatigued and left by the caravan mentioned above. They attacked and killed it, and, he said, they were so weakened by starvation that they just sat down and ate raw liver, not waiting to cook it. The dusky eye of the Oriental flashed as he recalled the joy that had come to him in this spot when the yak and traces of a caravan told him he was again approaching the haunts of human beings.

Wild onions grow in great quantities in these districts and are particularly welcome to travelers, for they grow in places along the caravan-trails, where there is no meat to be had, and where they are the only obtainable green for diet. We invariably tented when possible in what had previously been *kopas'* camps, and the deserted fireplaces, together with the small *obos* around on the hills, served as landmarks to point out the road, as the blazed trees did in pioneer times in our own country. The corpse of a man on the roadside told its own pathetic tale, how he had fallen sick and unable to keep up with his caravan, how he had been left behind with a supply of clothes and food, and had died alone when the food was all used. There, surrounded by his scattered and torn garments, lay his body, the flesh partly devoured by wild beasts and eagles. Rahim shuddered at the sight, and at the memory of his own escape from a similar fate; and our arrival at the Chumar river where he had first seen traces of the *kopas* who helped him, revived the memory of how kind *kismet* had been to him.

Having camped again near some *obos* made of large prayer-stones in a position east of a low ridge of hills, and after having crossed some sand-dunes, we forded the Chumar, one of the headwaters of the Yangtse; and even though at the ford the depth was less than elsewhere, we experienced considerable difficulty in crossing it, for there were several branches separated by small sandbars bearing tufts of grass. In the first branch our horses sank into the quicksand, and had Rahim not been an expert we would have lost several loads, while the last branch was very deep, all the horses having to swim. Then we passed through a shaking bog, which well-nigh exhausted our animals. It seemed that at every step the wavering foundations would give way and we would sink somewhere into the depths of the earth. Dead horses and camels strewn along the way gave evidence of the extreme difficulties of transport across this treacherous piece of country. In the entrance to the Koko-shili range on the southeast of the valley, we came to a spot where caravans had evidently stayed several days, and where a dog that had had its back broken was keeping guard over some dead horses, and resented Topsy's advent. The ascent of the Koho-shili is at first gradual, but near the top it is very steep. A violent snow-storm overtook us and we feared to lose the trail, but two *obos* indicated our arrival at the summit, and a careful descent brought us to a pretty camping ground. The transition from the area of a snow-storm around the summit of a pass with its irregular stony paths, its bleak peaks and *obos*, to sunshine, green grass and bright crystal streams below, gives one an exceedingly pleasant sensation, and makes the pulse throb with joy and a sense of satisfaction.

The next few days' traveling brought us to different branches of the Ulan Muren, and on to one of the branches of the Mur-ussu, another high water of the

Yangtse, called Mur-ussu by the Mongols and Dre Chu by the Tibetans. Here I make extracts from Mr. Rijnhart's diary which will give an adequate idea of the locality.

"August 10th. To-day fine and hot. Start at eight o'clock, travel through sand-hills covered sparingly with grass, pass along the east side of a lake, then turn southwest and enter between two lakes. On the north shore of the southern one are many large *obos*. Stop after traveling three and a half hours on the western extremity of a lake, north of the Mur-ussu, with directly south of us a snow-peak, Mt. Dorst, and southeast Mt. Djoma, also a snow-peak. Charlie is teething."

"August 11th. Charlie is a little better. Started with fine weather from the northeast corner of lake. In about an hour afterwards we reached a large branch of the Mur-ussu; on one of the largest streams horses swim; get many things wet, but did cross admirably. On the road have a fearful hail-storm; pass two small lakes, one east, one west of our track. Come in sight of largest branch of Mur-ussu, a source of the Yangtse; camp on right bank."

The main branch of the Mur-ussu is very large, flowing quietly in a deep bed, and it gave us a feeling of inability to ford, unless it spread to a greater width further on. We kept looking for that as we skirted its banks, when in the distance we spied yak, and Rahim announced that they were saddled. Rahim's vision was much keener than ours, for we could barely verify his words by means of our telescope. We were all on the *qui vive,* when suddenly we saw some white tents, and on nearer approach discovered that there were fourteen of them, having about 1,500 yak and many horses. Our way led through the center of the encampment and not having any fear we rode up and were received in a very friendly manner by the travelers, most of them knowing us. They had been just one month coming from Nagch'uk'a and were on their way to Tankar, so we sent messages with them to our friends. By their dripping yak, and everything being spread out in the sun to dry, we concluded that the river in front of us, and which they had just crossed, was very deep; and though they wanted us to camp beside them, we went on to ford the waters, which would probably give us such a wetting that we would need to stop on the other shore and get dried. There were five branches, and while the *kopas* watched our passage we crossed first one then another, the horses swimming at times. The only one who enjoyed the fording was Charlie, who shouted with joy, when we all called out to the horses to arouse their courage as well as our own. The sensation of camping across the river from friends was peculiar. The tents on the opposite bank looked like a town, but in the morning every vestige of the recent inhabitants with dwellings was gone, and we were again alone. We had the worst storm that night we had experienced on the road, and it seemed as if tent and everything would be blown away, but we steadied the poles, and in time all apparent danger was past. Later on some of the *kopas* must have visited our camp, for next morning, to our consternation, five of our best animals were gone. They had undoubtedly been stolen, as we traced them away down to a river-crossing with footsteps of another horse and dog. This event marked the beginning of sorrows, for Charlie had begun to cut his teeth, so was causing us no little anxiety, but we traveled very short stages and he seemed to improve, even though a gland in his neck was swollen. On the bank of a large river Rahim shot and killed a wild mule, some of whose flesh we were glad to use for food, having tasted no meat for many days.

In the most deserted region through which we had yet passed we found ourselves without guides, lost five of our ponies and saw the hand of affliction laid upon our little child.

CHAPTER XV.

DARKNESS.

Nearing the Dang Las—Death of our Little Son—The Lone Grave Under the Boulder.

Following the occidental road from the Ts'aidam we had ascended many passes, and though some of them were over 16,000 feet above the sea, on none of them did we find old snow, and hence the snow-line in that region cannot be lower than about 17,500 feet. Wild animals abounded in many localities, yak sometimes being visible from very near. One fine day we surprised a number of the latter which, on seeing us, dashed across a large stream, their huge tails high in the air, the spray from their headlong rush into the water rising in clouds, presenting a magnificent sight. Wild mules had been seen in large numbers, especially after we crossed the Mur-ussu river, while bears and antelopes were everyday sights. On August the twenty-first, after we had been ascending for several days, we found ourselves traveling directly south, following up to its source a beautiful stream full of stones, probably one of the Mur-ussu high waters. In front of us were the Dang La mountais, snow-clad and sunkissed, towering in their majesty, and, to us tenfold more interesting because immediately beyond them lay the Lhasa district of Tibet, in which the glad tidings of the gospel were unknown, and in which the Dalai Lama exercises supreme power, temporal and spiritual, over the people. Moreover, as we hoped to obtain permission to reside in that district as long as we did not attempt to enter the Capital, it seemed that our journeyings for the present were almost at an end. This hope, added to the fact that our darling's eight teeth, which had been struggling to get through, were now shining white above the gums, revived our spirits and we all sang for very joy, picking bouquets of bright pink leguminous flowers as we went along.

The morning of the darkest day in our history arose, bright, cheery, and full of promise, bearing no omen of the cloud that was about to fall upon us. Our breakfast was thoroughly enjoyed, Charlie ate more heartily than he had done for some days, and we resumed our journey full of hope. Riding along we talked of the future, its plans, its work, and its unknown successes and failures, of the possibility of going to the Indian border when our stay in the interior was over, and then of going home to America and Holland before we returned to Tankar, or the interior of Tibet again. Fondly our imagination followed the career of our little son; in a moment years were added to his stature and the infant had grown to the frolicking boy full of life and vigor, athirst for knowledge and worthy of the very best instruction we could give him. With what deliberation we decided to give his education our personal supervision, and what books we would procure for him—the very best and most scientific in English, French and German. "He must have a happy childhood," said his father. "He shall have all the blocks, trains, rocking-horses and other things that boys in the homeland have, so that when he shall have grown up he may not feel that because he was a missionary's son, he had missed the joys that brighten other boys' lives." How the tones of his baby voice rang out as we rode onward! I can still hear him shouting lustily at the horses in imitation of his father and Rahim.

Suddenly a herd of yak on the river bank near us tempted Rahim away to try a shot, but the animals, scenting danger, rushed off into the hills to our right; then across the river we saw other yak, apparently some isolated ones, coming towards us, but on closer examination we found they were tame yak driven by four mounted men accompanied by a big, white dog. The men evidently belonged to the locality, and we expected they would come to exchange with us ordinary civilities, but to our surprise when they saw us they quickly crossed our path, and studiously evading us, disappeared in the hills. This strange conduct on their part aroused in our minds suspicions as to their intentions. Carefully we selected a camping-place hidden by little hills; the river flowed in front and the pasture was good.

Though baby's voice had been heard just a few moments previous, Mr. Rijnhart said he had fallen asleep; so, as usual, Rahim dismounted and took him from his father's arms in order that he might not be disturbed until the tent was pitched and his food prepared. I had also dismounted and spread on the ground the comforter and pillow I carried on my saddle. Rahim very tenderly laid our lovely boy down, and, while I knelt ready to cover him comfortably, his appearance attracted my attention. I went to move him, and found that he was unconscious. A great fear chilled me and I called out to Mr. Rijnhart that I felt anxious for baby, and asked him to quickly get me the hypodermic syringe. Rahim asked me what was the matter, and on my reply a look of pain crossed his face, as he hastened to help my husband procure the hypodermic. In the meantime I loosened baby's garments, chafed his wrists, performed artificial respiration, though feeling almost sure that nothing would avail, but praying to Him who holds all life in His hands, to let us have our darling child. Did He not know how we loved him and could it be possible that the very joy of our life, the only human thing that made life and labor sweet amid the desolation and isolation of Tibet—could it be possible that even this—the child of our love should be snatched from us in that dreary mountain country—by the cold chill hand of Death? What availed our efforts to restore him? What availed our questionings? The blow had already fallen, and we realized that we clasped in our arms only the casket which had held our precious jewel; the jewel itself had been taken for a brighter setting in a brighter world; the little flower blooming on the bleak and barren Dang La had been plucked and transplanted on the Mountains Delectable to bask and bloom forever in the sunshine of God's love. But oh! what a void in our hearts!

How empty and desolate our tent, which in the meantime had been pitched and sorrowfully entered! Poor Rahim, who had so dearly loved the child, broke out in loud lamentations, wailing as only orientals can, but with real sorrow, for his life had become so entwined with the child's that he felt the snapping of the heart-strings. And what of the father, now bereft of his only son, his only child, which just a few moments before he had clapsed warm to his bosom, knowing not how faint the little heart-beat was growing? We tried to think of it euphemistically, we lifted our hearts in prayer, we tried to be submissive, but it was all so real—the one fact stared us in the face; it was written on the rocks; it reverberated through the mountain silence: Little Charlie was dead.

As I sat in the tent clasping the fair form of my darling, Mr. Rijnhart tenderly reminded me that the Tibetans do not bury their dead, but simply throw the body devoid of clothing out upon the hillside to be devoured by the beasts of the field and the fowls of the air. If the men whom so recently we had seen and whose actions were so suspicious, should come to rob us, they would, he feared, dispose of our darling's body as was their custom, and that would be to us a still greater trial than the loss of our goods; and so, reluctantly and tenderly he suggested, to avoid such a calamity, that our precious little boy should have a Christian sepulture on that very day. Kneeling together we prayed that God who loved us and whose children we were, would make us strong and brave. Our drug box, emptied of its contents, and lined with towels, served as a coffin, which I myself prepared, while Mr. Rijnhart and Rahim went to dig the grave. With hands whose every touch throbbed with tenderness I robed baby in white Japanese flannel, and laid him on his side in the coffin, where he looked so pure and calm as if he were in a sweet and restful sleep. In his hand was placed a little bunch of wild asters and blue poppies which Rahim gathered from the mountain side, and as the afternoon wore away he seemed to grow more beautiful and precious; but night was coming on and dangers threatened, and the last wrench must come. Many of his little belongings were put into the coffin, accompanied by our names written on a piece of linen and on cards. Then there was the agony of the last look. Our only child, who had brought such joy to our home, and who had done so much by his bright ways to make friends for us among the natives—to leave his body in such a cold, bleak place seemed more than we could endure. As the three of us stood over the grave, the little box was lowered. Mr. Rijnhart conducted the burial service in the native tongue, so that Rahim might understand, and the cold earth of Tibet, the great forbidden land, closed over the body of the first Christian child committed to its bosom—little Charles Carson Rijnhart, aged one year, one month and twenty-two days. Mr. Rijnhart and Rahim rolled a large boulder over the grave to keep wild animals from digging it up, and obliterated as well as possible all traces of a recent burial. There was another reason for this. The natives often bury goods when their transport animals break down, and robbers search for booty wherever they find the surface of the ground disturbed. If such should discover our little grave we knew they would disturb it, and in their disappointment desecrate it with wanton indifference. When the funeral was over we went to the tent, but could we eat food? could we drink tea? could we close our ears to the frenzied mourning of Rahim? We could only say, "Lord we are stricken with grief, we cannot see why this should be, but help us to say 'Thy will be done.'" Less than a month afterward we realized that the All Loving had dealt very kindly with us in taking our little darling when we were comfortable, when we had plenty of food for him, a tent to sleep in and horses to ride on; for later we found ourselves with barely enough common food to exist on for a few days, while we traveled on foot, Mr. Rijnhart carrying on his back a heavy load.

When night came on the sky was unusually dark. What more fitting than a nocturnal storm after the inward tumult of the day? The thunder rolled, the lightning flashed, while from the sable clouds in torrents fell the rain, which as the winds grew colder, was congealed into snow. We could not sleep. We could only think of our precious one and be thankful that the body from which the vital spark had fled, had no power to feel the chill of the mountain blast. The little fellow's bed had always been made of blankets and furs, while every precaution had been taken to exclude any draft from his corner, and now what need had we to be careful? No need, for he slept not with us, but in another world, free from all care, and future sorrowing. Dear child, now, as then, it is still well with thee. On arising the following morning how I missed him, for there was no little boy to dress, no one to joyously relish his food, watching the spoon go backwards and forwards for every fresh spoonful. When the time came for departure we took a sorrowful farewell of the little grave with its protecting boulder of strength. It seemed impossible to tear ourselves away, knowing that every step took us further from the spot that held our most precious treasure, with the conviction that we should probably never return there again. Before leaving we covenanted that by God's help we would seek to be instrumental in sending out another missionary to Tibet, in the name of our little boy. Mr. Rijnhart, instead of mounting first and having Baby handed to him as was his custom, tenderly placed me in the saddle, and all three of us sobbing, we tore ourselves away. Following the stream we saw some bears with their cubs digging for roots—and again we felt thankful for the strong boulder over the little grave. If Mr. Rijnhart could speak, he would wish to say some word in tribute to his little son, but since his voice is silent, what more fitting than to close this chapter by a quotation from his diary, dated August 23, the day of our departure, from this, to us, the most sacred spot in Tibet? It reads thus: "To-day we started with broken hearts, leaving the body of our precious one behind in regions of eternal snow, where the mother of the Yangtse Kiang flows tranquilly past. His grave is on the western bank of one of the southern branches of the Mur-ussu, at the foot of the Dang La mountains, a little over two hours north of the mineral springs of the Dang La, and about ten hours' travel from the nearest *kopa* encampment in the Lhasa district under Nagch'uk'a."

CHAPTER XVI.

BEYOND THE DANG LA.

Accosted by Official Spies—Our Escape—The Natives Buy Copies of the Scriptures—Our Escort to the Ponbo's Tent.

From the north it occupies a period of several days to climb slowly to the summit of the Dang La, and after the first sudden steep descent on the south the road leads down gradually for days, and is comparatively easy traveling for both man and animal. Though it was warm when the sun shone brightly, on the night of August 25 there was almost an inch of frost and the firewood was wet. Some of us had to go supperless to bed, and could not have any breakfast, but on the road Topsy caught a large hare, and in one-half hour we approached the first Tibetan encampment, on the opposite bank of the Dang Chu, whose downward course we had been following. After four hours we crossed it and campel on the west bank. Shortly before crossing two men heavily armed came over and rode up close behind us, then returned to the opposite bank, and as they did not speak to us, we presumed they had been spying our movements. A considerably lower altitude had provided abundance of fuel, and the day being warm we halted and took advantage of the welcome opportunity of making bread, and having a delicious meal of rice and hare. As Topsy had provided the latter she was not forgotten.

Although we had been seen by the people of the large encampments about us, no one came near us and we were not anxious to court interference, so stayed away from their tents. In the night one of our horses most inopportunely died, and the next morning Rahim and Mr. Rijnhart were compelled to walk and ride alternately. After having been on the road about three hours, we were met on a beautiful slope by eight mounted Tibetans, who were armed with guns and swords, and looked very different from any other Tibetans we had ever met. They were all very dirty, wore sheepskin gowns, girt so high that as they sat on horseback their knees were bare. Some of them had their hair done up in a queue ornamented with rings of ivory or silver set with coral, all bound around their heads; while others had their bushy locks hanging about their faces, giving them the appearance of wild men. They all used snuff, being very dirty about it, plastering it over the nostrils and upper lip. As we rode along they turned and rode with us, asking such questions as, "Have you any merchandise?" "Where are you going?" They were soon joined by two others from the valley who were both well dressed, but not any cleaner than their comrades. After having reviewed the situation two of them rode on ahead and in a short time were lost to sight, evidently having gone to report our advent to their chief, for we were satisfied that this was a small party of attachés of the government at Nagch'uk'a, who were watching to keep any foreigners from entering their domains. Mr. Rijnhart, Rahim and myself took care thenceforth as we traveled to converse only in a language which the Tibetans did not understand, and after discussing the situation, we decided to push on just as far as we were able that day. So not even stopping for lunch, on we went, until we were weary and tired, especially Rahim, who refused to ride in the presence of others while his master walked. When we neared a river, one of the men came to tell us that when we camped near its banks we were to remain until their two companions returned from Nagch'uk'a with permission for us to proceed; whereupon Mr. Rijnhart informed him that we were going to see the official, thus following a conviction established by much experience, that it is better to go to headquarters than deal with petty chiefs who, having no independent authority, are compelled to be obedient to their superiors and therefore arbitrary.

When we had forded the Shak Chu we camped about one hundred yards from the spot where the Tibetans had now pitched their ragged brown tent. They were all very friendly, for they came over and sat freely about our tent-fire, chatting with Rahim and through him with Mr. Rijnhart, who did not wish, under the circumstances, to be familiar with them, refraining from going either out to them or inviting them to come in. They told Rahim that no foreigner had ever passed that place, and they did not intend to allow us to. Their plans were not commensurate with their intentions, for in the dead of the night while they slept soundly, we arose quietly, packed our loads, took down our tent when we were just ready to start, and mounting our ponies, rode away. The moon gave enough light to avoid the pitfalls, with which were interspersed those small tufts of grass that make it so difficult to ride among them without plunging in the mire. Silently our little caravan ascended along a stony trail, the Khamlung La, and, as the blush of dawn overspread the landscape, we had begun the descent on the other side, scrambling through a very stony road with large boulders that made it hard for us to get our loaded horses past in safety. Presently we had reached a beautiful plain dotted with tents and merging into low hills, the whole clothed with green grass, a crystal stream flowing through it bubbling over its bed of small stones. A man well dressed in *pulu,* wearing ornaments enough to indicate wealth, as far as in this country a man can have wealth, rode up in a very friendly manner, informing us that the stream was the Sapo Chu, and that the district was called Sapo. He pointed to his tents, of which there were five, and invited us to stay near him, in order that we might do some trading, so we halted five hundred yards from his encampment. The population of Sapo is estimated at one hundred and fifty tents, and the chief, who lived west from our camp, pays tribute to the Chinese ambassador at Lhasa. When we first halted, the ground was very wet from the frost which glistened on every blade of grass, so we postponed pitching our tent until it was dry, and while we waited our guards of the previous night were seen galloping swiftly towards us. Having arrived they dismounted and throwing themselves on the ground beside us, they laughed heartily, telling us that we were smart to have escaped from them in that way. A wreath of smiles also covered Rahim's face, for he with ourselves felt a little dubious about they way they would receive our decamping as we did; but so thoroughly do the Tibetans enjoy outwitting their neighbors that though they were the sufferers they displayed their native characteristic in approval.

We spent two days in this locality, having pleasant intercourse with the inhabitants, and doing considerable bartering, for we were in need of meat, fresh butter and milk. For the first time among Tibetans we had brought to us for sale some legs of mutton. In the Koko-nor only the whole sheep, and never a part of it, can be bought. The most useful articles for bartering here were *Wuchai khatas* and red broadcloth, the latter being used for making collars, for trimming boots, and to adorn the headdress of the women. We traded some Tankar boots for the kind used in this locality, and Rahim bought a prayer-wheel, made of silver set with coral and stones.

We thought the people were very filthy as they presented the appearance of never washing their faces; but they brought their good horses to the river near us and after having driven them into a deep place where only their heads were above water, they gave them a thorough cleaning and left us to wonder why they did not consider water was good for human beings as well as for horses.

The clothing of Tibetan women in all parts of Tibet is made after the same pattern, so that little variation except in headdress is noticeable even in districts most widely separated. In some localities, however, aprons are worn and in others little sleeveless jackets. But the women here attracted our attention at once by a peculiar fashion of headdress. We had often read of the women smearing their faces with a repulsive cosmetic of black sticky paste in order that by their beauty they might not allure the lamas from their devotions, but these women here with the same purpose, instead of painting had their hair arranged so that it fell over the face, hiding it from view. Parted in the center it was woven in fine plaits from the middle of the forehead on either side, and the plaits were fastened together, forming meshes like a coarse veil, the two sides being separate. When they wished from coquetry or otherwise to cover the face, they pulled the veil of hair down, first one and then the other side, fastening the two sections opposite the chin by means of a button, making a distinctly original mask through which their bright eyes could see everything, but could not be seen. It was rather amusing to watch a good-looking young woman or girl in her *pulu* gown and ornaments, hastily pull her veil of plaits over her face when a lama or a stranger approached. Sometimes the action was a gesture of grace, accompanied by a smile which flashed across her face and in her eyes. A cheery, good-natured woman of about thirty-five came to offer for sale a little wooden bucketful of fresh milk, asking about three times as much for it as she expected to receive, while we offered as much less in the same proportion as we expected to give, whereupon, as was also the custom, she put it down and seated herself near the fire to enjoy the general conversation. After about an hour she took the .bucket up, thereby intimating that we were to complete the bargain, when, lifting the cover she discovered that the precious liquid had all leaked out. Everyone laughed at her and said she deserved the loss as she had asked too much for the milk; in fact she joined heartily in the laugh herself. The women came freely to our tent and sat around our camp-fire. As most of their own tents were across the stream they would, when going home, sit down beside the bank, remove their cloth boots and, gathering up their skirts, trip across on the stones, laughing and chatting merrily all the time. The men who came about us were, in common with their race, anxious to drive a bargain, but they were above the average in intelligence. A certain number of them were able to read and to our surprise manifested an ardent desire to secure copies of the Scriptures in the Tibetan character. In no other part of Tibet had we ever been offered money for the books, but here people came from far and near anxious to get them and offering in return silver, or anything else we might wish to ask. Many of Mrs. Grimke's text cards were here distributed, and I look back on our stay among those friendly people with great pleasure, remembering the promise that "My word * * * shall not return unto me void." The Word of God has been scattered for the first time among them, and we do not know what far-reaching results will follow.

The people in Sapo have a greater admiration and reverence for Jerimpoché, the great incarnation at Trashil'unpo, than they have for the Dalai Lama. From this district pilgrims go frequently to worship Jerimpoché, hence there is a highway leading directly across the country. The people suggested our following that route, saying that a lama was about to start for Shigatsze in a short time and we could go with him. However, we had told our guides that we were going to see the chief at Nagch'uk'a, and to deviate towards another place would give rise to suspicion, perhaps getting us into trouble; besides which this other road probably presented the same obstacles as the road we had at first intended to follow. While trading here we made use for the first time of the Tibetan coin called *chong ka,* a round beaten silver coin divided by lines into eight parts which are cut when small pieces are wanted. Eight of these coins are worth one Chinese tael. Rupees were also used in that locality, and nearly every man had a pretty leather purse, often set with corals, in which to carry coins.

While we journeyed the following day attended by three soldiers, it stormed furiously, and Mr. Rijnhart and Rahim walked the whole distance. We met several people on horseback who invariably stopped us, and inquired if we wished to buy any horses or sheep. We were reminded of the men who visited Huc and Gabet, and wanted to buy saddles of them but were really spies. We saw one man on horseback carrying a bright red umbrella, showing how Chinese civilization, in some of its varied forms, has found its way into remote corners of the great Empire.

From our road as we wearily journeyed along, we caught glimpses of the beautiful Chomora Lake at times hidden from view by the hills, but in its quiet recess, suggesting calmness and rest on its shores away from the toil of traveling, which since baby was gone had lost its charms. The journey became tedious and life had no longer for us the rosy hues that sweet childhood reflects upon it. Beautiful rivulets babbled near the roadside which skirted the hills, and finally we camped near tents, whose dwellers cheerfully gave Rahim some fuel in exchange for a *khata,* while near us without any tents camped our guards, now only two in number. The next morning when we had traveled about three hours, after crossing a low pass, we were suddenly confronted by nearly forty men, who had pitched a tent and were evidently awaiting our coming. Associating the tent with the removal of his load, our most lively horse went straight up to it, literally into the arms of the men, and Rahim went quickly to drive him back, but seeing that it was impossible Mr. Rijnhart also went over. The Tibetans gathered about him and one of them, well-dressed in *pulu,* having in his hand a prayer-wheel, profusely invited him to enter the tent to drink tea, the others seconding the invitation. Feeling that this was a ruse to have us stop, my husband laughingly passed it off, saying that we had our loaded horses to look after, and that in a short time we would be camping anyway. They then said their *ponbo,* or chief, was coming to see us, and received for reply that

TIBETAN CORACLE

we were on our way to see him. Only the great tact and finesse used at that time prevented collision. Mr. Rijnhart put them in good humor by giving one of the men's prayer-wheels a turn in the right direction, thereby showing his knowledge of their ceremonial. Thus amid the most pleasant politeness on either side, we went our way, leaving them kindly disposed, yet staring in consternation because we had passed a large outpost of soldiers designed to prevent our journeying further towards Nagch'uk'a. A man soon passed us on the gallop, and we presumed he was on his way to notify his *ponbo* that the *peling* or Englishman (the only name all foreigners are known by in that part of Tibet), had succeeded in getting beyond the guard, who had probably received orders not to use any violence towards us. After having gone some distance we were overtaken by several of the men who rode alongside us, and conversed pleasantly and agreeably. A violent hail-storm driving in our faces compelled us to allow the horses to stand, when they immediately turned their backs to it, sheltering the rider's face. Our companions dismounted and crouched down in the shelter of their horses, pulling their capacious gowns over their faces, thus improvising a wrap. Crossing a plain in which we had Lake Chomora on our left we saw many camels and yak, and clustered around the sheltered nooks of the hills the familiar black tents of the nomads. We knew we were approaching Nagch'uk'a, an important district of the province of Inner Tibet, governed directly from Lhasa, a fact which explained the vigilance that had been exercised over us since our coming. A blinding snowstorm towards evening necessitated our selecting a camp just before we had reached the houses of Nagch'uk'a village, and we tented in the midst of a large encampment on a small piece of sward surrounded by hummocks of grass. Some of the men we had previously seen at the outpost tent came around the fire and informed us that we were to remain tented there, because in the morning their two *ponbos* were coming to see us. Mr. Rijnhart replied that we would arise and have our breakfast, pack our loads, and if by that time the *ponbo* had not arrived we would slowly make our way to him, that it made no material difference where we met him, but we could not long await his pleasure.

CHAPTER XVII

NAGCH'UK'A

Government of Nagch'uk'a—Under Official Surveillance—Dealings With the Ponbo Ch'enpo—We Are Ordered to Return to China—Our Decision.

The village of Nagch'uk'a beside which we were camped is situated south of Chomora Lake in the Lhasa district and contains about sixty houses built of mud and brick, but most of its people live in black tents, preferring a nomadic life. The monastery of Shiabden adjoins the village, but the number of its priests we were unable to learn. Nagch'uk'a is governed by a lama who is the representative of the Dalai Lama and is changed every three years. Associated with him is also a lay official supposed to be Chinese. This latter has virtually little power of his own, everything of importance being settled according to the decree of the great dignitary from Lhasa. Though the well-dressed *kopas* who had endeavored to prevent our proceeding on our journey had exerted their utmost to convince us of their authority, we knew that as yet we had not met anyone who really had any power to stop us, as the *ponbo ch'enpo* of Nagch'uk'a is a man of too high rank to travel any distance from his home to meet two unknown persons with such a small, inconspicuous caravan as ours. The previous day's hard traveling had prepared us for an undisturbed night's rest, and the sun was shedding its warmth on our tent and over the tussocks of grass upon which hung diamonds from the snow and frost, when Rahim awakened to remember that we were expecting to see the *ponbo* that day, or very soon at least. An excited cry of *sahib* at our tent door aroused us, and the boy informed us that a large number of Tibetans were erecting a tent near by. Upon peering through the door we saw pitched first one beautiful white tent, and then another, amid the greatest commotion. While our tea was being boiled three of our traveling companions, or so-called guards, came to inform us that their official had ridden over and was in a neighboring tent, and invited us to *kali, kali, i. e.,* slowly visit him. At about ten o'clock, mounted on a noble chestnut horse richly caparisoned with red and gold, and accompanied by a large retinue, the *ponbo ch'enpo* of Nagch'uk'a rode from a black tent over to his own official one, where shortly afterwards we were invited to come to see him. We had in the interim discussed the wisdom of my being present at the interview, and had finally decided that we would both go, together with Rahim; accordingly we donned our best clothing and having mounted our ponies, rode over to the beautiful tents.

We were led to the larger of the two, a white one embroidered with dark blue and white with capacious awnings, altogether the best tent I have ever seen. On our arrival near the entrance several *kopas* dressed neatly in dark red *pulu,* with red boots came forward to meet us. Some grooms took charge of our ponies, and we were ushered into the tent, to find the furnishings of the interior in keeping with the exterior; beautiful rugs and mats lined the sides to the door, while the further end was completely covered with very rich Turkish rugs; upon a dais several inches in height, composed of mats filled with wool, sat the *ponbo ch'enpo,* and at his left side the second chief who is supposedly a Chinaman, but in this instance was not. The former was a handsome young lama about thirty-five years of age with fine cut features, small black moustache and shaven head. He was dressed in rich brocaded Chinese silks. The other was an old man with gray hair worn in a queue, a large gold earring pendant from his left ear. He also was dressed in rich silks, and wore a circular hat.

They invited us to take seats in front of which were little carved tables, and a good-looking, intelligent young *kopa* extended his hand, asking for our basins which we brought forth from our gowns. As a mark of honor the tea was poured into our basins from the same pot from which the *ponbo* received his. We presented to him a satin *khata* with pictures of three buddhas on it, which he accepted, looking a little surprised at our knowledge of the customs. He told us that no *peling* had ever been there before, that he could not permit us to go any further into Tibet, and that we must return over the same route we had come by. Mr. Rijnhart told him he was not English, that he was Dutch, that he was not a traveler just passing through the country, but had lived among the Tibetans for years and added that we would not return to China as he wished us to. The chief looked perplexed, but replied that he had no power to forcibly prevent our going on, but, did he allow us to proceed, he would be beheaded. In this way oriental officials endeavor to compel submission to their desires, taking it for granted that no one wishes to be the cause of a man's losing his life. At this Mr. Rijnhart laughed and said he was conversant with their customs, and that in their sacred books a man is forbidden to destroy life, even that of a louse, and remarked how much in unison with that teaching it would be for their Dalai Lama to have him beheaded, thereby destroying a life of such high degree! The young chief turned to his confreres and said how strange it was to see a foreigner so different from any *peling* they had ever seen before; we knew their customs, spoke their language, wore their clothes, and even had read their sacred literature. He said to us that did we go on, he would be required to send word ahead, and that a chief of greater power than he would meet us and have the authority to stop us. We told him we had no desire to visit Lhasa, that we were willing to be blindfolded when near the sacred city, as we had been informed at Tankar by officials from Lhasa, that we might go to within one day's journey of the capital and remain as long as we wished, provided we did not attempt to enter, nor cast our eyes upon the five-domed golden temple of the Dalai Lama. Our conference lasted a long time, the tea in our basins being renewed as politeness demanded; and when we rose to withdraw, nothing definite had been settled, except that we positively refused to retrace our steps, Mr. Rijnhart adding that he would prefer being beheaded to returning by the route over which we had come.

Almost immediately on our return to our own tent some of the *kopas* brought us a *khata,* a bag of rice, one of flour, two large bricks of good tea, and a skin containing four pounds of butter with a message from their *ponbo* informing us that the gifts were from his hand, and that as soon as the flocks were driven in a big fat sheep would also be given us. We bade the messengers thank their chief, and gave them as a return present for the time being, a beautifully bound copy of the Gospels, accompanied by a *khata.* That the book was accepted and prized was to us a source of satisfaction. Often my thoughts go back to the *ponbo* of Nagch'uk'a with the copy of the Gospels in his tent, and I wonder whether it has yet brought its message to him, and muse on the influence it may yet wield among the *ponbo's* people. That evening when it was growing dusk, a group of soldiers were stationed in front of our tent about a hundred feet from us, and shortly afterwards another group took their place the same distance away on the opposide side. The *ponbo* was evidently taking every precaution against our escaping in the night again, something we had not the slightest intention of attempting; and we felt thankful that we did not need to put the iron hobbles on our ponies, for they would not be stolen from us that night, as ourselves and all we possessed were being so thoroughly guarded by the official's soldiers.

Our tent was pitched in a level place which was lower than the surrounding hummocks, and would certainly be flooded should a storm arise. Besides, there being no running water near us, the following morning, watched from the *ponbo's* tents by his men, we packed our loads, took down our tents and moved to the bank of a pretty brook of circling course, upon whose edge we decided to settle down among the many tents already there. What a state of excitement the men were in when they saw us preparing to move, but as soon as our intention was plain to them they did not interfere. It was a beautiful morning. While all the preparations were being made, and some of the goods were being moved, I sat on a hillock enjoying the warm sunshine, while before us stretched green hills dotted with innumerable black tents, and behind were scattered groups of gaily dressed servants of the Lhasa government. Upon arrival at our new camping-ground, we pitched both our tents, and used our rugs to make us as comfortable as possible, expecting to stay for awhile and receive company. Some of the *ponbo's* men came over to inform us that their chief was glad we had moved our tent to a good place, as where we had been was low and unpleasant, but that we were not to move again until we started for China. This, they said, was the expressed wish and command of the chief. Evidently the tent dwellers in that vicinity had also received their instructions not to have any communication with us, because, contrary to our experience in other places, not a single man or woman from any of the black tents came to barter or chat with us; only the attachés of the government visited us and we realized that we were completely ostracised. Feeling that if we remained there, or pursued our journey further toward the south, we would be similarly treated, and as the object of our going had been to come into contact with the people, to study their needs and not merely to travel, we feared it would be frustrated by the orders of the chiefs. Had we considered it best we might have pushed on further for we had abundance of food, but the strain of always being guarded by soldiers and of being met by petty officials who endeavored to turn us back, would necessarily prove trying. Thus our desire to mingle freely with the people being unattainable, we decided either to winter in Nagch'uk'a could we gain permission, or yield to the *ponbo's* desire for us to return towards China and winter some place on the road. Having decided in this manner, when next we visited the *ponbo*, we were inclined to yield, but did not find him so polite as on our previous visit, though perhaps it was owing to our imagination. Our tea was now poured from a different tea-pot from that out of which his was poured, and Mr. Rijnhart remembered the custom of the lamas, praying a person to death with the aid of aconite, and consequently drank little. All our efforts to obtain permission to remain during the winter in that locality were in vain, but the chief agreed to our following the *Jalam* (tea road) towards Ta-chien-lu, though when we suggested fresh horses being given us for our tired ones, he said yak were best to use on that road. We left for our own tent again without having come to any definite arrangement. The chief even refused to allow Rahim, who was a Tibetan, to go towards Ladak to his home, but insisted that we must all three return together. On our return to our tent we had a conference and decided that we would not go again to see the *ponbo,* but that we would just stay indefinitely until he came to us, and arranged everything to suit our desires and not his own. In the meantime we and our horses would enjoy a refreshing rest.

The *kao-yeh,* or secretary of the *ponbo,* and a Tibetanized Chinaman came over the following day to ask us upon what condition we would journey towards Ta-chien-lu. We replied that we were to be provided with three guides who knew the road, our tired horses were to be exchanged for fresh ones, and we were to be given two extra ones, as we were setting out on a journey of several months which our own ponies would not stand unless we gave them a long rest. The result of our interview was that the next day four of our horses were traded and we received two extra ones, after which we were invited again to the chief's tent. During the conversation he informed us that he knew there were several *peling* countries, and telling them off on his fingers he gave us the extent of his knowledge of the geography of the outside world, composed, he said, of the following countries: England, London, Paris, France, Italy and Tien-chu-kiao, the latter being the Chinese name for the Roman Catholic religion! This from a lama and one of the highest officials in the land, is another sample of the deep and superior knowledge with which western Theosophists believe the lamas to be endowed. How ignorant must the mass of the population be who have never had the educational privileges of their exalted teachers, and how much in need of the education and knowledge that go hand in hand with the gospel of Christ! While we were supplying the secretary data for his report to Lhasa of our name, country, etc., several men came into the tent, each carrying one of the following: a bag of rice, one of flour, a very large bag of *tsamba,* a brick of tea, and several pounds of butter, and set them down before us. The chief then told us these were for our use on the journey, adding that two fat sheep would be brought us in the evening. We thanked him, but having all the food we could possibly require we accepted only the sheep and butter, so he added another lump of the latter. Shortly afterwards we arose to go, realizing that we had passed a very pleasant time with these chiefs, who really had been as kind to us as their superior at Lhasa would allow them to be, only being compelled to be apparently disagreeable in refusing us permission to remain or proceed.

We had told the *ponbo* that we would leave the day following, if our guides were ready, so we reckoned up with Rahim that evening, for according to agreement, he was to go on to Ladak if we were compelled to return to China. We gave him 40.65 ounces of silver, Tankar weight, a carbine and cartridges, a horse with a saddle, and as much food as he wanted. His plan was to travel with us the first day, then branch off towards Sapo, and from there to Trashil'unpo; for the chief absolutely refused to allow him to remain in Nagch'uk'a after we were gone, or to go from there towards his home, but he would allow him to go on with us half a month's journey to Tashi Gomba, then return to Nagch'uk'a with the guides, and proceed to Ladak if he wished. As Rahim considered a month's extra traveling as unnecessary as it was undesirable, he preferred adhering to his own plan.

CHAPTER XVIII

ON THE CARAVAN ROAD

The Start from Nagch'uk'a With New Guides—Farewell to Our Last Friend—Rahim Leaves for Ladak—Fording the Shak Chu Torrent—Reading the Gospels—A Day of Memories.

There are three great highways leading from Nagch'uk'a to China, the first being the *Chang-lam,* or long road, through the Ts'aidam to Tankar, which was formerly traversed by the tribute on its way to Pekin. This is the road we followed. In times past there was another road through the Ts'aidam to Tankar called the oriental road, the one that Huc and Gabet pursued. The second important highway runs to Jyékundo and through the Horba and Dergé provinces on to Ta-chien-lu, where it is known by the name of the *Pei-lu,* or northern road. The third highway is the one through Ch'amdo and Batang to Ta-chien-lu, called the tea road, though often caravans from Lhasa to China do not touch Nagch'uk'a, but go directly to Ch'amdo. This is the road taken now by the tribute from Lhasa and also from Nepaul. There are two other roads to Jyékundo, and another going south of Ch'amdo, but joining with the third of the above mentioned highways at Ichu.

On account of its more direct route we had expected to go towards Ta-chien-lu along this third road, but the *ponbo* rather desired us to pursue our journey by way of Jyékundo, and we felt it made little difference to us which highway we followed, as our plan was to winter some place *en route*. Having insisted upon being provided with three reliable guides, and having been promised them, we did not prepare to depart until they had made their appearance. About eleven o'clock on the morning of September 6, they came, mounted on three small graceful ponies, each leading another pony upon which was a pack saddle with food and pots. They also had two sheep which with ours would provide us with fresh meat for some time. In the presence of a large interested crowd of spectators, Nyerpa, the *ponbo's* steward, told the three guides what was expected of them, that they were to take us to the lamasery of Tashi Gomba (or as they called it, Tashi la bu Gomba) where they were, if possible, to obtain permission from the *kanpo* for us to remain all winter, whence they themselves were to return to their homes. Could they not procure the desired permission, they were to proceed to Jyékundo with us, and upon arrival there, we would give them food for the return journey and a present of money if they served us well. When all was understood and agreed to, Nyerpa introduced our men to us, and told us the oldest of the three was a *mamba,* that he was the leader, hence responsible for the other two. Immediately every one began to help us prepare for departure, so we had no opportunity to do more than take a hasty glance at our guides, but noticed they were alert and quick in their movements. The chief came out to say good-bye, and watched our departure in a blinding snow-storm until we were beyond his ken.

Our caravan now consisted of ourselves well mounted on fresh ponies, our three guides, our seven loaded animals and two sheep, while Rahim rode along to avoid any one's suspicion that he intended to do other than to accompany us toward China. Our route lay first east for four hours and a half, then north across the Tzar Chu, a small stream flowing southward, passing in its course Shiabden Gomba. We camped some distance east from Chomora Lake, in a quiet plain, scattered over which were tents and to some of them one of our men betook himself for fuel.

The three guides were dressed in sheepskin, and had extra *pulu* gowns for use in storms to protect themselves from rain and hail. The *mamba* was about forty years of age, a thin, short, wiry man with a wizened face wearing a subdued expression; his hair was hanging about his shoulders, a brass case full of medicines across his bosom, and a bell at his back. He wore a broad-brimmed hat with a peaked crown, made of a light frame-work covered with cloth, and tied under the chin with narrow strips of red cotton. He was a man of remarkable energy, as lively as a little boy, and was almost incessantly mumbling prayers and turning his prayer-wheel as he rode along, while he watched the earth for peculiar stones to make medicines of, asking us to give him hints on points of medical science with which he was not conversant. The other guides were younger, we judged about twenty years of age; one of them was poor, but so willing to help to work and so agreeable in every way, even when working hard looking so pleasant, that we called him the "nice boy." The second one was better dressed, but so unwilling to do anything when it could be avoided that we called him "the lazy one." As the passing days made us more cognizant of his qualities even this appellation, we thought, was too good for him, for in addition to being lazy he was the filthiest of the filthy in his actions and about his food, even putting sausage meat into the casings when the latter had been simply turned but not washed. All the guides were armed with guns and swords. There was a quiet about our hearts that evening, which could only be explained by the fact that it was the last day of Rahim's company and service, but we overcame the tendency to be sad, and discussed our journey together. Rahim impressed upon our three guides how advantageous it would prove to them if they put forth every effort to help us on the road, and retold his desire to reach his far-away home without any unnecessary wanderings; hence his determination to cut across country and reach Shigatsze.

The following morning we arose early, and after tea was partaken of we prepared ourselves as well as we could for another heart-wrench. Words seemed powerless to express our feelings. We could but grasp the hand of the last friend we had in the interior of the great lone land, listen to his "good-bye" and with tear-dimmed eyes watch him retire from us, polite to the last, making his salaams as he led his horse loaded with bedding, clothing, food, a pot and a Tibetan bellows, away towards the Chomora Lake, around which he intended to travel, always keeping it between himself and Nagch'uk'a, and then make his way across to Sapo. There he hoped to remain until he found company with which to journey to Shigatsze. He had many misgivings that he might be murdered for his money, but on the whole was cheerful and hopeful, though lonely. And could he be more lonely than we, as we realized that another link which bound us to the sweet past at Tankar was to be broken? Our two Chinese had long since deserted us, and now we were to be separated from our faithful Rahim who, from the day he reached our northern home, had never ceased to ingratiate himself into our hearts. The boy whose nature had been mellowed by the love of our dear little Charlie, the boy who had accompanied us amid dangers innumerable through the Ts'aidam desert, across treacherous marshes and rivers, and over laborious passes, and who had helped to share our sorrow around the lone little grave north of the Dang La mountains, and had mingled his bitter tears with ours—the last friend we had, it was hard to see him go. Trusty Rahim, with thy dark honest face and flashing eyes, among all the followers of the Prophet thou wert to us the most precious jewel! God grant the Truth may ripen in thy heart, that thou mayest yet be numbered among the disciples of the Christ. The last sight we caught of him was as he disappeared around a little hillock waving his hand. Did he ever succeed in crossing Tibet and reaching his home in far-away Ladak? I do not know; but I have fondly believed he did, and have pictured to myself his joyful meeting once more with his friends who had long since mourned him as dead.

Hastily we prepared to depart in an opposite direction, with nothing human to comfort us—only our dog Topsy and three horses remained to us of all the caravan that left Tankar. We went on into a strange country with strange guides, feeling that our lives were in the Father's hands, whose work we had come to do, and willing that He should dispose of us according to His will.

We met immense caravans of yak with loads of tea from Jyékundo, as many as 1,500 and 2,000 yak in each caravan, with the merchants well-dressed and well-mounted, and drivers some of whom were women and girls. We passed an encampment of traders on their way to Lhasa, at the foot of Karma Kumbum, a large mountain; the hills around were covered with saddled yak, all black, about two thousand of them, while on the pretty plain was a village of large white tents, or more properly, of awnings which were spread out over the tea. We threaded our way through the encampment while the natives in their picturesque garbs of *pulu,* and varied headdresses, held the large dogs in check, or drove our horses from among theirs; then we climbed a steep, stony pass over the afore-mentioned mountains. The usual storm with vivid lightning and hail swept past that day, and while we stood during the severest part, our "nice boy," his horse and sheep all rolled together on the ground, and the hairpins in my hair stung my head. We expected to see the boy unable to rise, believing he had been killed by lightning, but presently he and the animals were restored to their normal position and upon asking him what had happened, he said his horse had been frightened and had fallen. On camping that evening one of our guides on the way to some tents for fuel saw eight robbers heavily armed, and was warned against them by the nomads in the tent, so we put hobbles on our horses that night, but we were not disturbed.

September ninth presents some of the most vivid reminiscences of the two weeks' journey with those guides, and on account of their stupidity at fording rivers is intimately associated with the robber disaster a few days afterwards. It was a beautiful day, the sun bright and warm peeping over the hills into the valley along which we were traveling, hanging drops of silver on the grass. Pursuing our way we reached the Shak Chu at its confluence with the Dang Chu, the former small, but the latter flowing quiet and deep, indicating a difficult ford. The guides looked across and, judging from the little pathways on the opposite side, concluded that sometimes the two streams were forded separately. To do so now, however, was impracticable, so we followed down the Dang Chu which boiled and foamed in a narrow gorge seemingly angry at being thus confined by the rocks, until our path along its edge became difficult and finally, for the horses, impassable on account of the rocks that stood in our way. Ordinarily there would have been a passage between the rocks and the river, but the latter being much swollen had extended its waters right up to the rocks. The *mamba* said we must turn back and cross the two rivers at all hazards, but Mr. Rijnhart not favoring this proposal, crept over the rocks to see what was beyond, and returned to say that we were on the proper trail, that the river was unusually high and that since the horses could not scale the rocks, they would have to be driven into the water and made to swim around to reach level ground on the other side. Feeling it was somewhat risky to trust our riding and loaded animals in the boiling torrent, Mr. Rijnhart made an experiment with his own horse. Tying a long rope to the horse, he retained one end of it himself and crawled again over the rocks as the horse made its way through the seething waters, prepared to pull the animal ashore should it be swept off its feet. The experiment was successful, both landing on the other side of the rocks in safety.

Mr. Rijnhart came back to announce the result and the difficult place was soon passed by all, though the river was not as yet crossed; but we soon reached a spot where this was necessary and where apparently caravans were accustomed to ford. The *mamba* and the two guides said it was impossible to cross a large river where the waters were confined in so small a space, but there was no way of returning or going forward. He sat still on the horse's back to tell over his beads to divine whether we would cross in safety or not, and in the meantime we drove our ponies in, while his horse, being evidently of the same mind as its rider, barely stepped into the water and then stood still. My horse took his cue from the *mamba's,* going only a few steps from the bank and then

CROSSING A ROPE BRIDGE

refusing to move farther, until Mr. Rijnhart, having reached the opposite bank with our loaded animals, came back for me. Dragging our two sheep behind us, while the *mamba* dragged his, we urged on the horses, which, striking out into the current, had to swim hard to keep from being swept down. This was among the most difficult rivers we had forded, and glad were we when all were safely across. While drinking tea, and attempting to dry our clothing, we were amazed and disgusted to see two of our loaded horses across the river quietly grazing. In a moment when we were not watching them, the perverse creatures had recrossed the river, and we happened to look up in time to notice that two others were just about to follow their example. Mr. Rijnhart had to ford the boiling torrent again to bring them back. It will scarcely be wondered at, that we soon began to associate rivers with disasters, and contemplated the crossing of them with little pleasure, seeing that our guides, as they themselves confessed, were unaccustomed to them, living as they did in a place near which there were no streams of any size, and never having forded rivers where the horses had to swim.

Resuming the journey we crossed a high mountain, the Shalop Chercho, and camped on the descent where we had the view of a snowrange, the Sokdee. On the eleventh we ascended another mountain but kept on climbing to cross a higher one still, the Wang-ma-la, with snow peaks on either flank, encountering during the ascent a severe snowstorm through which nothing was visible, and·in which we had the greatest difficulty not to lose one another. We shortly afterwards crossed the Pon Chu, a river worthy of notice on our maps (for I observe it is not marked on that of the Royal Geographical Society) and encamped near a caravan from which eignt horses had been stolen during the night. Here we could find no fuel to boil tea either in the evening or morning. On the twelfth we reached a large tributary of the Sok Chu, which we crossed, and then followed up the main river which was on our right, meeting parts of a caravan of yak upon arrival at the regular ford. As a large portion of the caravan proceeded at once to ford this apparently large river, we sat down to watch them. The foremost yak stood on the river's edge until the whole number came rushing down the incline to the bank, crowding and crashing their loads together. The men shouted and threw stones, some large dogs took to the water, and the first yak plunged awkwardly into the stream, the others following. When they had passed the deepest part of the river they stood still, letting the cool water lave their sides heated with the day's march, not knowing or caring if their precious burden of tea did get wet, or of greater moment still, if they kept their companions behind plunging in deep waters, endeavoring to reach a comfortable standing-place where they too might enjoy the cool stream, and avoid the stones of the drivers. How thankful we were that we had none of these stupid, perverse animals in our caravan. Just when they should be quick they lazily stand still, and where caution is expedient they push and crowd over large boulders and through narrow places, each one trying to occupy the identical place for which another is aiming, all rushing promiscuously with their loads, threatening to smash to pieces everything breakable. The ford was gradually freed for us, the last yak carrying over the drivers who had patiently stood shouting and throwing stones, and we were ready to cross, having first taken off our boots and stockings that they might be kept dry. Holding our feet high up to the saddle, we crossed in safety, and none too soon, for it began to snow, and we could barely find the road. Further on, the caravans we met at intervals left the trail very distinct, and seeing black tents to our left we camped near them, a short distance from the Sok Chu, and succeeded in procuring milk, *sho* and fuel.

I had been almost unfit for traveling for several days; so, although our guides had emphatically refused to rest, we halted at that beautiful place. The snow was deep the next morning, and we could see the women and children come out to look after the flocks and herds. Having only boots and gowns on, and with the soles almost worn off the former, they were shivering with the cold. If they could be taught to prepare the wool and knit comfortable garments for winter wear, how much easier life would be for them, for they must suffer severely in the winter months at altitudes where there is so much snow and intense cold. This, I believe after careful study, is responsible in a large measure for the small families, for many children, not being able to withstand the severity of the weather, succumb.

Our next camping-place was on the banks of the

Teng-nga river, near, though not within sight of, the Teng-nga Gomba. From the latter there were several lamas at the tents near which we were camped. The people were very kind to us there, bringing us milk, etc., warning us also of robbers on our next few days' journey. They accepted with alacrity some Gospels we gave them, sitting around reading them with the *mamba* and Mr. Rijnhart. A nun with her shaven head and plain garb minus many of the ornaments the Tibetan women are so lavish of, took a copy of the Gospels, but could not read a word. Our *mamba* doctored a man there and our guides left one of their sheep, so that they might have meat for their return journey. Brigands must be very numerous just there, because on the following day we heard of fifty of them having killed several men and driven off their yak with loads; moreover the tea merchants we met and camped near, numbered over fifty in the one caravan, such a large company indicating that there are dangers of attack on the road. After following the Ta-o Chu through an immense plain, we camped on September fifteenth in a deserted tenting-place, the remains of the stone and clay ranges all about telling us that the nomadic people favored the green sward near the little stream, for their sheep and cattle. They were evidently either away in the hills on account of robbers, or, because the winter was approaching, they were seeking more sheltered spots for their homes. How welcome was the opportunity to rest on that auspicious day, September fifteenth, for it was the fourth anniversary of our marriage. We had no comfortable parlors into which we could invite our friends, and no friends to invite, yet the day meant so much to us that we must celebrate it even amid the silence, desolation and dangers that surrounded us. For a time we forgot all about robbers and prepared a feast—a rice pudding with sultanas, sugar and butter in it, which we shared with our guides. What memories came trooping up from the past, of our friends in America, of Kumbum and Tankar, of Charlie, and of all the joys and sorrows that had come to us since hand in hand we had gone forth to fulfil the mission to which we had been called. How tenderly my husband spoke of the mysterious dealings of Providence, and of his faith in that unchanging love which he had learned to trust, even where he could not trace. And can I ever forget his words of comfort and assurance to me, words which the poet has thrown into music:

> "My wife, my life! Oh, we will walk this world,
> Yoked in all exercise of noble end,
> And so through those dark gates across the wild
> Which no man knows!"

Little did I realize how soon he was to pass into those dark gates leaving me on the dreary wild alone. Even that happy day was marred by an accident which happened to Mr. Rijnhart, who trod on the rusty buckle of a saddle and as a result suffered intense pain, which was much augmented when the time came that he had to journey on foot. The weather was perfect and we enjoyed talking of our prospects when we reached Tashi Gomba, where the *mamba* said he was almost sure we would be allowed to spend the winter. The following day we crossed another large plain at the eastern extremity of which we forded the Dam Chu, a beautiful river, very clear, every pebble in the bottom of which we could distinctly see. Before we started, wolves in large packs howled around our tent, and we met individual ones on the road. Topsy chased a bear only a hundred yards from us, while a large herd of wild cattle were scattered around us. On September 18 we had snow, hail and rain while we crossed a mountain called Gerchen tsang mo la, and camped near a large stream of which the *mamba* did not know the name. None of our guides had ever been this far on the road before, but had received directions as to how to find the lamasery we were looking for, and as the *Ja-lam* we were following was a large trail, we had little fear of losing our way. Our three guides had served us faithfully and our days together had been profitable to both them and Mr. Rijnhart, to the latter especially in the language and character. Every day when evening came, the *mamba* had taken his bell, little drum and a book, and, sitting in the far corner of the tent that Rahim had used, had chanted prayers for two hours or more. The "lazy boy" had not improved on acquaintance, but was bearable, the other two more than making up for his disagreeable manner, which sometimes even amounted to sulkiness. The unexpected manner in which even these guides were lost to us will be told in the next chapter.

CHAPTER XIX

ATTACKED BY MOUNTAIN ROBBERS

We Cross the Tsa Chu—Suspicious Visitors—A Shower of Bullets and Boulders—Loss of our Animals—Our Guides Disappear—The Dread Night by the River.

The last tent people and caravans which we met had told our guides that we were approaching a large river, the Tsa Chu, and had given the directions we were to follow, in order to reach Tashi Gomba, which they informed us was on the bank of the above river, assuring us of the truth of the statement by saying that the lamas carried water from the river to make their tea. Having traveled over one rocky mountain after another and across two streams flowing south, we camped on September nineteenth within sight of a large range of mountains east of us. How imposing these latter were, perpendicular and bare, rugged and severe, giving us the impression that along their edge flowed a large river. This was also the *mamba's* opinion, for he remarked that probably at their base was the mighty Tsa Chu. Next morning we reached a little stream which the guides said was a feeder of the Tsa Chu. Following it a long distance by the side of rugged mountains whose peaks were barren rocks lost in the clouds, we passed a large mineral stream spreading out and flowing down the hillside, leaving dark brown stains on the rock and stones wherever it had coursed, and eventually reached the Tsa Chu, where a large tributary flowed into it. Having crossed the latter with very little difficulty, notwithstanding the fact that large masses of rock half concealed by the water almost caused the loss of some of our ponies, we halted on the bank of the main river, tightened our girths, gauged the best spot for fording, and all dashed into the water shouting lustily to encourage ourselves and the horses. Though very wide, the river was not more than two and a half feet deep, and the current was neither rushing nor strong as in some other rivers we had recently crossed, hence we congratulated ourselves on our good fortune in having left behind us the last large river to be forded until we should pass the lamasery. As the caravan road did not skirt the river, we turned aside from it to the right and followed a bridle path along the bank, the people having given the information that in half a day's journey down the river from the ford, yak could easily reach the lamasery of which we were in search.

Our march that day had been a wearisome one for us all, and we immediately looked for a suitable place to camp where there was good fodder; half an hour after fording we found one, a level sward, with hills behind us covered with grass and firewood, and in front of us the Tsa Chu. Having pitched our tents on the northeast of the river, we roamed about enjoying the gorgeous view that presented itself to us. The valley from which we had just emerged was narrow; the hills and mountains on either side were ranged against the horizon in glittering masses, rugged, fantastic and multiform in outline, and of varied tints, the brilliant green of the sloping pasture land mounting gradually and fading into the delicate purple and grey of the rocky summits; the river in its placid onward course suggested peace and power; the hillocks close to its edge across from us, seemed with their side garments of deep verdure tapering off into rocky, sun-gilded crests, like monarchs of a lower rank reflecting the splendor of the kingly giant-like elevations whose heads, towering far above, were crowned with azure and gold. Behind us again, were other hills clothed with beauty in minute detail, from the massive rocks with their clinging lichens, to the pretty low shrubs covered with small leaves and yellow flowers like miniature roses. The little paths intersecting one another and running in all directions suggested our proximity to a lamasery or encampment, and in anticipation of reaching it soon we were happy.

Toward nightfall two men on white horses emerged from the valley we ourselves had just quitted, and, instead of fording the river, skirted the bank, arriving at a spot opposite us, where they reined in their horses to hold converse with our men. The lazy boy went to the river's edge and talked with them, during which time Mr. Rijnhart leisurely took a good look at them through the telescope. They were heavily armed with guns, spears, and swords, had no saddle bags, hence were not travelers, and one of them had his face painted red and yellow. While they talked they indulged in snuff, and looked too closely at our ponies to make us feel altogether comfortable, the *mamba* standing near us being of the same opinion as ourselves. Having satisfied their curiosity they disappeared over the hills diagonally from the river down stream. Immediately the guides came to caution us about their probable intention to rob us that night, and themselves prepared to meet the enemy by taking down their tent, intending to sleep outside so that they could watch their six horses. We put the iron hobbles on ours, tied Topsy behind them, and Mr. Rijnhart slept in the door of the tent with both revolvers ready to frighten anyone who should come about during the night. It was the very last time we used a tent. The night passed but no noise was heard, and in the morning, feeling that we might have been unduly alarmed, we bent our thoughts and hopes on the lamasery, the very sound of Tashi Gomba having now become as music in our ears. We could find no proper road—only a bridle path that now skirted the river's edge, then led up to well-nigh inaccessible places and circled on the slopes of steep hills. The riding was unsafe and often we had to rest our horses. One of them fell and his entire load had to be removed before he would attempt to rise, even then remaining complacently as he had fallen until we forcibly aided him to use his feet.

About noon we followed a road down to the river to a grassy place where was apparently a yak-trail, but beyond which the rocks looked as if thy jutted into the river. To avoid having to retrace our steps should we find it thus, we sent the lazy boy ahead to see, and as he did not return we concluded the road was passable; so drove our animals across the grass, over a little hillock, to find the boy sitting playing with pebbles beside the river, near a spot where the water boiled against a cliff that rose steep and straight and impassable from its watery depths. Mr. Rijnhart suggested fording the river and refording further on, but the *mamba* said that our horses, especially the one that had fallen, tired out with the day's travel, would be unable to stem the flood, and it would be best to return, rest there on that grassy spot while we drank tea, and then go up over the hills, and so past the difficult place. Knowing the wisdom of his advice, we acquiesced, and, having arrived, took the loads off our horses; then the men got three stones to rest the pot on, gathered fuel and began to prepare our lunch. The river flowed in front of us, while behind, a distance of seventy feet from the former, rose cliffs and rocks at the foot of which were traces of old camps, such as ashes on the ground and smoke on the stones. We reclined in the shade of the cliff until the tea would be ready, and Mr. Rijnhart said suddenly that he thought he heard men whistling in the characteristic way in which they drive yak. We all listened, but heard nothing, when, without any warning, a shot rang through the air, the bullet falling in the water. At the command of the *mamba* the two boys jumped up and ran to drive the horses into the shelter of the cliff, where they could be prevented from stampeding on the little road leading up to the robbers. The "nice boy" was shot almost immediately through the right upper arm, whereupon we all promiscuously sought cover at the side of the cliff. Bullets continued to fall like rain. Immense boulders were hurled down from the heights, any one of which striking us would have crushed us beyond recognition, while accompanying both the shooting and the hurling of the rocks there were yells, piercing and hideous, which only Tibetan robbers know how to utter. Mr. Rijnhart, determined to ascertain the direction from which the bullets were coming, and who was firing them, stepped out from under the cliff towards the river's edge and looked up, only to be greeted by a bullet which, as he suddenly stooped, struck the ground behind him. He quickly returned to shelter, but in his haste ran into the nook where the guides were crouched, so that he was hidden from me, as a projecting angle separated my nook from theirs. There I was alone, not knowing at the time whether my husband had been killed or wounded, or whether he had taken refuge somewhere under the cliff. There had always been an implicit understanding between us that I was to remain just where he left me in case of peril or danger, relying on his care over me even when absent. So, straining myself as close to the rocks as possible, I waited breathing a prayer for the protection of our lives, for I thought my husband and the guides had gone to parley with the robbers. After what seemed a long time, the firing almost ceased, then a final volley of quick shots and a few deafening yells, followed by shouts dying away in the distance, told us that for the immediate present the danger was over. Mr. Rijnhart then came up and threw himself in exhaustion on the ground, saying: "Well, we have lost all our horses except three." What a sigh of intense relief I heaved! I was so thankful to see him unharmed after my dreading his being killed. "Have you made peace with them?" I asked. "Why," he replied, "I have never seen them, except when I went to look up and saw three men behind a rock with their guns resting ready aimed; the powder flashed in the pan; involuntarily I stooped, and then sought and remained in shelter, attending to the poor boy's arm, all torn and bleeding."

He then took me by the hand, and carefully keeping close to the rocks, we crept to where the guides were, and saw that three of the horses that were apparently saved had been shot, one being already dead, while another was shot through the backbone and could not rise. Some of our horses had absolutely refused to be frightened by the bullets and boulders that were cleverly directed by the wily robbers, to divide us from our horses and prevent our saving them; but the last shots had despatched three of these four, so that we might not be able to pursue or trace the thieves. The guides, who understood the tactics, had managed to save three of their ponies, exposing themselves to fire thereby, but we, ignorant of the natives' way of robbing, imagined they would come down from above, and did not try to save our horses, though it is manifest that we would have been shot had we interfered. A sorrowful, frightened little band we were, grouped together in the cover afforded us by the friendly rocks, the wounded boy tenderly nursing his arm, on which the blood had left marks little darker than the skin, and whose face bore besides the expression of pain, that of hurt surprise that he should have been the only one to be injured. We managed to drag the pot of tea into shelter, where we quenched our thirst and ministered to the "nice boy," who was faint from loss of blood. The *mamba* said: "Buddha knows that the men will return for our baggage, kill us all, and throw us in the river." Mr. Rijnhart walked up a little distance to drive back the old grey horse which was straying in the direction his companions had gone, and quickly the three guides prepared for departure. The lazy boy shouldered his own and his wounded comrade's gun. They helped the latter to a seat on a pack-saddle, their riding saddles all having been stolen but one, and, only delaying a moment to answer my inquiry, "Where are you going?" by replying, "To the monastery for many men to come with us to find the robbers," they started off to the river. Having said they had better stay until their leader returned, I called Mr. Rijnhart, but when he arrived at the spot they were half way across the river, and he had no horse with which to follow them.

Quietly we dragged our possessions into the shelter of the cliffs, tied our grey horse near them, and sat down to drink tea. The feeling uppermost in our minds was one of thankfulness that our lives were spared, and that we were unhurt and had our food and bedding left us. One dead horse was already a prey to the vultures, while the pretty black horse lay not far away, paralyzed from an injury through the spine. He had my riding saddle on him, the only native saddle I had ever found comfortable, and suitable for long journeys. The chestnut horse, shot through a vital spot, and in pain, wandered to the grey horse for comfort, lay down near him, neighed good-byes to the black horse, laid down his head and died. We were now alone with our grey horse, the poorest of the caravan, the one that had fallen that same morning, and was really the cause of our having halted at that grassy place. Suddenly we missed Topsy, and, upon comparing our knowledge of her movements, we found that we had last seen her rushing toward the road when the shots were fired. She had always been accustomed to run after an animal when Rahim went to have some sport with the gun, and we feared she had gone off with our horses, but hoped she would discover her mistake and return. It was about two o'clock in the afternoon, and, talking it all over we decided to stay in that place until the next day to see if our guides were true or not, though we had a very strong suspicion they were not, and even that they were in league with the robbers, and had deliberately led us into ambush. One point was certain, either they had been treacherous or they had not known the road, and unconsciously led us along that bridle path. In either case, the *ponbo* of Nagch'uk'a would be held responsible for the trouble, because as long as we were on the Caravan Road no harm had come to us, and Tashi Gomba is, as far as I can learn, on that highway; but the guides had purposely or unwittingly led us astray. Owing to this uncertainty of the intention of the guides, we concluded to await their return until next day about noon, and then, if they came not, to prepare to travel on foot until we reached the lamasery. But then came the question, where was the lamasery? Were we on the correct road or not? How far away from it were we? As the afternoon wore away we kept, by means of the telescope, a fairly good lookout for the approach of human beings, whether enemies or otherwise; but evening came on and we had seen no one, though we had a very strong feeling that we were being watched all the time, while sounds of the recent shots rang in our ears.

The robbers were well aware of the fact that we had seven loads of baggage for which we had no means of transport, as were also the guides, and we had no doubt that our movements were being spied from the hills or cliffs about us; hence we had some fears that they might return to possess themselves of the valuables. Our loads were not of such great value to us that we cared to risk our lives defending them, and the place had such associations as to give us uncanny feelings, so we decided to abandon the cliffs for the night, when darkness obscured our movements. Silently, not speaking above a whisper, we took our bedding to the edge of the river, where there was a margin of stones six feet wide between the water and a shelving bank two feet high. Spreading our rugs and blankets down, and covering ourselves well, we rested where the water almost laved our feet. Rain fell gently most of the night, but we were protected by our rubber sheeting. We had always carried on our persons money in the form of *sycee,* bullion silver ingots of various weights, and if we had been discovered that night, we intended to take to the water, and upon reaching the other bank, make our way to tents for aid. The night was very long and dark, no object being discernible, and no sound heard but the rippling of the water over the stones, and the cry of some animal or bird unknown to us, that seemed to come from above among the cliffs, and like a sentry's call and answer re-echoed through the mountain silence. Towards morning it ceased raining; a grey light overspread the sky and transformed the river into a second sky, but we did not know the dawn was breaking, thinking the increasing light was due to the clouds dispersing. Then the grey light slowly suffused the whole atmosphere, and we could discover rocks and cliffs and hills standing out, first indistinctly against the heavens, and then in dark relief. As the horizontal streaks of light began to take their places in the clouds over the mountains we arose and, dragging our bedding back to the cliff, were welcomed by our grey horse, and found all as we had left it. We wrapped some blankets about us and crouched down until it was breakfast time, when we gathered some firewood and made our tea.

We both realized the magnitude of the misfortune that had befallen us, and each endeavored to make light of it, and the result was a predominance of brightness rather than gloom; although we were almost certain that our guides had deserted us, and that we would very soon have to find our way on foot either to the lamasery or to an encampment where we might hope to hire some animals. Midday came with bright sunshine, so we undid all our baggage and separated from it what we wished to take with us, not of course all we wanted, but what we could take along, because our one remaining horse was incapable of carrying a heavy load. It was very difficult to reject our most cherished possessions, and when our Bibles of years' use, our instruments and many things that had become a part of our being had to be laid aside, we felt it; but necessity is a stern master, and it had to be. We selected enough food to last fifteen days, all the bedding needed, one large and one small pot, some dessicated soups, beef tea and condensed milk, a change of clothing and the diary of the journey, Mr. Rijnhart's Bible with a few papers, two or three cherished belongings that had been loved and handled by our darling little boy, and a few sundries. Everything else that was valuable we buried under stones at the foot of the cliff, and left in one corner the tents, pack-saddles, etc., hoping that we might meet some one who would come back with us to get the things, and yet feeling all the time so sure that the robbers were watching us, ready to swoop down like eagles after their prey as soon as we had gone. The afternoon wore away, the sun sank behind the hills, and the shades of evening brought no guides, but did bring us an indefinable aversion to spending another night in that place, associated, as it was, with robbers, where sleep would be altogether out of the question. We placed our riding saddle on our grey horse, and on it piled as much of the baggage we had selected as he could possibly carry. Mr. Rijnhart shouldered the remainder, and each taking in hand a staff composed of half a tent-pole, we said good-bye to the cliffs and retraced our steps to follow the same road, up which the horses had stampeded. As we were passing the black horse he tried hard to join us and neighed farewell as far as we could see him. Mr. Rijnhart would have shot him out of mercy, but I begged him not to, for I could not bear the sound of the revolver to ring out, perhaps to give notice of our whereabouts to some travelers overhead, thereby entailing more trouble. Cowardly, it is true, the feeling was, but for long afterwards the sound of shooting brought anything but pleasant memories to my mind.

CHAPTER XX

OUR LAST DAYS TOGETHER

The Robbers' Ambush—The Worst Ford of All—Footmarks and a False Hope—A Deserted Camp—The Bed Under the Snow—Mr. Rijnhart Goes to Native Tents for Aid, Never to Return.

The grassy spot beside the cliff was an ideal camping place, affording shelter from the cold, bleak, piercing winds, or from the hot rays of the noonday sun on warm days; but the recent occurrence had removed all the charms nature had previously possessed for us, and we were glad to tread our way slowly up the trail we had come down the day before. Ascending even so insignificant an incline was laborious, for instead of having our sturdy ponies to carry us up, we had to walk, while Mr. Rijnhart, in addition to shouldering a heavy burden, had to drag along the almost spent horse with his load, an impossible task had I not been behind to urge the poor animal on with my staff. Soon we were at the top, passing the robbers' ambush of the day before, and a beautiful spot it was behind the rocks, a pretty little hollow having served to shelter their horses while they busied themselves in obtaining ours. How many men there had been we could not tell, but we

PETRUS RIJNHART

supposed there were ten or twelve, and they had probably been following and watching us all the morning before a good opportunity for robbing us without danger presented itself. It had now grown dark, but there was sufficient light to enable us to pursue our way a short distance, when we stopped to camp, because we were not sure whether shadows that lay across our path were gullies or not, and we did not wish to lose our bearings. We unloaded our horse, which now seemed so precious to us, tethered him near by, arranged our food in little packages at our heads, to prevent a wild animal snapping at us without warning, and lay down exhausted but much more at ease in our minds than had we remained below the cliffs. The queen of the night slowly wended her way across the star-dotted heavens, diffusing light and shadows about us while we rested, but slept very little. Arising at dawn we found everything that had been exposed to the atmosphere stiff and covered with thick frost, and were astonished to discover ourselves on the edge of a deep gully, into which we would have fallen had we made a few more steps the previous night. We had no idea that we were in the vicinity of such a place, much less so near it.

The next difficulty we encountered was our inability to make a fire, having no fuel except the *argols,* and not being proficient in the use of the Tibetan bellows (a goatskin tied at one end to a round iron pipe fourteen inches long, and about one inch in diameter), which are manipulated by a peculiar motion of the hands. Although Mr. Rijnhart had had considerable practice with the bellows while sitting with the natives around a well-blazing fire, he found it quite another matter to start one when so little force was required, so that at first he succeeded only in extinguishing the blaze instead of increasing it. It took our combined ingenuity and efforts to finally get the fire started that morning, and then I gathered fuel while he plied the awkward bellows. During the tea drinking we discussed our plans, and knowing the over-weight of our loads, both that of the horse and the one under which my husband was obliged to trudge with his sore foot, and considering, besides this, my own poor health, we felt we must not wander aimlessly around. We planned to follow the river down for two days, and then if we failed to find traces of the lamasery or tents, branch off to the left, to again strike the Caravan Road; for, according to our compass and knowledge of the general direction, we were not just then deviating very much from the latter. Having found a path along the little stream on which we had camped, leading toward the Tsa Chu, we followed it around a hill, and soon were beside the obstructing rocks beyond which our boy had been sitting on the day of the robbery, and where we commanded a view of the river and its opposite bank stretching away into open and level country.

After traveling three hours along steep slopes, we reached an overhanging ledge where we must either ford the river or branch in over the hills. Surveying the latter, we saw them rise one tier above another endlessly, and felt that in our circumstances neither we nor our horse were able to undertake any more mountain climbing. Visually measuring the width of the river with its volume and current, we shrank from crossing, but Mr. Rijnhart said he was able to swim in any current and did not fear to undertake it. After due deliberation we decided that the best place to ford was a short distance above the junction of a tributary from the other side and opposite a sandbar which divided the river. Just above the sandbar the waters swept around a curve, while immediately below it were rocks. Mr. Rijnhart, donning some thin garments, loaded the food, pots and sundries on the horse, and started off, intending to make a return trip for me and the bedding. He led the horse across the first part of the river, which was about two feet deep, then let him go, and both swam over. It had begun to rain, and Mr. Rijnhart shivered while he unloaded the animal's burden on the other side, mounted and returned for me. His teeth chattered as he tied the blankets to the back of the saddle and I mounted. As I carried considerable weight in my gown, about ten pounds of silver, our two revolvers, the telescope, our silver-lined *tsamba* basins and dry stockings for us both, Mr. Rijnhart cautioned me not to fall off, for with such impedimenta about me he could do nothing to save me. Taking the long rope in his hand and leading the horse as far up the sandbar as he could without swimming, he then let go and stood to watch us. The current caught the rope and swept it down; the horse, thinking he was being led, turned his head and began to swim down the stream. My husband called to me to pull the right rein, which I had done instinctively. The horse turned suddenly, the rushing water caught underneath the bedding and swept me, saddle and all, almost into the river. Realizing my peril I threw myself over to the opposite side, and so hanging on to the horse's mane with my weight in the right stirrup, by sheer force I kept the whole balanced and reached the bank in safety. The old horse, tired out, sat down in the stream, not being able to step up on the bank; so I dismounted in the water. Almost everything was saturated. Mr. Rijnhart plunged again into the current and crossed successfully, though chilled through from the icy water. Now that all our garments had got wet we were in sore straits. Owing to the rain it was with difficulty we secured sufficient fuel to prepare some hot soup, and as soon as the shower passed off, after spreading our blankets out to dry, we roamed some distance away in search of larger quantities of fuel. Suddenly we discovered the fresh footprints of three horses and a dog. Were they traces of our guides and Topsy? On what slender threads the drooping heart is prepared to hang out a new hope! Wet and cold and forsaken as we were, a tremor of joy awoke in us as we thought of the possibility of help from the old *mamba* and the two boys who had left us on the day of the robbery. Had we misjudged them, and were they still faithful to us? We tarried the night and divined our hope was a vain one; we must therefore press on.

The morning of the following day we almost immediately had to cross a tributary of the Tsa Chu, not a large stream, but the bottom was covered with big stones, and the current was very strong. Not willing to have any more delay than was necessary, we managed to wade across hand in hand, but had great difficulty to hold ourselves erect against the force of almost three feet of water and the tendency to slip on the uneven stones in the bed. The question of river crossing had become harder than ever to solve, with only one horse and not a single native with us, and we tried to think that perhaps we would not be compelled to cross any more. In a pretty ravine we found a deserted camp, in one corner of which we saw three stones that had just recently served as a fireplace, and a small bit of paper and string that we judged had held some medicine used by the *mamba* for the wounded boy's arm. This was the last trace of our guides that we saw. After threading our way through dales and over hillocks we reached a level place on the river's edge, where were remains of several mud and stone ranges, indicating a tenting ground; and as there was good grass and abundance of fuel, we rested for lunch. Looking about carefully we saw what presented the appearance of cattle, and upon taking the telescope discovered immense flocks and herds and tents away down the river, but on the opposite side! Some rocks obstructed our way along the river's edge, necessitating probably a long detour over the hills in order to progress in the direction of those tents, but how welcome the sight and what rejoicing it brought to us! It seemed as if our difficulties were all ended, and feeling no fear to remain alone, but knowing the horse's inability to successfully ford the river again, I would have Mr. Rijnhart cross then and there and go to the tents for aid, leaving me to await his return.

He looked at me a moment, then said: "No, I could not leave you here alone—travelers may come along and find you, and you are a woman. We must stay together as long as we can, and when we have reached a place opposite the tents I can watch you while I am gone."

To that end we left the river and went at right angles to it over steep hills, one rising above another, but each one hidden from view until we had gained the crown of the first, and passing some magnificent rocks we reached the basin of a limpid mountain stream which we followed. Numerous traces of tents were found in this spot hidden among the hills, an admirable place for robber bands to escape detection and yet be near the highway. Large flakes of snow announced an approaching storm, and in order that we might appease our hunger before night came on, we gathered fuel in the skirts of our gowns as we walked along, a practice we had learned from the natives. At dusk we were not yet out of the ravine, but were almost at the summit from which the rivulet sprang, and there we camped. Was it the coming disaster that weighed us down and crushed our bright spirits, or was it that we were in a glen where crime had left its stain? An indescribable feeling of uncanniness seemed to seize us both, so that we scarcely spoke above a whisper, while we selected a spot near an old fireplace. With our one staff, some pieces of string and two pegs, we put our rubber sheeting up for shelter, and crept beneath it. Eight inches of snow fell during the night, making us as warm as when in well-heated apartments; but in the morning it was almost an impossibility to creep out from beneath the weight, even after we had summoned courage to decide that we wanted to. The weather looked threatening and the bulk of snow would tend to make the walking hard, besides wetting our Tibetan boots and consequently our feet. The only dark object we saw far or near was a large brown bear with a white ring around his neck, prowling and shuffling about just a few yards from us. Our pony was the first to stir. He had already brushed the snow away with his lips in order to reach the luscious grass, and at last we, too, with a desperate effort threw off our lethargy and with it our blankets, and crawled out to breakfast on *tsamba* and snow. With fingers biting and aching from the cold, we fastened on the horse's load, Mr. Rijnhart shouldered his, and off we started again, bruin watching us with perhaps more than friendly interest. My husband left me with the horse while he went to reconnoiter a little, so that we might not unnecessarily climb hills, and hence get too far away from the river bank. He found that we had passed the rocks, so we walked around the steep slopes of the hills until we were overlooking the river again; but the walking was inconceivably bad, and in turns we fell on the slippery snow and grass. The horse would slip and struggle, the load would fall off, and then with cold fingers and endless trouble the saddle and all would have to be readjusted and the whole start be made again. Finally, when high up among brushwood on the side of a very steep hill above the river, the horse slipped and rolled over and over down the hillside, until we feared he might only be stayed on his headlong course when he reached the water. When he did come to a stop we felt, even though we were not much nearer the tents on the opposite bank than we had been the morning previous, we could not possibly manage to proceed another step; so, scraping the snow away from a little piece of ground more level than the remaining part, we sat down and made a fire with some of the brushwood growing in the locality.

Some men from the tents were within hailing distance. We shouted; they answered, but would not come near enough to hold any conversation with us, and ran about very much excited on the hills. A Chinaman's curiosity would have induced him to come near enough to find out at least who we were, but a Tibetan's is not so great.

The sun shone brightly, and the snow melted quickly, while we felt that it was too late in the afternoon for Mr. Rijnhart to attempt to go on foot to the tents, as at nightfall he would not have had time to return; so he tried to ford the river on our horse, but it was impossible. Having talked of, thought about, and prayed for guidance in the matter of reaching the tents, we concluded that it would be best to spend the night where we were, and that in the morning Mr. Rijnhart would swim over, hire animals, and at the same time find out our whereabouts in reference to the lamasery. How sore our faces were that night from the sun and snow, and how severely our eyes smarted! Neither of us having any thought of the impending calamity, we rose on the morning of September 26, had breakfast, and my husband prepared for departure. Cutting our rubber sheeting in two, he used part of it to wrap about his dry underwear, jacket, trousers, a piece of silver, five ounces in weight, some *khatas,* and my light revolver. Binding the whole tightly, he strapped it on his back and, taking the staff in his hand to deal with the dogs when he reached the tents, started away cheerfully, telling me not to be afraid, but to use his big revolver, which he had given me in place of my small one, if any one went to harm me. He said he would return before dark, if possible; but if not, he would call out when near me, so that I would not be frightened. When a few steps away he turned to wave his hand and said "ta-ta." Reaching the river's edge he threw off on the bank his heavy wadded Chinese jacket of dark blue cloth, and entered the river. Wading half across, he put out his arms to make the first stroke, but suddenly turned around and walked back again to the bank where he had first entered the water. Shouting something up to me which I did not hear on account of the rushing river, he walked up-stream in the opposite direction to the tents he had set out for. Then he followed a little path around the rocks that had obstructed our way the day before, until out of sight, and *I never saw him again.*

CHAPTER XXI

LOST AND ALONE

Waiting and Watching—Conviction of Mr. Rijnhart's Fate—Refuge Among Strange Tibetans—Their Cruel Treatment—The Start for Jyékundo for Official Aid.

To swim across a river along both banks of which are numerous overhanging cliffs, and which pursues a serpentine course, is by no means easy, for the current carries a swimmer down sometimes to a place where he cannot land. When Mr. Rijnhart turned and waded back to the place at which he had entered, I hastily concluded that he intended to make another trial higher up, where the landing was level and good; for opposite us there were rocks that were in places almost a complete barrier to his getting a footing on shore. I watched for him to enter the water again beyond the large rock behind which he had disappeared; but not seeing him at once I took the telescope and walked a distance down the hill, so that my range of vision should command the bank. To my great surprise I saw flocks of sheep and numbers of cattle just beyond the rocks, on the same side of the river that I was on, and only a short distance away, almost near enough

THE AUTHOR IN TIBETAN COSTUME

for me to have thrown a stone at them. I knew then that Mr. Rijnhart, when he turned about in the water so suddenly, had caught a glimpse of these tents in our vicinity, and had hailed the sight with gladness, feeling that going to them he would need to be away from me only a short time, in comparison with that which he would necessarily occupy in crossing the river, and making his way down to the tents he had first proposed to visit. I also was much pleased at our discovery, for I expected him back perhaps in an hour or so with some of the natives, and at least felt sure that he would not be away until dark. Varied were the thoughts that passed through my mind, for in my imagination I saw him in his clothing wet from wading in the water, as he had not waited a moment to divest himself of the wet garments, nor to pick up and throw about him his warm jacket which he had left on the bank; but accompanying that came a scene beside the fires of the tent where he was probably drinking steaming tea, while he explained his mission to the owners of those sheep and cattle, and bargained with them for animals. A thought of his meeting with trouble did not enter my mind until the hours sped on and he came not; but even then I did not fear, for we had always been treated with the greatest kindness and hospitality whenever we had met the people at their homes, although it is understood by all that the natives are robbers when away from home. He himself had not thought of difficulty, for he did not wait to remove from his bundle the revolver that might have had a moral effect over the tent people; but went around the rock buoyantly and sure that I would no longer have to walk, and that his heavy burden would be carried by strong yak, and doubtless entertaining the hope of being able to get aid from the abbot of Tashi Gomba in tracing our lost horses, resulting perhaps in their recovery.

Soon the sun went down over the top of the hill on which I sat, and the shadows grew longer and longer. Four bears gamboled about on the hillside until the shade fell on them and they shuffled away. I prayed for strength to be quiet, for God to give me freedom from anxiety as the time passed on and there was no appearance of him for whom I had watched all day. The cattle and the sheep across the river were rounded up and driven home to be tethered near the tents, but, besides the bears and my horse, there was not a sign of any living creature on the same bank where I was, for the flocks and herds towards which my husband had gone had long since disappeared.

Knowing that the Tibetans are sometimes dilatory and hard to manage, I tried to think that the tents were some distance away, that the natives refused to help us unless my husband would remain until morning, and so I consoled myself with the thought that daylight would bring him to me. Reason told me he had fallen prey to wicked men, but I would not, because I had no desire to, listen to it, and my heart hoped against hope. Dusk settled into darkness, and a desolate solitude reigned over hill and valley, almost chilling me to the heart as I sat alone in the stillness of that oriental night, broken by no sound of human voice, with no sympathy of friends to fall back upon, not even the companionship of the faithful Topsy. I thought of the possible strain both physical and mental of him who had gone so cheerfully around the rock that day. What he must have suffered did he have time to think of his wife alone and in danger! I knew that, unless he had hopes of helping me himself, every thought was a prayer that his loving Father would tenderly care for the one alone on the hillside. I tied my horse among the bushes and lay down, more for protection from the cold than from any desire to sleep, and spent a quiet, peaceful, though slumberless night, in a mood not to be surprised if the sound of that precious voice rang out my name through the deathly stillness, remembering what he had said about calling to me if he should return after dark—but in vain. Morning came, and with it I rose to use the telescope once more, and wait for the hoped and longed for return of my husband. The cattle and sheep spread out over the hills across the river, and all nature basked in the sunshine, but as the hours of the second day sped on and no trace of him was seen, my heart almost ceased beating. Well it was that we had learned to trust God in hard and difficult places. What else supported me through the leaden hours of that day but the thought that I was in God's hands?

> "Nothing before, nothing behind,
>   The steps of faith
> Fall on the seeming void, and find
>   The rock beneath."

But I must admit it was a faith amidst a darkness

so thick and black that I could not enjoy the sunshine. Evening found me still alone with God, just as I had been the night before. My undefined fear had shaped itself into almost a certainty, leaving me with scarcely any hope of ever seeing my husband again, and with just as little, probably, of my getting away from the same people who had seemingly murdered him, and indeed, I must confess I had no desire to leave that hill. The conviction that the tents beyond those rocks belonged to the robbers who had stolen our horses was forced upon me, and I concluded also that when Mr. Rijnhart suddenly came into their presence they thought he had come for his horses, and would accuse them to their chief, thus causing the loss of the goods they had; and so, to avoid trouble, they had shot him and thrown his body into the river. Some days' journey from there the celebrated traveler Dutreuil de Rhins had been killed in 1894 and the Tibetans had thrown his body into the river, but were compelled to pay dearly for it in silver, and a lama had been beheaded for the crime. This was all well known to the men near us, and if I am correct in my surmise that these were the robbers, my brave and fearless husband had fallen a prey to their distrust and fear. M. Grenard, who was Dutreuil's *compagnon-de-voyage* on the expedition on which the former was killed, as soon as he heard of Mr. Rijnhart's disappearance, wrote that the tribes in the locality where we had met our trouble were the most hostile they had seen, refusing to sell them anything even for large sums of money—and Miss Annie Taylor just avoided being stoned as a witch by the people of Tashi Gomba. These circumstances add weight to what I myself had thought at the time.

The second night I lay awake watching the stars that twinkled joyously, meditating and praying for some light as to my future, and asking God not to permit me to be rash and make mistakes. Oh! if I could only have helped Mr. Rijnhart! Morning came, and with it no solution of the impenetrable difficulty, and it seemed to me that I must stay on and wait indefinitely for some one to come. About ten o'clock I stood scanning the landscape with the telescope, when suddenly I heard a shout from behind me on the hill. My heart bounded with delight under the impulse of the moment, for I concluded it was the voice I so longed to hear, and that the yak I saw were some he had hired to help us. Therefore I was only the more disappointed to see that they belonged to two lamas and several armed Tibetans coming from the opposite direction. I shouted to them, and as the lamas came down the hill I went up towards them, and we sat down to converse while their comrades went on with their yak. After the usual civilities had been exchanged they asked me where my husband was, and I replied that he had gone to some tents and had as yet not returned. They inquired if I were not afraid to stay alone; and for answer I showed them my revolver, explaining that I could easily fire six shots from it before a native could fire one from his gun, and that each bullet could go through three men; whereupon they remarked to each other that no one had better try to harm me, as I could wound eighteen men before I could be touched. They were traveling, they said, to a place three days' journey away, and as they were apparently friendly, I at first thought of journeying with them in the hope of enlisting their help, but gave that up as impossible. Then I asked them to take me across the river on their yak, and in answer they inquired if I had money. I said yes, I would pay them well for it. They jumped up, and, saying they would go for the yak, ran up the hill and out of sight in the direction of the tents to which my husband had gone.

I waited in the same place all that day, but there was no sign of Mr. Rijnhart, nor did the men return when the sun had gone down. I felt that my life would not be worth anything if I remained there all night, and that I must get away from that place; but whither I was to go I did not know. I tried to cross the river on my horse, but he would not venture into the water. Then I dragged him up the hill, sat down once more and reviewed the situation, when the thought came: "Why! I can never get away from here safely anyway. I will never be able to get out of the country, I am so far from the border; I may as well be killed first as last, and so I will go where my precious husband has gone." And once more I pulled my horse down the hill intending to go around the rock. But I was not to go. The impression grew upon me that it was rash to rush into almost certain death, and thus neither be any help to my husband, nor leave any trace of the three of us who had left Tankar in such good spirits, thereby bringing untold sorrow and suspense to our home friends. Then there was the thought of future work. Had we not both consecrated ourselves to the evangelization of Tibet, and now that my dear husband had fallen, was the work and its responsibility any the less mine? Eventually I walked along the river down stream toward the tents Mr. Rijnhart had first in view, with a strong desire to get help to take me to the lamasery or to the chief of the tribe, but with a vague feeling of unrest and of doubt as to what would happen. On reaching the river's edge opposite those tents I called so loudly to the people that a man and a boy came to the nearest place to me, so I asked them to come over the river with two yak, holding up a *khata;* but that was not enough to tempt them, so I showed a piece of silver which I would give them for taking me across the river, and they ran away to return with two yak upon one of which there was a pack saddle. I was amazed to see them drive the fierce looking brutes into the water with stones and shouts. I saw that they expected me to catch them, put my bedding on one, saddle and mount the other, a task that was utterly impossible, for I had no experience with these strange wild burden-bearers—all my life, in fact, I had been possessed of an inordinate fear even of domestic cattle. I shouted over that if a man did not come with the yak they need not send them, as I could not manage them; then they stopped throwing stones and the two unwieldly creatures returned to their homes, while the man said I could stay where I was. I made ready to spend the night there, directly across from those tents, feeling a little more secure when I was so near people whom I did not know were treacherous, so I partook of some *tsamba* and cold water, tied my horse where he could easily be watched, and lay down on the snow. It snowed nearly all night, and it was difficult to be peaceful. How would it all end? Would the people help me in the morning? These were only a few of the many disquieting thoughts that swayed through my mind, while deep down in my heart a voice whispered, "Be still, sad heart, and lean upon thy God, who knoweth the end from the beginning."

When morning dawned I called again, and was glad to see several women and children come to the water's edge, for I thought I could manage them better than I could the men. I soon saw that they would do nothing for me until I had proved that my horse would not take me across, so I put my bedding on him and mounted. The women shouted, threw stones, and waved their hands, while I did my best to persuade him to cross, but he knew his weakness better than we did and not one step would he take, so *Achi* called out for me to dismount, which I did. I then asked what they would do for me. Finally a lama said if I would wait a while he would go to some tents near by and bring a horse over, and I could then cross in safety. About ten o'clock a man and six yak came over for me. The Tibetan was submitted to a careful scrutiny, for on him so much depended, and I saw a man with a dirty face, ragged hair and clothing, but there was an expression in his eyes that made me trust him. He tied my horse to one of the yak, put my things on another and my saddle on a third. He then gave me his own and my riding animals to hold by the rope through their noses, while he drove the other four into the water, amid the clamor of a large party of onlookers on the bank opposite. My horse at first refused to go, but at last launched forth and dragged the yak to which he was tied down the river so far that all feared they would both be lost, though they did succeed in landing far down the stream. I felt anything but comfortable in this, my first, attempt at riding the yak, especially to cross such a large river, but there was nothing else to do; so while my rough-looking guide held the huge black ox by the horns I mounted, and then my companion mounted his. Having no bridle, I had expected my guide to lead mine by the rope, but the two black, bulky animals plunged awkwardly into the water, and I clung convulsively to the saddle, with difficulty keeping my balance, while we swayed with the motion of the animal swimming, and the current which was very strong. When we arrived on the other side, all wet, for oxen swim lower in the water than horses, I expected to go into the tent, change my wet garments, and warm myself before a genial fire; but no, the Tibetans had other plans, and I felt it should be my first aim to make an agreeable impression on these people. Amidst such remarks as, "She is not Chinese, she is a foreigner," they opened up every thing I had with me, and thankful I was that there was nothing among the things that could arouse their suspicion except the revolver, of which they had an intense fear. One man plunged his dirty hand into the bottom of my *tsamba* bag to see if there were anything secreted there, and found a dessert spoon which I gave the one who had brought me over the river, the silver and *khata* having been taken possession of by a man, whom I afterwards learned was a doctor. When the inspection was concluded I then took one of the women by the hand and asked her to come into the tent with me, as I was shivering with the cold, for I had on my wet garments, and the ground was covered with snow. One of the men pointed to a spot in the open a little distance from the tents, and said I could put my things there and sleep. I firmly held to my purpose of not sleeping out-of-doors if I could in any way help it, and besought them to let me have a common tent, or put up a little shelter for me, and finally they led me to the entrance of a narrow cave where a sick cow was lying, and, driving the cow out, they allowed me to put my things there and stay. I quickly availed myself of the shelter, and was soon comfortable in dry garments, sipping hot tea, the first I had had for three days. I thought I had never tasted anything so delicious in my life before as that Tibetan tea, for hunger and cold are efficient appetizers. My efforts to conciliate these people were eminently successful, and we were soon on the best of terms, chatting freely, but deep in my heart lurked the awful fear of my husband's fate, and despair of getting aid. They told me that the lamasery of Tashi Gomba was two days' journey away; the abbot had been beheaded, and all the people were fighting, so nothing would induce the men to go with me there, and the chief of the tribe was three days' journey distant, so that I could not find my way to him. Though I did not tell them what I thought had happened to my husband, they suspected that there was something amiss, and they knew I had been robbed, also that I could not have come there alone; so they would not aid me to reach any person of authority, because they might then be interfering in their neighbors' escapades, thereby making of their nearest tent-dwellers lifelong enemies. One Tibetan will not openly betray another, but sometimes very secretly for a large sum of money he will tell the owner of horses that have been stolen at whose tent the latter may be found; but the fact that the information has been given him by another is never to be made known, not even to the chief. This was the secret of the Tibetans in that locality not helping me, for if they had it would have spoiled their lives. They told me that Jyékundo, a good-sized town, could be reached in ten days by horseback and in fifteen by yak. As a Chinese official is stationed at Jyékundo I prepared to go there to meet him. I knew he could send letters to Ta-chien-lu for me, and could also send soldiers back with me to find out what had happened to Mr. Rijnhart. But the natives refused to go all the way, and asked so much money to go five days with me that we could not come to terms, so I remained four days in that little cave.

At night the sick cow lay outside and ground her teeth, while I put my saddle and traps in the entrance to prevent her walking in upon me. The men and women visited me freely, bringing me butter and meat for sale, and always wanting the same things in exchange, viz.: the green stones that are used so profusely to decorate headdresses. I went the afternoon of the first day to a spot on the river across from the place where I had sat those days waiting and waiting. How sad I felt when I saw on the bank, just where he had left it, my husband's wadded jacket. The third day two lamas on horseback, and I on a yak, went again, the former going across the river to get the things that I had left there, because I was not able to take them all when I had gone towards the tents. I watched them through the telescope, and my heart sank when I saw all the things in the same condition in which I had left them, for I knew no one had been near the place, and my last atom of hope for the return of the absent one was gone. With a weary heart I urged the men to start on the five days' journey toward Jyékundo, but they were slow in promising to leave. Finally, from some superstition or fear, they did not wish to have me near their tents any longer, perhaps because they thought I might bring harm to them, so we soon came to terms and started away. Almost everything I had, they managed with great sleight-of-hand to steal from me, and it was only upon my refusal to go without my own bridle, which was a good one, that it was forthcoming. I also demanded a wadded garment that would be sadly needed in the cold. A man had hidden it under a stone, but brought it out when I told the woman I must have it. Leaving the place where my baby was buried, and setting out alone with these Tibetans from the locality where I had lost my husband, stand out prominently as the two events in my life that have called forth the greatest effort, accompanied by sorrow too deep for expression.

CHAPTER XXII

WICKED TIBETAN GUIDES

The Apa and the Murder of Dutreuil de Rhins—Conference with a Chief—New Guides, Treacherous and Corrupt—The Night Camp in the Marsh—We Are Taken for Robbers—A Lamasery Fair.

The district along that portion of the Tsa Chu where Mr. Rijnhart disappeared is called Ga-Je, and is governed by native chiefs under the jurisdiction of the Amban at Sining, whose nearest representative is the Chinese official at Jyékundo; so that though the necessity of traveling towards the latter was painful, my heart was full of hope that I might there enlist help, accuse the guilty, and perhaps be able to return with soldiers. The three men whom I had engaged to accompany me five days' journey with yak were to receive ten ounces of silver besides a valuable garment, and they were to arrange with other men to take me another five days' journey towards my goal. The oldest man was about fifty, had almost grey hair, was very dirty, but his manner was so full of simple dignity and kindness that I felt attracted to him, and called him *apa,* a title which pleased him very much. One of his companions was the man who had brought me across the river, and though he ate raw meat with such keen enjoyment as to remind me of cannibalism, and killed a small animal his dog had driven from its shelter, by battering its head against a stone, I did not fear him. About the third there was nothing unusual except that it was he who always held communication with new-comers, and bargained when such was necessary. They each had a sword but no spear; only one carried a gun, while all three walked, driving along three yak, one with my things, one for me to ride, and the other to carry their food, which consisted almost entirely of meat, with a very little butter and *tsamba.* My horse was led by one of the guides, and must have rejoiced in his freedom from even a saddle, after his journey of so many months. The evening before we started on our five days' journey we went a short distance through the hills to some tents belonging to relatives of the guides. The three men slept inside the tents, while I remained out-of-doors on the edge of a hill, where they made a good fire for me, procuring from the tents fuel enough to burn the greater part of the night. Not once again was I ever allowed to enter a tent, or the living room after I had reached the agricultural districts, where the people occupy houses made of stone; for the natives have, besides their superstition and prejudices against all foreigners, a peculiar custom which does not permit women other than those of the family to enter the home. These three guides in their own way were exceedingly kind to me, and though I could not trust them implicitly, my mind was comparatively free from fear.

A TIBETAN HOUSE

The yak I first rode was untrained for riding purposes and, though led by one of the men, made such sudden lurches down the hill that twice the saddle turned and I was violently thrown off, fortunately, towards the ascent and not downwards; but, after the second fall, I insisted on having a larger, though more quiet, animal, and found him much better. My guides succeeded in trading my jaded horse for a fresh one, and when the owner of the latter came to complete the deal he happened to spy my last towel, and nothing would do but I must give him that—not that he would use it much, but he coveted it, and I could not find any substitute acceptable to him; so, feeling that I might not have any other opportunity to make a trade, I let him have what I had hitherto considered a necessity to my existence; but a horse that could carry me over the road was of infinitely more service to me than even a towel.

The three men expressed their satisfaction and pleasure that I was again riding a horse, for they seemed to take quite an interest in me; but no offer I made would induce them to consent to go any further with me than the five days' journey, so much afraid of robbers they were when outside their own district. The *apa* told me there was a large amount of brigandage practised in the locality through which we were then traveling, also in that through which we would have to pursue the journey towards Jyékundo; and therein lay the reason why they had come unmounted and unarmed, for anyone meeting them would at once conclude that they had nothing of value, looking as they did, like beggars. While we were camped one night in a barren valley on the caravan road, between Nagch'uk'a and Jyékundo, on the bank of a little mountain stream, near which the horse was tethered with a long rope so that he might graze the while, suddenly one of the men told us to be still, as the horse heard something. We looked and noticed that his attitude was one of attention, his ears strained to locate a sound. One of the guides immediately untied him, led him to me, and, putting the rope into my hand, told me not to allow him to be taken away on any pretext whatever, but, if necessary, to threaten with my revolver. Soon two horsemen quietly approached, and one of my men went to converse with them, with the result that one of the two went on, and the other stayed during the night with us. He was a well-dressed lama, and, though very inquisitive, was quite harmless; so, after a little anxiety at the beginning, I did not have any reason to object to his presence.

My guides had no small difficulty to hire other men and animals to journey with me when they would leave, but I was so anxious not to be compelled to make a start alone again that I offered them five extra ounces of silver of they succeeded. This was quite an inducement, and, on the night of the fifth day, I had six men with nine yak to stay beside me in the narrow ravine, but I did not feel so comfortable or easy in mind as I had done when alone with my first three guides. The *apa* and I had often sat by the fire chatting freely, while the others gathered fuel and carried water, and I felt as if I were parting with a friend. He told me about the killing of the Frenchman, Dutreuil de Rhins; said that he was there and helped do the firing. I do not credit that, though the fact that he so nonchalantly gave the details, upholding the conduct of those who had taken part in the murder of the gallant French explorer, made me feel anything but secure in the hands of those who think so lightly of killing a foreigner. The morning came for parting with my guides who had been, on the whole, so kind and thoughtful, really having successfully set the ball rolling for me towards Jyékundo. Having received their money, they made me presents of some food, and off they went. We had talked freely of baby, of my husband and of the robbers, and as they had shown me some sympathy I was really lonely when they were gone, and I felt their departure the more keenly bceause they were returning towards the place where my heart had been so strained, and where my thoughts were yet centered, while I was going always further away.

Of my three fresh guides, one was a man of about forty, whom I also pleased by giving the name of *apa;* the youngest was a boy of about seventeen, with a pleasant face, his well-combed and greased hair hanging down behind with an evenly cut fringe in front. He had a new sheepskin gown, white and clean except where his well-oiled hair had soiled it at the back. The third was sneaky both in appearance and action, and was the only one I feared or mistrusted. They were all armed with gun and sword, and, on the whole, we jogged along very harmoniously together. But, strangely enough, they studiously avoided camping near the people, though they agreed to secure the services of three more men to travel the remainder of the way to Jyékundo with me when they themselves had to return. On the morning of the fourth day, as we were following the road high up on a slope, we suddenly saw a chief's tent in the valley at the foot of the hill. I immediately decided to repair to it, and ask for an escort of men with horses, because the yak were so slow and the men were making as little progress as they possibly could each day, in order that they should get only a short distance away from home. When I considered the rate at which we were traveling I felt dubious about the ultimate success of my efforts, for my money would not be sufficient to meet the necessary expense for transport and food; but when I made known to the men my intention they firmly objected, saying they were afraid, for this was their own chief. I took the initiative and dragged my horse down, bidding them follow, which they reluctantly did. Soon the old man and I were calling to the servants around the tent.

On our approach the chief's steward came to converse with us, so I gave him a beautiful *khata* for the *ponbo*, and asked for an interview. He returned the *khata* and said because I was a woman I could not enter into the august presence of his master, but that he himself would act as middleman. I refused to accept the *khata*, and, showing him our Chinese passports, I informed him that we had been robbed some distance away, that this was the first chief I had been able to find, and that I desired an escort with horses to take me to Jyékundo, expressing my willingness to pay for it. He withdrew to the tent to make known my wishes to his master, and returned presently to say there was another chief near by who would give me what I wanted, but that he himself could not. I replied that my present guides were not responsible to anyone for my safety, and that I would not leave the place where I now was without an escort, and that I would stay indefinitely depending upon him for my food, and for the safety of my horse; if I died the government would in time trace me to that spot, and the *ponbo* would get into trouble. This was sufficient to move the chief, and we very soon came to terms; but I was to wait until next day so that the escort might make preparations for the journey. As the five days were not yet up, I retained my three guides until the following morning when, paying them their full amount of money, I permitted them to leave. The subordinates of the chief came about freely, trying to buy my revolver, and particularly the telescope. The *ponbo* did not forget his dignity enough to speak to me, but he sent to ask the loan of my telescope, with which it was evident he was as pleased as a child, for he was anxious to buy it; but, feeling that he would not give me very much for it, I said that if the escort he provided took me to Jyékundo I would send it back with them as a present for him. Several times he sent messengers to ascertain if I meant what I said, to each one of whom I gave the answer that if they returned without it, it would be because *they* had not fulfilled the agreement.

In the evening the two men destined as guides were introduced to me. I noticed that one of them had a very wicked face and a shaven head, while the other was just an ordinary lay Tibetan. I had given the *ponbo* a piece of silver as payment for the escort, and, fearing it was not good all the way through, I presume, they asked if they might cut it in two, and upon permission they did so, each taking a half. They then requested me to travel at night, but I emphasized the fact that I never traveled after dark, and that settled the question. The chief had already sent me presents of butter and cheese, and the next morning we set off, the two men carrying my things on their saddles so that they might not have a third horse to delay us on our way. I had an easy heart, thinking that the chief's men would be quite an improvement over the ones I had hired myself. But what a change! Instead of security I found myself in imminent danger, for two very bad men had been given me, and only the promise to send the telescope to their chief secured any help from them. There are no worse men in the penitentiaries to-day than were those men with whom I traveled for some time, for they planned to kill, to rob me, and did succeed in cheating me. Not for one instant did they escape my surveillance except when they went inside a tent, and even then I watched to see them again at once when they emerged. The one who carried my food on his saddle went to his own tent for the necessaries for the journey, and when gone stole half my little supply of *tsamba* and butter. How despicably mean I thought he was to take from me, a lone woman, my only food, when I was in a hostile country among strangers; but it served to put me on my guard.

The first night we spent beside the other man's tent, and my soul revolts when I think of the suggestions he made to me, and yet he only treated me as if I were a Tibetan woman, not knowing that women in our land are in a widely different position from those in Tibet. When that man—the very thought of whom makes me shudder—was leaving to go to sleep inside the tent, I reiterated what I had already said, that if anything approached me during the night, I would fire my revolver at whatever it was, whereupon he told me to be careful not to kill the dog! In the morning as we started on the big caravan road towards Jyékundo, my treacherous guides caused me to feel more uncomfortable than ever, but they found out that I was to be treated with respect, and that I would not tolerate either familiar language or gesture, being ready with my revolver to resist any impudence. Oh! how I thanked my husband for his thoughtful care in giving me that protective revolver, for it was the only instrument to keep in control the abusive and insulting tendencies of those men. I have never seen any other Tibetans or Chinese who even approached them in wickedness of every description, and sometimes can scarcely realize that I spent days and nights alone with them.

They assured me that women were so low and degraded that they were ashamed to be seen traveling with me, and when we were near people, I was not to open my lips to utter a word, for if I did it would be known I was not one of the nobler sex *like them* and they would not go another step with me. They wished to appear very kind and wanted to relieve me of the heavy telescope, which they offered to carry, but I preferred retaining that myself in the blouse of my gown. As long as I had it, they were to a certain extent in my power, for it would almost mean the loss of their heads did they return to their chief without it. They soon found that I was on the alert against being cheated in a simple manner, so they planned on an extensive scale to get me within their control, but I was in the hands of the great, good Father, and He protected me.

About noon the more wicked of the two complained of a severe pain in his stomach, which grew worse until he was apparently almost unable to proceed. They asked me if I had any medicines that would relieve pain, and I replied in the affirmative, for I had my hypodermic syringe with tablets of morphia which I knew would relieve him, if he were really suffering, something I very much doubted. He asked me if the medicine were Chinese or English, and upon my replying that it was the latter, he said he dare not take it, for though English medicine might be all right for us and the Chinese, it would certainly kill a Tibetan. Seeing tents in the distance to the left of the road, he said we would spend the night beside them, and he would secure the services of a lama who could give him medicine and say prayers for his recovery, so we went towards them. When we had arrived at a place near the last ones, we sat down; they indulged in snuff and conferred together, while I several times suggested that we should make our way over towards the tent and settle down for the night, for we were exhausted and needed rest, while the sick man could go and place himself in the care of the *mamba*. But soon I saw that they were making other plans, for we started on again and left the tents behind us, because, so they tried to make me believe, the inhabitants were very bad robbers, and it would be dangerous for us to remain near them.

I dared not quarrel with them, for it would have ended in their telling the people I was wicked and should be killed, which would probably result in my death, so I felt it was better policy for me to be on my guard and yet not incense my guides. We passed old sites of tents, where were mounds of fuel laid up for future use, and reached an immense marsh through which we traveled for hours, our horses having difficulty to pick their way, and where human beings had in all likelihood never been before. Reaching a little stream we followed it until we found a place where our horses could jump; here we crossed and then followed it back into a right angle, where they dismounted to camp. We had the black, miry stream on two sides of us, and were hemmed in by very marshy ground that extended miles away to the base of some hills. I noticed that the men carefully concealed the fire in order that the flames should not be seen in the distance, and as it was long after dark, we prepared to rest as soon as we had our evening meal. They frequently assured me of the safety of our camping ground, where we could all sleep soundly without any danger of robbers, for we could not be reached without the plunging in the bog betraying the approach of an enemy. They lay down with their guns ready, and their heads beside the smouldering fire, while I spread my rubber sheeting in the driest place I could find a few yards from them, With my revolver in my hand I spent the night, now looking at the stars to glean some hope from their bright twinkle, now at the horses—praying for strength to keep awake that I might watch with unerring and unfaltering eye every movement of the two bad men beside me; for though they had told me so kindly to sleep without fear, they yet called me very softly six times during the night, when I promptly answered so that they might know I was not to be caught napping. What their purpose was I could not discern, but their leading me away from human haunts into the center of that extensive marsh, bidding me have no care for we could all safely sleep, and then calling me so frequently, made me realize that their actions boded no good, and that I might have found a last resting-place in that forsaken spot without a trace being left. Men may plan, but it was not to be as they wished. When the morning dawned the man's pain had vanished, and with it even the appearance of kindness; probably they were angry that a woman was so unexpectedly on her guard. We saddled our horses—I had to saddle my own—and before the sun had as yet risen over the hills, we were on the way back to the main road which we had quitted the day before, trotting along quickly until we reached a place where there were two roads.

Here the guides hesitated, saying they were not certain which of the roads led to Jyékundo, but eventually they took the smaller one, and I suggested our doing what the nomads always do, ask at some adjacent tents for directions as to the proper road; so while I stayed as I had usually done at one side on account of the dogs, they sought information from the tent dwellers. Soon they came to me, asking if I knew what smallpox was, and saying that there was an epidemic of it at Jyékundo, and they would not go. It was not difficult for me to realize what that meant, for Tibetans are very much afraid of that dread disease, and flee from it as we would from yellow fever or cholera. But I said that I was not afraid, and that they must go with me or they could not have the telescope for their chief; whereupon they intimated that it would be better to be killed by the *ponbo* while among their own friends, than to die of smallpox among strangers! It was of no avail for me to say that when we arrived within sight of Jyékundo they might return, and I would proceed alone, for they would not take another step in that direction. I felt that they were only endeavoring again to cheat me, so I suggested having breakfast there near the tents, for I was faint with the long horseback ride, the severe strain of watching the men, and the almost hopeless task of balking them in their wicked designs. I did not dare to tell them I would dispense with their services, for that would at once have turned them into bitter enemies, leaving me to again make my way alone and unknown to tents, where they probably would have scattered calumny. I could scarcely restrain the feeling of desperation that forced itself upon me, and it was difficult to keep the guides from thinking that I was almost nonplussed to know what was the most expedient course to pursue. Any attempts to induce them to go to Jyékundo proved futile, and I concluded to accept their offer to guide me along the caravan road to where there was a Chinaman, for I felt if only I could see one of the Chinese merchants so common near Tibetan towns, that he would certainly help me, a surmise which afterward proved correct. After considerable bargaining and almost a fight between the two men, one of them drawing his sword at the other (whereupon I acted as peacemaker—an important personage in all oriental disturbances), I gave them ten ounces of silver, and promised them the telescope when we found a Chinaman. It is as a rule very poor policy to pay all the money down to guides, and I refused to do it, but they would not stir from the place until I had, though of course I held a firm hold over them through the telescope. At the first tent we came to, they inquired the whereabouts of the Chinese merchants, and led me off the road along a little foot-path, by following which we would find some in two days. My whole nature revolted against traveling with them, for I knew they were bad men trying to cheat me, but it was best to be patient, and so I tried to keep my thoughts on the brightest side of things.

We camped in one of nature's loveliest spots that night—in a little recess among the hills where many tents were pitched on pretty grassy strips, where flocks and herds were peacefully grazing, and where babbled winding brooks, on the bank of one of which we made a fire. The bad men spent the evening in a black tent, but I was almost petrified when they said we were approaching a lamasery where there was an intense hatred of foreigners, and that if it were discovered that I was a foreigner we would all be killed; so that everything that would betray my nationality must be destroyed. I shall never forget the struggle I had when my husband's Bible that he had used for years—his most precious possession—and his diary, were condemned to be destroyed by being buried in a miry stream with stones piled on them; but I had to accede to their requests or face further trouble. The next day we went on, the men acting most mysteriously when the shades of night overwhelmed us, leading the way high up into a sort of cauldron in the hills, far from some tents in the valley, where we could apparently have so peacefully remained. We found just enough water to make a little tea, and then lay down to rest. Suddenly a voice near us rang out in the darkness, the men hushed up their dog, hastily arose, donned their sheepskins, ignited the fuses for their guns, and stood ready to defend their horses, while I prayed for protection. The shouting continued, but slowly died away in the distance, when one of the men remarked that they must be searching for us, or it was some one who was lost, so he in his turn called, and soon, guided by the voice, the stranger made his way to the fire, and the three talked together. I heard him ask who I was, and the guides replied that I was a Chinaman who was going to join his companions at the lamasery, but I did not know the language at all, so he need not address me, a very artful way indeed to prevent his finding out that I was a foreign woman. Presently he went away, and returned almost immediately with three men. I felt that there was something amiss, but soon discovered that owing to our suspicious actions we had been taken for robbers, and they were a deputation sent by the chief to investigate. On their departure they had taken with them one of the guns belonging to my men, as security that we would molest no one during the night. I was painfully weary but dared not sleep, and rejoiced that we would probably reach the lamasery of Rashi Gomba the following morning when I would let the men go back to their homes. I hope no other travelers will ever fall into their hands.

At daybreak a young lama brought back the gun, and as I had the seal of silence on my lips he believed that I was a Chinaman. My hat and fur collar concealed the most of my face, which was far from white, and my garments were by no means unlike those worn by a merchant of the Celestial Empire, especially my big straw hat, which the guides implored me to wear in order to cover my face and hair. How beautiful was the country through which we wended our way on that bright day! Evergreen trees dotted the grassy hillsides and were welcomed as old friends, for I had seen none for many months. Was it because hope sang in my heart, that nature looked bright and inviting? Or was it that breezes whispered the same stories through the boughs as I had often listened to in far-away Canada? Or perhaps the secret lay in the fact that in a few hours I should have parted company with the worst men I had ever had the misfortune to come in contact with. The tents, nestled in snug corners of the valleys, looked inviting, and I would not have had any fear to make my way to them, for where Chinese merchants are common, Tibetans are as a rule tolerant and liberal. Presently we came in sight of a small lamasery which was, as is usual with these villages, built partly on the slopes of hills and partly in the valley beside a river, and though the houses were not many in number they were very substantial and looked well. There were hundreds of tents of different kinds scattered around the lamas' abodes, and I realized there was a fair in progress, thus accounting for the large number of people in gay apparel whom we had seen journeying in our direction. A Tibetan fair is the last place foreigners should go to when they are unknown, for a rabble of people drinking and carousing is unreliable, and just as likely to be hostile as friendly. The men found a Chinese merchant who had rooms in a lama's house, so to him we went, and as I was debarred from entering the lamasery because I was a woman, he came out to see me. The guides merely told him that I was a Chinese woman from Sining, and immediately made off, telescope and all, but I breathed a sigh of relief even though I had as yet to make a friendly atmosphere for myself in my new surroundings.

CHAPTER XXIII

A FRIENDLY CHINAMAN

A Protector at Last—I Receive a Passport from the Abbot of Rashi Gomba—A Lama Guide—Battle With Fierce Dogs—Arrival at Jyékundo—No Official Aid.

Near the entrance in the mud-brick wall around the house stood a group of lamas, conspicuous among whom was a Chinaman about fifty years old, with pock-marked face and typical Chinese features, who wore the ordinary Chinese garb, not omitting even the little circular black hat with the red button. There was nothing in my cursory glance at him to give me cause for either hope or fear, though his first words might seal my fate, for he could wield as he chose the curious and idle crowd that was quickly gathering about and hemming us in. What would be his first hasty thought? Would he be unfriendly and so increase the innate prejudice of the unruly and armed Tibetans? or would he grasp the situation and thus save me?

I addressed him as *lao-yeh* (a very respectful title to give an old man or one of rank), in my Sining dialect of the Chinese, which would tally with the announcement of the guides that I was a Chinese woman from

Sining; but his first sentence told me that he had pierced my identity with his careful scrutiny, and knew that I was a European, for he said, "How is it that you are here all alone like this?" He had recognized the bond between us of our being the only "strangers in a strange land," and though several Tibetans said that I was not Chinese but *peling,* he gave them no heed; while I opened my heart to him and told him of the fate of our caravan, of our little son's death, of our being robbed, and then of the awful separation from my husband—with the subsequent necessity of my traveling alone. He was touched—the death of a son always comes with sorrow to a Chinaman —and he said, "You have eaten much bitterness. Quiet your heart, for now that you are with us Chinese you are all right. The Tibetans are bad, but we are all travelers alike." Some of the lamas brought me a pitcher of tea which was indeed welcome, while we two conversed in a language which the Tibetans did not understand, and he communicated to them as much of the information as he deemed wise, withholding the fact that I was not a Chinese woman, though had they looked at my feet they might have known.

It was with a great shock of disappointment that I learned of the absence from Jyékundo of the Chinese official, for the representative of the Amban had left that place in the summer, and no one would come to fill the office until the following year. Thus my hopes of aid from that source were crushed, but the merchant said there was no small-pox there. He had a depot for trade in that town, and when the five days of the fair were ended, he would be returning, and he offered me the escort of himself and his men if I would wait and go with them. In the meantime the lamas erected a comfortable shelter near the doorway where I could remain until we were ready to leave; but, though kindness and sincerity had prompted the act, I felt that I, a woman alone, was not safe. So I made known my misgivings to Kia *Chong-kuei-teh,* the Chinaman, saying that if only I were near other women, or could procure an escort to Jyékundo where I might rest until he came, I would feel safer than at the fair where I would have to remain five days, each day increasing the turbulent crowd. There was little possibility of being able to persuade anyone to leave the fair just at its commencement, but he clearly saw the reasons for my fears, so towards evening I was taken to the proximity of a black tent where there were Buddhist nuns, in which I was to have quarters. I could scarcely realize the transition from such deep fear when with those guides, to the sense of peace that resulted from the care, respect and friendly interest manifested by that Chinaman and the priests. As evening settled down, one of the lamas took my horse to his home where I would have no anxiety concerning him, and as I drank in the delight of the peaceful shepherd scenes about me, my troubled heart was lulled into a calm. The black cattle came slowly in, glad to see their young again, the sheep pattered along bleating, horses whinnied joyfully, women carried water from the clear mountain stream, while a short distance away the visitors to the fair in their gay garments were busy piling up near the white or blue tents their merchandise, and tethering their transport yak, or mules and horses where they could exercise vigilance over them during the night.

Early the following morning a messenger came to inform me that I was to leave that day for Jyékundo. Kia *Chong-kuei-teh* had, contrary to his most sanguine expectations, received from the abbot of Rashi Gomba, the lamasery where I was staying, a passport duly signed and sealed by the same, which said that I was a Chinese woman from Sining sent by the officials of Nagch'uk'a, and that I was to have *ula* and escort to Jyékundo. Presently a lama brought my horse which he saddled, putting my load on it, and then led me into the presence of the Chinaman, who communicated his plan for my safety, saying that a lama would go with me until we reached a chief in the Jyékundo district who would provide an escort to the town itself, where I was to inquire for his home, and stay there until he arrived. He also tried to have a piece of silver changed into Indian rupees, but the abbot not having any use for my *sycee* wanted too much discount, so the merchant himself changed it without loss to me. It is only fair to pay a tribute to this man, a perfect stranger, who treated me in as kind and thoughtful a manner as any European could have done, not expecting to receive the smallest compensation for his pains either. It is not pleasant to hear wholesale condemnation of the Chinese race from people who know very little about them; all Chinese are not Boxers, and if my experience with that merchant will tend somewhat to modify anyone's opinion about them, I shall be satisfied. The old lama who was to accompany me to the nearest section under Jyékundo jurisdiction intimated that he was ready, so I bade good-bye to those who had befriended me, and winding our way around a high wall built entirely of white *mani* stones, inscribed with the mystic formula, *O mani padme hum,* we paused before the old man's house to tell his relatives where he was going. After that we followed the crystal stream a short distance, and then, crossing it, stopped beside a tent. I was given an abiding place in the shelter of a huge stone which protected me from the cold, while the sun shed its genial warmth about me, and, as almost all the natives were at the fair, I had no idlers lounging around from curiosity. Thus for hours I sat alone reviewing the past days and planning the future ones, still enjoying the respite from strain, and having no fear of such treachery as had almost led to my doom the last time I had received an escort from a chief. The old lama boiled my tea, and, with kindness supreme, brought his rug out and, settling himself not far from me for the night, guarded me from harm and danger. This may have been due to the respect and civility shown those who are traveling on a passport, for when a traveler has *ula,* the people are supposed to watch over him and his belongings to insure safety against thieves.

Jyékundo is two days' journey from Rashi Gomba, but we spent three days after we left the old man's tents in reaching the town, and I did not at all object. The first day was a long one, for we traveled from early morning until almost dark, through beautiful country

MANI STONE WITH INSCRIBED PRAYER

in places dotted with trees and alternately mountainous and level. We lunched in the afternoon with two travelers known to my lama, one a well-to-do merchant, the other a nun, good-looking, sprightly, and apparently very devotional, diligently mumbling prayers, but ready whenever the desired opportunity came to take her share in the conversation. They were on their way to the fair, but were camping for the night; so they had piled up their baggage, mostly *tsamba* and tea, and taken shelter beside it. They were both well-dressed, had silver *tsamba* basins, silver mounted knives, etc., and were on very familiar terms with each other; while Moggie, as the men called the nun, coquettishly resented the teasing she received from one of those who had accompanied me.

Another interesting woman played an important part in our evening's entertainment, for, having passed through tangled copsewood, we reached a group of tents, at one of which the men called and in answer a woman came forth. She was about fifty years of age, with an intensely pleasant face and characteristic manner, her head crowned with discs of amber, her hair with streaks of silver in it, her hands decked with jewels. Her husband, the government steward, was away, so she held the reins of authority, and when my passport had been examined amidst considerable friendly discussion, during which the Rashi lama was often mentioned, she invited us to select a camping spot. Meanwhile she repaired to her tent, almost immediately returning with a brass teapot wrought in curious and elaborate design, filled with milk tea which she proffered for our refreshment. The old lama then gave me over to her care, adjuring her to make sure that I should be protected from the dogs, and when all was amicably settled she withdrew to the tents. The three of us made ourselves as comfortable as possible for the night, although we were much startled by dogs and people running about in an excited manner, because, as we learned from one of our men who went to inquire, there were people camped beyond the copse who were supposed to be robbers, and the chief had ordered an investigation to be made by the tent-dwellers in the vicinity; hence the confusion. In the morning my two guides having returned to Rashi Gomba, I was supplied with an escort consisting of a man and his son who, as is the custom with *ula,* led me to the tents where the latter was to be supplied, and in their turn left me with strangers in an extensive plain. That night was as uncomfortable as any I ever spent among the Tibetans. It was raining and snowing, and as the natives did not wish to sleep out-of-doors beside me, they provided me with a large heavy native woolen rug, and went themselves into their tents to sleep, leaving me outside entirely alone, though that is unusual when one has *ula.* The dogs, over a dozen in number, large and ferocious, soon discovered that I was a foreign element near their home, and came at intervals during the night, barking around me, scratching at my blankets and jumping upon me, while I kept well covered, with a hand grasping the bellows to strike one if he ventured too near my head. I felt like some one who is being hunted to the death, and called aloud for help; but, though the people heard the dogs and understood what was wrong, they heeded me not, and I could hear them laughing and talking. As far as they were concerned I might have been torn and bitten, but morning found me safe. Soon afterward I left with one man and a yak for Jyékundo, and, having traveled about three hours, we suddenly saw cultivated fields, which to me were the harbingers of peace and safety. A great joy possessed my heart, for months had passed since last I saw such marks of civilization.

The town of Jyékundo was not far from the little farms. Turning abruptly into another valley we saw the bright walls of the lamasery on the summit of a steep hill, at the foot of which was the secular part of the town, made up of houses substantially built of mud-brick, with flat roofs, the whole reminding one of a beehive, for the natives were busy ascending and descending the incline between the town and a clear placid river flowing below it. The valley was level and fairly green, droves of yak were resting and grazing in it, while throngs of travelers were coming and going all the time, all reminding me of the old scenes at Tankar. We wended our way across a little bridge spanning the river, and up into a street upon which opened courtyards and a few shops.

The Tibetan with me did not know the whereabouts of Kia *Chong-kuei-teh's* house, so he stopped in the center of the street, and quickly a crowd of Tibetan men, women and children, with a few Chinese, surrounded me. I could get no one to direct me to the merchant's home, as all seemed afraid to help me, so I showed my passport from the Rashi lama, and asked for a room to dwell in for a few days, the man who was my escort seconding the demand because he was in a hurry to leave, and yet could not dump my bedding, which was carried on his yak, into the street. The abbot of Rashi Gomba seemed to be much respected, and several of the natives endeavored to find someone willing to give me a lodging, succeeding eventually in securing a room in the home of an old man to whom I promised two rupees for the use of it—every Chinaman around helping to *kiang* the price. Followed by a motley crowd, I made my way to the house, the rooms of which were built around a central courtyard, on one side two-storied, on all the other sides flat roofed. I found that a corner room had been allotted to me. Around the walls hung quarters of beef and dressed sheep, on one side were heaped heads of animals and piles of wool; but when the room had been swept and my rug spread on the floor, though there was no window and no furniture, I felt that I had, at least for a few days, a resting place. One never knows how the evil intentions of men may be transformed into blessings, when the ultimate issue of their actions has been made known. When the guides led me, not to Jyékundo, but to Rashi Gomba in order to cheat me, I did not realize that only good would be the outcome, but I was thankful when I stood for two hours in the streets of Jyékundo endeavoring to get an abiding place, that I had not been brought there by those two men. In that case I should have been without the passport that really proved to be the *sesame*.

Among the people crowding about were two Tibetan

women of great beauty, white skin, rosy cheeks, good features, pleasant manners, well dressed in cloth gowns and bedecked with jewels. They were great favorites with the Chinese merchants, who admired them, and, contrary to the custom in the latter's own country, were familiar with them. The house I lodged in belonged in part, if not wholly, to one of these women, who could speak considerable Chinese, and who had been much liked by the Chinese official who had been stationed there.

This town has many different names. I have heard it called Kegedo, Jédo and Jyéku, though Jyékundo is, I believe, the correct name. It has an altitude of 12,935 feet according to Rockhill, is situated at the confluence of two streams whose waters empty into the Dre Chu not far from it, and, together with the lamasery, has a settled population of nearly one thousand, and a floating one of several hundred. It is of great commercial importance, built, as it is, at the junction of several large roads, radiating in different directions, the principal one of which leads to Ta-Chien-lu, the second to Nagch'uk'a, while others lead to Ch'amdo, Sungpan, Sining and Taocheo. The Chinese merchants who reside at Jyékundo import flour, tea, tobacco, chinaware, cotton cloth, thread, buttons and red leather, exchanging them for furs, gold dust, musk, drugs, deer horns and wool. They find the trade profitable, but do not enjoy life at Jyékundo on account of the cold weather and the precarious position of all foreigners among the Tibetans, who are so changeable and often violent.

In this town W. W. Rockhill met with no little trouble, for the chief informed the natives that if they sold him food the money he gave them in payment would, through the foreigner's subtle power, be drawn back to himself; hence they were forbidden to have any communication until he, the *ponbo,* should return from a conference with another chief as to what course they should pursue towards the unexpected and unwelcome stranger. In the meantime the friendly Chinese persuaded Rockhill to leave for Ta-Chien-lu, before the chief's reappearance, otherwise he would assuredly be compelled, however unwilling he might be, to retrace his steps to the Ts'aidam.

Eminently different was my sojourn in Jyékundo. The Chinese merchants accepted me as one of their own countrymen, and vied with one another in endeavoring to make me as comfortable as circumstances would permit, one of them sending me by his servant a large dish of *m'ien* with meat and vegetables.

The morning after my arrival, amid considerable confusion, my room was entered by a man whose face betrayed at once that he was a Mongol, looking very familiar among the Tibetans who had accompanied him. To my astonishment and great pleasure, he addressed me in Sining Chinese, and when I had answered him in the same tongue he turned triumphantly to the bystanders, saying, "She is indeed from Sining, for her words are Sining words." He then told me that he had been absent from home when I arrived the day previous, and had quite resented the information given him that a Chinese woman from Sining was in Jyékundo, and having come expressly to prove that I was not from Sining, was amazed to recognize my dialect. His home was near Tankar, and he had come to Jyékundo as interpreter to the Chinese official, had married a Tibetan woman, to whom he had become so attached that the thought of parting brought him pain, and he was waiting until she and their small family of children could accompany him to his old home. In the meantime he had official rank, and was acting in connection with the Amban's government at Jyékundo. Calling me his relative and guest, he constituted himself my protector and friend, thereby rendering me services that can never be adequately acknowledged. We had scores of acquaintances in common, for his ancestral home was in a little lamasery on the Hsi-ho in the vicinity of our old home, and I was able to give him the first reliable account that he had had of the Mohammedan rebellion, the devastation by the rebels, and the wonderful foreign guns and torpedoes which helped so efficiently to quench the ardor of the *Huei-huei.*

In the absence of the Chinese official the abbot of the lamasery was almost supreme in authority, but my desire to personally interview him did not prevail against the stringent laws forbidding women to enter the lamasery except once, annually, for the purpose of worship; so my conferences were carried on through my Mongol friend, for such he assuredly proved himself to be. I gave him particulars concerning the robbery, and Mr. Rijnhart's mysterious disappearance, which he considered due to his having been murdered, for he said the natives of Ga-Je have a reputation for being difficult to restrain, cruel and treacherous to an extreme. When I asked that an investigation should be made in the latter locality the chief said he had no responsibility or authority in that region, and during the absence of the Chinese official nothing could be done, that Sining would have to be notified, and the Amban would personally send an expedition. By sending up my two Chinese passports and the Tibetan one I had received from the Rashi lama, I impressed upon him my right to an escort, and asked him to provide me with means to travel in safety back to my home in Tankar; but he said that he was sorry that such an arrangement was beyond his power, for the road was so infested by brigands that a very large escort would be required to protect me, besides the fact that the trails are impassable in winter.

The districts under the jurisdiction of the Sining Amban extend only to Kansa, two days' journey from Jyékundo on the road to Ta-chien-lu, hence the Tibetan chief could not be responsible for my being kindly treated in the provinces of Dergé and Horba, which are under Sze Chuan government. I had to adopt careful tactics to induce or compel him to make provision for my safe journey, and emphatically said that unless he would give me a good passport and an order for *ula,* I would wait in Jyékundo until the Chinese official arrived from Sining. As the trouble caused by the Frenchman's murder was fresh in their minds, and my husband's fate was unknown, the abbot would not have me remain in his locality for any consideration, so with the aid of my Mongol friend, devised means for my traveling in safety to China. The Chinese merchants were all in the midst of their most profitable trade, and none of their caravans were leaving except one, that was to be sent on from place to place by agents in the various towns along the route, and might be delayed a month in a place waiting for transport animals; so they, even Kia *Chong-kuei-teh,* could give me no help. The chief sent me presents of *tsamba,* butter, straw for my horse and meat that I had to give away because from its odor it did not promise to be very palatable, and manifested his interest in my welfare by not permitting me to pay any rent for the room, as I was considered an official guest. Soon a passport was ready for me, and literally translated read as follows: "Passport.—This foreign lady, traveling to Ta-Chien-lu, by the supreme order of the above great person, the chief of every place through which her way leads must diligently see to it that she is provided with escort to accompany her. The lady has no horse. She arrived at Jédo on the first of ninth moon, and leaves on the tenth of tenth moon. Passport and *ula* given by three chiefs to Sze Chuan Kansa." The seals of three chiefs were to be affixed to the document to give it greater weight, and the chief said that no one on the road would assume the responsibility of refusing to conduct me safely beyond his section, so I would reach my destination in perfect security. Having changed enough of my bullion silver to give me a sufficient number of rupees for my journey, he sent me his best wishes for peace on the way, and the interpreter, the escort with the *ula,* and myself rode out of the town, across the river and beautiful plain into the main road leading from Jyékundo to Ta-chien-lu, a very large wide trail. Varied were my experiences during the month I spent in reaching the Chinese border, sometimes so thrilling that I doubted whether I should even yet meet my death in Tibetan wilds, separated by long stretches of country from the two who had been so much to me.

CHAPTER XXIV

MORE ROBBERS

From Jyékundo to Kansa—Difficulties with Ula—At the Home of the Gimbi—Corrupt Lamas—Attacked by Drunken Robbers—Deliverance.

The parallel upon which Jyékundo is situated marks approximately the boundary line between the districts of Tibet governed by the Amban at Sining and those under the jurisdiction of the Governor-General of Sze Chuan, and though Jyékundo is the most northerly military post there are several to the south; three of these are on the road which I was to follow to Ta-chien-lu, one at Kanzé, one at Dao, and one at Tai-lin. A colonel with a small number of soldiers is stationed at each post. Though they have no authority over the Tibetan chiefs they report to Ta-chien-lu on the condition of the country, so that should there be any difficulty brewing troops might be dispatched, and thus avoid a struggle that might end in great bloodshed. In the district governed by Sze Chuan the position of the Chinese officials is a very precarious one, and great tact must be used by them in dealing with the natives who consider the Chinese as inferiors in courage and endurance; but, in the portion under Sining supervision the natives fear the Amban and the Chinese soldiers to a surprising extent; hence it is that the Amban's authority is unquestioned. Nevertheless the Chinese *Tung Shih* always exercises the utmost prudence in settling any trouble among the Tibetans when the Chinese government acts as arbitrator, or when it exerts its authority or exacts indemnities. My Mongol friend at Jyékundo assured me that the affair of Dutreuil de Rhins' death had caused the Amban and his stewards great trouble, for the Tibetans thought they should not be compelled to pay such a large indemnity as was demanded, especially as it reduced them almost to penury. But the Amban is supreme.

Kansa, or Sze Chuan Kansa, as the natives frequently call it to distinguish it from the town Kanzé in the Horba district, which is often called Ho Kanzé, was the destination of the interpreter who accompanied me. Being all well mounted, we rode quickly along a fertile valley, where some of the natives, men and women alike, were in the fields doing harvest work, looking after flocks and gathering fuel. That day I saw for the first time a Tibetan woman able to read. My Mongol friend had to get the seal of a chief stamped on my passport as we traveled, but instead of finding him camped where he supposedly was, we found the men of his tribe were moving his tents and goods to another spot, for we met part of the cavalcade on their way. The chief had gone ahead, but his wife was there, a rosy-checked, good-looking young woman with a profusion of ornaments on her hair and hands, and mounted on a black horse with several men in attendance. The interpreter introduced me to her, gave her the passport and also a letter from the Amban at Sining, which had just arrived, relative to some tribal difficulties not far away, in which his representatives were asked to be arbitrators. She read them both, commented in an intelligent manner upon them, nodded good-bye and rode on to overtake the remainder of the caravan, taking with her the passport, which the chief stamped and sent back to us in the evening. We spent the night in a miserable, dirty little shanty, minus doors and windows, near a large house over which floated prayer-flags galore, and not far away was a small lamasery. We had to wait some time for tea and fuel, because the women were all away digging *choma,* and the men would not under any consideration lower their dignity by carrying water.

The chief sent me presents of *tsamba* and butter, at which the interpreter was much pleased, for he said it augured well for my journey to get full dishes of anything the first day. The women came home late in the afternoon, tall, swarthy-cheeked, and skin-robed, but kind and friendly without that tiresome curiosity that characterizes the Chinese. That night I had five of them sleeping just outside the door of my room in accordance with the custom that travelers with *ula* must have a proper guard, but the interpreter said I was honored in having so many, information which I doubted a little, for might it not have been a belief that numbers increase safety that led so many to spend the night beside the foreigner? Their merry voices were heard long after we had retired, a custom which we found common among the Tibetans, and finally I had to interfere, or their excitement in guarding me would have prevented my slumbers. Fear of them I had none. In the morning our *ula* horses were tardy in coming, but at last we were started away, having been joined by a good-natured, genial lama, who was also to have *ula* because he was traveling with letters from a buddha which demanded haste, and he promised the interpreter to help me on the road so far as he could. There is in the valley through which we passed an *obo* that marks the exact border between Sining and Sze Chuan territory, and there robbers have been accustomed to dart out of the hills on either side upon caravans unfortunate enough not to be well guarded. The approach to Kansa is through a narrow valley through which courses a stream lined on either side by evergreen-dotted hills, while in the sequestered nooks nestle the black tents of the sparse inhabitants. The place itself, which we reached in the afternoon of the second day, is a mere hamlet containing several mud-brick houses, conspicuous among which were the trading depots of Chinese and Horba merchants. Here through my Mongol friend I received *ula,* which in this instance was a young girl who shouldered my whole load and trudged away with me to a large house some distance down the stream, where another woman acted as escort. The lama that had *ula* went ahead of me and left orders at every stage for my *ula,* so there was no delay whatever with the change. Our road lay along the Dre Chu, quiet and strong, pursuing its course towards the Yangtse and thence to the sea at Shanghai. Had I at last come upon the sight of waters that made their way to the same Pacific that washed the shores of my native land? Though the latter was still thousands of miles distant, yet civilization and safety began to feel near, and I was glad. Sometimes we were on precipitous hills hundreds of feet above the river, the narrow path wherever shaded being covered with ice in places, to prevent a fatal slip on which the natives had scattered ashes. At other times our pathway led us through glens of marvelous beauty, where trees, mosses, ferns and creepers united to make bowers and castles that our imagination peopled to suit itself, while we quickly wound in and out, zig-zag, among high rocks and boulders. Just below one of these beautiful spots we passed over part of the country that the year previous had been the scene of tragedy through on earthquake, in which a large monastery and several small hamlets had been completely buried. The harm had been almost completely confined to the south bank of the river, which had to a certain extent made a new bed for itself; for the whole mountain side with large trees and tons of earth had, without warning and with loud crashes like thunder, sped on its headlong course straight to the beautiful, calm river. Hundreds of people were killed in that catastrophe, of which the natives spoke in subdued voice and with tender pity for the lives and houses that had been lost. In the general demolition the great caravan road was destroyed for miles, and as there is no provision for the repair or making of roads in Tibetan economy, travelers had succeeded in wearing a little footpath in the midst of the upturned trees, great rocks and other debris, crowning the climax of difficulty by an almost perpendicular ascent to the summit of a hill; for the whole side of the road along the river had disappeared, leaving no space for even a footpath on the bank.

The day's travel was thus unexpectedly difficult and *ula* had been changed several times. At dark I reached a village where I expected to remain over night, but though the man who was traveling with *ula* was resting in one of the homes the natives refused to allow me to remain, but sent me quickly along the river with a small boy and girl, saying that not far away there were some farm houses where I could find shelter. The moon was shining just the same as she formerly shone at Tankar, and the remembrance of the tender thought and care exercised over me in those days made the refusal of refuge at dark all the more painful. As we journeyed on the girl told me that there were no houses until we had passed the mountain that looked to be miles away, so I risked all and returned to the village where I had received the *ula,* the children guiding me to the house where was the man who had helped me on from Kansa. Evidently there was some unusual antipathy to Europeans there, for he quietly told me not to say a word, but interceded with the natives to give me shelter in the straw room, to which they brought for my use a little fire in a shallow earthenware dish and some tea, while an old white-haired man brought a felt rug and lay down near me for the night. The following day it was many

A WALL OF TEA BALES

hours before I reached a house, the road was partly destroyed and so dangerous as to necessitate walking all the way, and I realized the depth to which the villagers had meant to harm me in sending me after dark along that mountain, for nearly the whole night would have been spent before reaching the other side in safety, if I could have accomplished it at all. The first house we sighted was the home of the ferryman, and was built on a perpendicular bluff in a sheltered corner where the Drushi Chu winds on its way to the Dre Chu. We had come into the region of boats and bridges which to us were welcome heralds of greater facilities of transit than are found in the interior. The ferry consisted of a coracle shaped like a tub, about five feet in diameter, composed of a flimsy framework over which were drawn yak hides, and manipulated by a Tibetan with a broad, straight paddle. A large pile of tea, done up in raw hides, was waiting for yak to come and carry it to Kansa, while some men and sheep were being ferried over the river in a second coracle. My friend was busy making his terms with the ferryman when I arrived, and upon reading my passport the latter refused to carry me across because there were no houses in the vicinity on the other side of the river, hence no *ula,* and he did not wish to take any responsibility concerning me. He accordingly sent me up to his home on the bluff, where I remained for two days, while he found out what course to pursue with regard to taking me across the river. A little bird with a red breast made itself at home chirping fearlessly about the straw on the veranda where I slept, but it was the only friend that made overtures, for the women were busy, and except for occasional visits to bring me delicious tea, they remained in their own apartments. After that brief rest I departed with *ula* which was changed at a well-to-do farmer's house, where were several lamas and good-looking women, who all treated me with profound respect upon the perusal of my passport, and after having given me tea and *tsamba,* one of the latter set out with me for the chief's home.

Following the Dre Chu we reached the village where lived the *ponbo,* who alone had authority to give me *ula* for the other side of the river. He was building a new house, and an army of workers, singing as they toiled, were busy carrying the sand for the walls and roof. There I had to pay a small toll for my pass across the river, and order for *ula* on the other side. The next morning with an old nun I made my way down to the ferry on which some lamas were being taken over with several loads of baggage, among which were some beautiful cushions and rugs such as we had seen in Kumbum. I entered the boat with the priest, to do which we had to remove our boots and step into water over our knees; moreover, I was not permitted to wear my hat during the crossing, probably from some superstition regarding it. Having been paddled out to the center of the river the frail structure was caught by the current, wafted to the other shore, and was then carried on the ferryman's back a certain distance up the stream to balance that which the current had wafted it down. The passengers had paid their fares by means of butter, *churma* and tea, which the boatman's family quarreled over while I sat waiting for my *ula*, which presently arrived in the unexpected form of a donkey, an animal which is in common use in that part of Tibet.

I was now fairly started on my journey with *ula* along the north of the Dre Chu towards Ta-chien-lu, and the days sped on, one almost the counterpart of another. The nomads and villagers were exceedingly friendly, and, though I was never permitted to enter their homes, they gave me a corner on a veranda or in a straw room, and adequately made up for their apparent inhospitality by supplying me with an abundance of tea and some coals in a shallow dish to keep it warm, all of which came through the influence of my passports. But if *ula* is good for one's purse and increases one's safety, it is more than trying to one's patience, for the Tibetans, having no idea of time, are in the habit of starting in the morning on a journey. When I reached their homes at mid-day they made all sorts of excuses to have me stay till the following morning. Though sometimes my *ula* was changed as frequently as three or four times in a day, sometimes just as often, when I had only been on the road two or three hours, my escort placed me in the hands of others at a tent or house and returned to their own homes. Though I used all my powers of persuasion it was impossible to move the imperturbable calmness of the natives, who said there could be no *ula* until the day following, and so I had to be content to spend the largest part of the day, when I should have been traveling, in waiting, waiting. My food consisted only of butter, *tsamba* and tea, and my strength was fast waning, so much so that I felt a little more speed was imperative if I were ever to reach Ta-chien-lu alive.

The province through which I was traveling was Dergé, the wealthiest and most fertile of Eastern Tibet, for there the natives are skilled in metal work, and the seals, bells, teapots and other articles manufactured by them find a ready sale and command high prices. They are almost independent of either China or Lhasa, and have a particular antipathy to the Chinese, who find residence in the province almost impossible, in fact the Imperial government has had difficulty in keeping peace in that part of its dominion. A Tibetan official from Lhasa was on his way through the province at the same time as I was myself, and it was rather significant to see the natives keep away from the highways to avoid falling in with his retinue, for the soldiers with him would demand everything they could see, even the very swords and horses they used on the road. Thus authority was repudiated. My *ula* people were most frequently women, but occasionally a whole group of young boys and girls came along with me, taking the very best care of me, and returning to their homes with other ideas of foreigners than they had previously had. Some of the official rest-houses along the road had no people living in them, and, as a rule, my escort took me to inhabited homes, where the little children and the women shed some pleasure into my lonely heart. Occasionally I had a little difficulty with my escort, and where this was so, as a rule, the people where I stopped were not overly kind. Two young boys, one of whom was a lama, resented traveling with me, and everyone we met at first was stopped and told slurring things about the foreigner; but when I asserted my authority and compelled them to go straight past all travelers on the road, they were very angry, but dared not object. That night I had a nicely painted room with a raised bed to sleep on, and some of the women begged several of the buttons off my gown in exchange for butter. The following day the same boy traveled with me from early morning until dusk, for all people on the road refused to accept the responsibility for *ula,* and though he did not wish to travel so far, I did not dare allow him to return. Without stopping even for tea by the roadside, we passed on through pretty glens and valleys, past villages and lamaseries to Gosa Gomba, a large monastery with prayer-wheels around the outside, where he placed me in a large house in the hands of an old man, *gimbi,* a name given to the one who manages *ula* in a place. There lived the chief of a new district, to whom the *gimbi* submitted my passports. I remained there two days, and was glad to escape, for there was great difficulty in restraining the lamas, particularly the younger ones, who came in crowds up the stairway and threatened to push curiosity and impudence into violence, a danger that was averted by the *gimbi* and several old nuns who lived with some of their children in the rooms not far from me.

The morning I left Gosa Gomba was beautiful, the sun shining brightly on the frosty grass, and playing upon the gilded turrets, tiled roofs, and painted walls and prayer-wheels about the monastery. Rustic bridges spanning the streams, where were clustered the homes of farmers, on which prayer-flags were waving in the breeze, added an unwonted charm that was enhanced by the long piles of white *mani* stones, the stacks of straw and the flocks of goats and sheep making their honeycomb paths all over the hillsides. A lama rode beside me for a space, with drum and bell on his back, on his way to some village to chant prayers and "beat the drum." Soon my escort led me past an immense *chorten* at the junction of four valleys, to a large farm house perched high on a hill whence no persuasive powers of mine could procure a continuance of my journey that day. Imagine my feelings when, in conversation with some women, I learned that the *gimbi* had sent me along a little footpath instead of on the big caravan road, and that by pursuing this path I would be months in reaching the Chinese border! My strength was waning and, fearing it would prove insufficient for such a long journey, I went with my *ula* the following morning back to the *gimbi,* who was absent when I arrived. While I awaited his return a young lama amused a crowd who stood about us by ridiculing foreigners, especially myself, even molding *tsamba* into obscene forms that I refused to notice, and I was thankful when I saw the *gimbi* appear, though he was surprised to see me. Having ordered straw for my horse and tea for myself, he listened patiently while I told him my reasons for returning to Gosa, and showed him the map, pointing out to him several places on the large caravan road that I wished to pursue. I refused to go the small road, where I was entirely dependent on the people, who could send me wherever they wished, as I would not know where I was. He insisted that he could not give me *ula* on the big road, but I was equally insistent upon going that road; so, towards afternoon, afraid on account of the turbulent lamas, as corrupt men as I had ever seen, to allow me to remain over night, he started me off to a little village on the big road and the escort took me to his own home. Here men were threshing barley in the courtyard, two on each side with their flails, who alternately sang *Om mani padme hum* as they raised and let fall the old-fashioned threshing instrument. It was a pretty harvest scene, which the children enjoyed as much as I did, as I sat in my quarters under a veranda in one corner of the courtyard, deciding to wait for one of my escort's relatives whose home was in Kanzé in the Horba district, and to which place he would go with me in order to manage my *ula* more quickly than I could myself. That same day a dark-faced, strong Chinaman walked into the courtyard to hire oxen to travel with him and his companions over the pass to Zochen Gomba. I called him to me and, after some conversation, he brought his father, uncle and their apprentices, all journeymen-smiths on their way from Jyékundo to Tai-lin, three days' journey from Ta-chien-lu. They had spent the summer in Tibet, but were going to China for the cold winter months. The old man was kind and full of sympathy, and was inclined to acquiesce in my desire for one of them to travel with me, but, owing to the fear of robbers, concluded we had better remain together until we had passed the dangerous places, and in the meanwhile they would help me manage my *ula.*

One whole day and part of another day's traveling together brought us to an encampment of fifty tents where a local chief lived, and where my *ula* was to be changed while my Chinese friends went on to Zochen Gomba. The unexpected happened just then, for the chief said unless I went three days' journey away to get the seal of the Dergé official stamped on my passport he had no power to give me *ula,* and, notwithstanding bluff attempts and gentle persuasion, I found that my passport was of no value there. Feeling that the Chinese smiths were ready to help me, I abandoned all hopes of *ula,* knowing that speed would more than compensate me for the loss of my official escort, and made my way to the house where the Chinese had quarters on a veranda, a corner of which they yielded to me for my occupation. This house was one of a cluster of stone and log structures, the homes of some Chinese and natives, built on a small stream by which several prayer-wheels in little wooden houses along its course were revolved. High up almost perpendicular paths is the lamasery of Zochen Gomba, where reside over two thousand lamas. The landlady slept out on the veranda, accompanied by her young son, a lama, who insisted upon his mother singing many songs, entertaining us with sweet, weird music away into the night, as well as giving her son pleasure, that, on account of his life as a lama he could very rarely have. Everything was now changed for me, and the Chinese vied with one another in trying to make me comfortable. This to me was proof that the loving Father was caring for His lonely little child that the very day that my passport was refused recognition, two Chinamen had agreed to travel with me down to Ta-chien-lu. This would reduce not only my danger, for those smiths had been years in the country, and I had implicit confidence in the Chinese, but would also reduce the length of my journey perhaps by a month.

The weather was extremely cold, and several nights we had to sleep outdoors. One night I had my feet frost-bitten, and as a result I suffered for nearly a year. The men were carrying all their tools, bedding, etc., on their back, and, as we journeyed in company with a large party of traders across a high mountain pass which is infested with robbers, the two who were to go ahead with me shouldered my goods, though we all remained together until we reached Rong batsa, where my six men regaled themselves freely with wine, filling my heart with terror, as they and the Tibetans in the house became very drunk. Before the carousal my Chinamen had securely fastened their money in scarfs about their necks, and the landlady, as each one became overpowered by the liquor, gave them their sleeping places, and there was no longer any fear.

In that locality we crossed the Za Chu and followed our way straight across the country through villages, meeting on the way thousands of yak, loaded with tea, and passing some carrying hides and other articles of trade on their way to Ta-chien-dao, as the natives there called Ta-chien-lu. The men were well dressed, and their horses were decorated with bright, gay trappings. We met frequently processions of lamas, one of whom, dressed in yellow satin with yellow hat and having a large retinue, betrayed his rank of "living buddha." The country was dotted with villages and small lamaseries, and cultivated fields worked by primitive wooden plows in the hands of men and women, attested the industry of the people. On top of the promontory or steep hill jutting out into a bend of the Za Chu was seen the beautiful gilded roof of the Nyara Gomba, and a little further on, beyond some deep cuts in the road, is Kanzé, a large place composed of the homes of laymen, and a large lamasery, Kanzego, with a beautiful Chinese temple. Here W. W. Rockhill had met with trouble from the turbulency of the lamas, and my guides led me straight past the place, for they said there were such strained relations between Tibetans and Chinese that the latter were almost *en masse* compelled to withdraw. This place is one of the largest in the Horba states, which are next in wealth and size to Dergé, in Eastern Tibet. Notwithstanding the antagonism of the natives to Chinese and foreigners, they were very interesting, and withal even charming. They were better looking and as a rule better dressed than natives in other parts, wearing a profusion of ornaments in silver and gold. The men are dressed in *pulu,* or colored drilling, have their hair mainly done in a great queue which they adorn with bright rings and twist about their heads. The breach of their gun and the sheath of their sword are decorated with silver, coral and green stones. The women often wear a large disc of silver on their forehead and sometimes on the back of their head, and both sexes carry from their girdles silver needle cases, flint and steel boxes and occasionally an embroidered cloth case for their *tsamba* bowl. They are exceedingly hostile to the Chinese, who have never until late years been allowed to live even in comparative peace among them, and though Chinese officials are stationed at Kanzé, Chang-ko and Dawo, they have practically little power, and for their cowardice are despised by the Tibetans, who disdainfully hold up the little finger, which designates the height of inferiority, and say that the Chinese official at Dawo is afraid even to step outside of his own door for fear of a dog.

The first town of importance we reached after passing Kanzé was Chango, which is built on a steep slope overlooking the Nya Chu, while on the hills above lies the Chango Gomba, inhabited by over two thousand lamas who enjoy the reputation of being desperately unruly and bad. On account of the prediliction of these lamas to quarrel, my guides led me around this place, after having stopped at a small lamasery to buy some extra tea, because tea leaves are so highly prized by the natives in this locality, that most travelers use them instead of money to pay for fodder and lodging, as you can obtain more for a little tea than for ten times its value in silver. Shortly after leaving Chango we saw on the road several drunken Tibetans, who were extorting money from some poor travelers, whose valuable large dog the former had in their possession. They were six of a body of fifty soldiers who had been summoned to compel the natives of Chango to pay their taxes, and had that morning been disbanded, but before leaving the town they had imbibed too freely, and as a result were an unspeakable terror to all travelers who fell into their clutches. My guides congratulated themselves upon having thus easily escaped them, but their gladness was premature, for while we sat in front of a rude farm-house we saw them passing along the road, and when we were again on the way we saw them sitting in a little grassy spot, drinking more wine while their ponies rested on the grass. Soon afterwards, looking back, I saw them galloping toward us, and a great fear possessed me, for Tibetans are very quarrelsome when they are drunk, and woe betide the poor traveler who is unfortunate enough to fall into their hands! The older one of my guides said he would drop behind, and if we should be attacked one of us might have a chance to escape. Presently they reached us, and while four of them stopped to see what the one boy had, the other two rode up opposite to myself and the second boy, and, halting, one of them said, "*choh kana du?*" (where are you going?). The boy answered that we were just going over yonder, which was a polite answer, but it seemed to incense the man, for, grinding his teeth in rage, he drew from its sheath his sword and made for the boy. His companion, who was not so intoxicated, endeavored to restrain him, but in a moment the six of them were beside us, and one of them caught me roughly by the arm and tried to pull me off my horse, asking me where I was going. In a moment all six dismounted, and while some of them dragged my boy by the queue this way and that, others opened up his load, scattering everything about the ground. My revolver was worse than useless, for they all were heavily armed, and to have incensed them meant that my life would have been taken sooner or later as a result. Anxiously I sat in my saddle, knowing that just as soon as they were through with the boy they would turn their attention to me. One of them, who was more sober than the others, motioned to me with his chin to go towards the other boy, and I turned my horse and followed his advice, but my safety was short-lived, for one of the Tibetans remounted and came up in a moment behind me. I rode astride, as all Tibetan women do, and as he rode along beside me his knee brushed against mine, and, taking his sword from its scabbard, he held the naked blade over me, bidding me dismount and give him my horse. I looked into his face, that was very near to me, saw his eyes glassy from alcohol, realized that he was scarcely responsible for his actions, and my heart was convulsed. As a child would call his father, I called aloud, "Oh God! Oh God!" and in Tibetan said, "*Mari, mari,*" which means "no, no." A strange expression crossed the man's face, and he put his sword away, turned and joined his companions, and in a moment all had galloped down the river, and not only was my life spared, but I had not lost anything; whereas had I been compelled to dismount my horse and my bedding would have been taken, for the latter was on my saddle. Quite unexpectedly, too, my Tibetan gown and pot were not lost, for they were in the load of the boy who sat on the roadside, while the other one's load had been thrown about and only the tea leaves taken, but he himself lost a valuable sword, his *tsamba* basin and purse, containing thirty rupees.

As we sat on the grass I was almost overpowered with thankfulness and joy that my life and the things needful had thus been saved, nor can I doubt that my deliverance was due to the care of the Heavenly Father, who neither slumbers nor sleeps.

CHAPTER XXV

SAFE AT LAST

The Approach to Ta-chien-lu—My Pony Becomes Exhausted—Long Marches with Blistered Feet—Chinese Conception of Europeans—Among Friends Once More—Conclusion.

With the disappearance down the river of the brightly accoutred horses and their riders came a great perplexity, for my boys had a desire to follow them and endeavor to regain some of their lost property. In the drunken, unaccountable condition of the Tibetans such a course could only have been attended by more calamity. Feeling the force of this they desired to return to Chango and accuse the guilty ones before the magistrates; but, upon remembering that the men were unknown to them, and also that it would necessitate great delay in reaching Ta-chien-lu, and not having enough money to reimburse their loss, I told them I was willing to return to Chango with them—they would still, however, have to accompany me to the border, according to agreement, as the money had already been paid to their father. They appreciated my offer, and also the necessity of fulfilling their father's agreement with me, and upon receiving my promise to supply them with food for the journey, they decided to push on to Ta-chien-lu.

With characteristically national desire to avoid meddling in other people's affairs, a Tibetan, whose house was near us though hidden by a hillock from view, came up after the fracas, and offered us the hospitality of his home. This we gladly accepted, as I felt it was better not to risk meeting those men again until the effects of the liquor had worn away, as well as from the fact that it was late in the afternoon, and quite time to rest.

The scenery along the road down the river for several miles from Chango is beautifully refreshing, the country being very fertile and dotted with hamlets; then, as the river bends southward, our way diverged, to return again to pursue its course through magnificent forests of large timber on the sides of mountains towering as far as the eye could see above us. Another day's journey brought us to Dawo, with its large lamasery, the Ninchung Gomba, with gilded roofs and its secular part with two-storied houses built on either side of a stream, over which are a number of gristmills. The lamas are about one thousand in number, and the population of the town is nearly as many more, of which over 10 per cent. are Chinese, some of them being workers in metal. Houses dot the valley to its close below Dawo, and to avoid intricacies that might prove bewildering if not dangerous, the older boy and myself went past the town to a farmer's house at the foot of the hills, while the other went up into the town to buy tea. He brought us, on his return, some bread, which was to us a delicacy of delicacies, though it had no leaven of any kind, for the staff of life had been absent from even the sight of our eyes for months. In almost every village there were Chinese, most of whom have become almost naturalized Tibetans in clothing, customs and even religion, murmuring the mystic six-syllabled prayer quite as faithfully as the natives themselves. On the road a large proportion of the travelers whom we met were also Chinese, among whom were even the indefatigable beggars, who apparently would have been much wiser to have remained in their own country; they were in all probability exiles on account of some crime. though many of them were very young. All these Celestials made us realize that we were every day getting nearer to Ta-chien-lu, and as my physical strength waned my heart grew more buoyant at the probability of our reaching the longed-for goal.

Signs of earthquakes are not wanting in the valley, almost every house being in ruins, only parts of the stone walls standing. We passed the corner of the hill near Tai-lin, having pursued the road which leads over the Jéto pass, as it was better and shorter than the one through Tai-lin, which place is largely Chinese. The second day before reaching Ta-chien-lu just after we had started from one of two houses where we had spent the night in a corner of a courtyard, I was compelled to walk as my horse became unfit to carry me, and soon so slow in his gait that he himself was a burden. After having walked some distance on my already sore feet, whose only protection was a pair of Tibetan boots, with simply one layer of untanned leather for the sole, we rested amidst the snow that covered the ground thickly, to boil some tea for our pony; for the natives give their horses liquid tea, tea leaves, *tsamba, churma* and at times raw meat to increase their strength and render them able to pursue their journey. Sitting on some stones waiting while the horse devoured from our pot his stimulating meal, we felt the small, rumbling shock of an earthquake. A great wave of disappointment swept over me as I thought of the possibility of being buried by a landslide and not realizing after all, the recently born hopes of refuge and safety in the great border town.

The stage that day was a long one, and I walked thirty miles just as quickly as I could with my spent strength and blistered feet, for the soles of my boots had worn through in places. The guides urged me on, for we could find no shelter until we were beyond the Jéto pass, which is about fourteen thousand feet in height. Wearily we climbed and climbed, the ascent being at first gradual, one dragging the old horse while another urged him on with my little whip. It wrung my heart to see the faithful, patient brute goaded like that, but unless we abandoned him on the road there was no help for it. I would fain care for the noble animal that had carried me without a falter or stumble, far from the regions of trouble and disaster. Nearing the summit of the Jéto pass, we saw the road to Lit'ang, winding past hamlets through a beautiful valley. The last part of the ascent was very steep and difficult. We found the top crowned with a huge *obo,* and if natives thank the spirits joyfully for aid in climbing I rendered sincere praise to my Father that, though weary to almost an extreme, my strength had not faltered, and I was beyond the most laborious stage of the ascent. It had begun to snow heavily and darkness settled down upon us, but the ground on either side was so rough that there was no place where we might lie down to rest; for stones, large and numerous, dotted either side of the road, while a rocky stream and a dense growth of large underbrush added to the difficulty of choosing a suitable camping place. Here and there we saw campfires near which were tethered large droves of yak, whose presence was betrayed by their black forms on the white background of snow. Feeling the extent to which the horse delayed us, two of us went more quickly on ahead, leaving one of the guides to drag along the poor animal, which had just as much difficulty on the stony road as myself. Presently we reached a little shanty a few feet square, in the center of a yard enclosed by a low stone fence, behind which we saw a large number of saddled yak. My guide asked for shelter during the night—it was denied us for want of space, but, after passing on, we decided to return and ask again, for the road was dangerous, being simply a running stream over rough and uneven stones. The boy told me to walk straight into the shanty because I was so well dressed that I would have more influence than he, who was just a shabby *peh-tsi*. Making my way through a gap in the fence to an opening in the side of the shanty, which was only three feet in height, I stooped low and entered, calling out *ta-ko.* A Chinaman, poorly dressed and dirty as a Tibetan, stepped up, and I told him that we were going to spend the night in the shanty, for our horse was tired out and unable to proceed any further. He objected on the score that the shanty was too small for any more occupants. When I said he was a good, kind man, that I was thoroughly tired out, that I had walked thirty miles that day and my feet were too sore to go another step, he invited us to be seated beside a huge blazing fire in the far corner; for he knew that did he not allow us to remain until morning we would still have to walk several miles through the slush and snow. I have, as a general rule, found the Chinese kind-hearted, and inclined to help those in distress. The little shanty was only a few feet square. The "entrance," devoid of a door, took up one side of it, being supplemented by a pigsty, where wallowed an immense hog. In the other side was the rude fireplace, just a hollow in the ground, and having on either side of it barely room enough to crouch down to rest.

Our feet were soaking, and while a half dozen Tibetans drank their tea and watched us furtively, we three endeavored to get dried, while the two Chinese lumbermen told us all about the different foreigners who were living at Ta-chien-lu. It is not surprising that there are Boxer riots in China instigated for the purpose of driving from their empire the foreigners, whom they believe capable of such atrocities as those men ascribed to our countrymen in the border town. We had heard before leaving Tankar that several members of Miss Annie R. Taylor's Tibetan Mission Band, under the leadership of Mr. Cecil Polhill-Turner, had taken up work at Ta-chien-lu, and I carefully questioned those two men to learn whether this were a fact or not. They informed me that there were several families of foreigners living there, all of whom had large houses, one with men only outside the north gate, another of the same kind outside the south gate, and one entirely with women inside the town; all of which were Roman Catholic establishments, the last mentioned being a school kept by Chinese Roman Catholic nuns. There was yet another family, they said, who had just arrived, with a lady and some children. These, I decided, were Mr. and Mrs. Turner and their co-workers. The men then proceeded to tell me what the people said of the foreigners, how their servants bought children on the streets and took them to the foreign home, whence they were never seen again; how the strange men could look at Chinese brass coins and change them with their evil eyes into rupees with the head of a woman on them. No one, they added, was allowed to enter the house to see what was within. I think, on the whole, in new places it is wise for missionaries to have their homes open so that natives may at times see into the smallest corners, and thus, as "seeing is believing," crush at the outset any ideas of mystery which heathen people are only too ready to entertain.

In the quiet of that lumber shanty my two Chinese guides told the others many things they had learned of foreigners from me, and the impression they had received of the only foreigner they had ever seen. They explained the purpose of missionaries in coming to and settling in a far-away country, and said their support did not come from magic, but from people in the homeland, who sent them so much salary a year. Nevertheless the strange tales that they had heard did not lessen their dread of entering the home of foreigners whom none of us knew, for of course I did not even know the Chinese name of a single missionary in Ta-chien-lu, and I felt really sorry for the men, their dread was so genuine, but they had implicit confidence in me and would have gone any place with me. I told them when in the future they heard anything disparaging about missionaries to just remember that they were all as good as I was, to say the very least that could be said about them.

One of the lumbermen told us of a foreigner who had gone past their shanty a few days previous on his way up country, walking and carrying a chest of carpenter's tools on his back, while one Chinese servant accompanied him. The foreigner had given him some medicine for rheumatism, and could speak Chinese and Lhasa Tibetan. I wondered who it could have been, and found, when I reached the mission station, that it was one of the Tibetan mission band, the talented, bright Mr. Amundsen, who had endeavored to become like a native himself, and in an unpretentious way was seeking to gain a foothold among them. He was unfortunately attacked by a drunken Tibetan, who concluded that his box was full of silver. Having been robbed of almost everything, he had returned by another route to his home in Ta-chien-lu.

When we had had our tea and were thoroughly dried, we made ready to spend the night, and soon in the very small space, around the hollow fireplace, were crouched six men and myself, while in the yard were several Tibetans. My own two men were closest to me, but all were within touching distance, and yet I had not a tremor of fear of them, so great was the difference between the Chinese and Tibetans, that to be with the former meant perfect freedom from fear and anxiety; even though these lumbermen were rough and uncultured, they were kind, and made me feel their sympathy. A common danger made us all akin in the little shanty, for at intervals was heard and felt the great rumbling noise of earthquake shocks, which were sometimes strong enough to shake the roof. The lumbermen recited on and off, tales of landslides and earthquakes in the valleys near, painting in glowing words the beauty of the homes so suddenly destroyed and the great piety and devotion of lamas who had been crushed. These recitals subdued me with quiet awe, and I was thankful after the sleepless night to see the first streaks of dawn, though with them came the most violent shock of all.

The sun was well up before we started to walk again, and its heat quickly melted the snow which had fallen to a depth of several inches. The road was virtually a stream of running water, in places almost half a foot deep, but I cheerfully splashed through it, knowing that I would, after a twenty-mile walk, reach a Chinese inn or the mission station, either of which would prove a haven of rest. The road was a gradual descent, though here and there were sharp ascents which taxed my strength to the utmost, and at times made me almost despair of reaching Ta-chien-lu that day. But on we trudged over the stony road skirted on either side now by rocks, now by clusters of holly and rhododendrons to me unspeakably beautiful, indications of the return of summer with its blue skies and balmy mountain air. We passed luxuriant valleys, and groups of houses, Chinese in appearance and so different from the homes of Tibetan agriculturalists, reposing on the hillsides looking so neat and inviting. My physical weakness and sore feet took away much of the poetry and all the pleasure of the walk. The Chinese boys kept urging me on, not willing that I should rest every little distance on a stone by the roadside, as I felt compelled to do. Thirty miles' walk the day before and twenty that day could not be accomplished by my already exhausted strength without acute suffering; but the goal was safety, peace and rest, and on I went.

Past a picturesque lamasery with red buildings surrounded by tall trees, on over an arched bridge, we wended our way toward the south gate of the town. My escort persuaded me to mount my poor, tired horse and ride into the place "in state." Just outside the gate we paused at the massive doors of the Roman Catholic Mission to inquire the whereabouts of Mr. Turner's house. It was certainly amusing and yet pitiful to see my boy edge away from the door after knocking. He had a mortal fear of foreigners, and evidently expected something to spring out of the door at him. A Chinaman answered our inquiry and informed us that Mr. Turner lived across the river. As we went on we attracted very little attention even in the crowded, narrow streets, for Ta-chien-lu has a motley population, and no one suspected that I was other than a Tibetan. After we had crossed the bridge a young Chinaman ran up and told me to hide my knife and chopsticks that hung by my girdle, as thieves might steal them. He then led us through a narrow, dark alley underneath a house, where I dismounted, as a lama called out in stentorian voice, "What are you doing mounted here?" Our guide was the cook who, upon arrival at the Fu-ing-tang (China Inland Mission House), rushed into the young men's room telling them a man had come, not knowing whether I was a Tibetan or a European. In response to his excitedly given information, two missionaries, Messrs. Amundsen and Moyes, stood in the outer courtyard when I walked through the entrance. How clean they looked in Chinese garb, and how white their faces! I knew I was not clean, yet, conscious of my dirtiness and rags, I stood in their presence waiting to be addressed. But no, I must speak first; so I said in English, "Is this Mr. Turner's?" and Mr. Moyes replied "Yes." How the word thrilled me through and through. It was the first English word I had heard since that never-to-be-forgotten morning two months before when my husband disappeared around the rock, and the speaker was the first white stranger I had seen since before we left Tankar. There was another pause, for I was well nigh overcome with emotion; then I said, "I am Dr. Rijnhart." Mr. Amundsen then invited me upstairs to Mrs. Turner's apartments. They had been so dumbfounded to hear the voice of an Englishwoman come from such a Tibetanized person that at first they could not speak at all. Upon reaching the door of the dining-room Mrs. Turner arose while Mr. Amundsen introduced me. Dear Mrs. Turner asked, "Are you alone?" "When have you had anything to eat?" Such thoughtful, beautiful care! Then she said, "Come into the nursery and cook will bring you some tea." I looked at the clean matting, so spotless, and then at my boots, which oozed at every step, leaving dirty marks behind, and I protested that I was too dirty to go into such a clean room. But that did not matter, I was ushered in only to have my heart torn by the sight of little Kenneth, just about the size of my darling baby boy, for whom I mourned. Tea in a dainty cup and some cookies were given me for refreshment, and then Mrs. Turner offered me a place to rest until supper; but it was impossible for me to sit down to a clean table with cleanly people, and I asked for a bath and some underwear, in response to which request every member of the household contributed towards my change of raiment.

I had arrived in Ta-chien-lu just two months after Mr. Rijnhart's disappearance. Could it be possible that I had survived that long and perilous journey alone over mountains and rivers, surrounded by hostile people and subjected to hourly danger from those who professed to be my guides? Was I really once more in a Christian home, surrounded by kind friends and comforts? Yes, at last, and the realization of it grew upon me when I saw myself delivered from the dirt and vermin of weeks, and lay down to rest once more on a clean bed. Gratitude filled my heart, and with the Psalmist I could say:

Bless the Lord, O my soul!
And all that is within me, bless his holy name. * * *
Who redeemeth thy life from destruction;
Who crowneth thee with loving-kindness and tender mercies;
Who satisfieth thy mouth with good things;
So that thy youth is renewed like the eagle's.

At the supper table Mr. Turner asked me what I would like to know first about the outside world, since I had been isolated so long. Scarcely knowing where to begin, I stammered out the question, "Is Queen Victoria still alive?"

Disappointed at not finding an official at Jyékundo, I now hoped to be able to ascertain through official means some definite news about my husband's fate. I prepared a statement of the case and sent it to the British Consul at Chong-King, requesting him to forward the same to the Dutch and British ministers at Pekin, to be presented by them to the Tsung-li Yamen. For six months I waited in Ta-chien-lu in the hope that some reliable reports would come down from the interior of Tibet, but I waited in vain. On my arrival at Ta-chien-lu I had not a cent of money, but kind friends in America responded generously to my need, and I was able to get down to Shanghai, thence to

Tien tsin, where I interviewed Mr. Knobel, Minister for the Netherlands, who assured me that he would do everything in his power to induce the Chinese government to make an investigation, and added that Sir Claude Macdonald, the British Minister, was acting jointly with him in the matter. I would fain have remained in China to await the result, but my health was undermined, friends were pressing me to return to America, and Mr. Knobel assured me that my presence was not necessary, that the government would do everything that could be done. Under date of May 2, 1900, Mr. Knobel received a report from the Tsung-li Yamen, of which the following is a translation:

"With regard to Mr. Rijnhart's case, our yamen has repeatedly corresponded with the Governor of Szechuen, the Imperial Resident in Tibet, and the Imperial Agent at Sining, who were all instructed to investigate and report upon the matter. We wrote you already to this effect on March 8th, last. We since received, on April 21st, a dispatch from the Imperial Agent at Sining, reading:

"'About this matter, telegrams have come to hand from the Tsung-li Yamen and the Governor of Szechuen instructing me to hold an investigation. The necessary orders have been given. According to information received from the English missionary Lo Tcheng (Laughton), living at Sining in the Fu yin tan, the Dutch missionary "Lin" is the same as Mr. Rijnhart. He is said to have disappeared while traveling.

"'The missionary Lo had found a priest by the

name of I-shi-ni-ma, who made inquiries for him. Upon reaching the bank of the river he heard that the murder was committed by an inhabitant of "To-chia" by the name of "Chia-li-ya-sa."

"'Whereupon I (the Agent) sent two competent persons from my yamen with the priest "I-shi-ni-ma" to "To-chia," and gave them an escort of civil and military officials and soldiers. Their report is:

"'According to the people of "To-chia," the oldest inhabitants of the place, together with the priest "I-shi-ni-ma" had gone from house to house, but man nor woman, old nor young, knew anything about a murder committed upon a Dutch missionary; also they did not know "Chia-li-ya-sa." We, the people of "To-chia," number three hundred families, large and small, and are all good subjects. If it should be discovered hereafter that a murderer of a European is among us, we are willing to suffer punishment.

"'I (the Agent) feared that all this might not be quite true, so I sent successively again a major, Li Chih Chung, and an official writer, "Yen Ling," to the said place in order to make new investigation. The major and others reported that they received a petition from Penk'o, the chief of the village, which was to the same effect as above. This is the result of my investigation.'

"As soon as we receive the reply from Szechuen and Tibet, we will inform your Excellency.

"PEKIN, May 2nd, 1900."

No further news except vague native reports has

been received; nor is it likely that I shall ever hear anything more definite.

The reader will recognize in the above report the name of Ishinima, our Tibetan teacher at Kumbum. With all his faults he had a sympathetic heart, for as soon as he heard that our caravan had come to grief in the interior and that Mr. Rijnhart had been killed, he offered his services to the official at Sining, and made the long journey to the interior in search of authentic information concerning his friend. Dear old Ishinima! On this page, which will forever to him be sealed and unknown, I cannot refrain from making some slight acknowledgment of his services. The sweet associations of our residence in the lamasery will never be forgotten either by me or by him, and although his dream of some day visiting America with the "foreign teacher" is now shattered, yet it comforts me to know that he has heard the name of Jesus, is acquainted with the teachings of the Bible, and prays to the "Heavenly Ruler" as well as to his brazen idol. While I think of him gratefully and pray for him earnestly I know that from time to time his thought will wander to the far interior of his native land, where sleeps the dust of two whom he loved—and also to me in the distant land so full of wonders, lying across the deep blue ocean.

It is natural to weigh our sacrifices against their results, although the process brings little consolation, for so often in our superficial view the results are minified beyond our vision and the sacrifice fills the whole horizon. Since my return to America many have raised the question, "Was the cause worth the suffering and have results justified it?" Critics of missions ask it—those who lift up their hands of disapproval when a life is given for the sake of the Gospel and the spiritual uplifting of a benighted people, yet lustily applaud the soldier who spills his blood on the battlefield in the cause of territorial expansion or national aggrandizement. To such it is sufficient to say that Christ also has his soldiers who are willing to die for his cause if need be, in the belief that his cause is the sublimest among men, and who are content to leave the results with him knowing that the Great Captain of their Salvation will in his own time lead his hosts unto ultimate victory and a kingdom universal. Such is the optimism of the Gospel and such the faith and courage it generates.

Kind Christian friends have questioned our wisdom in entering Tibet. Why not have waited, they ask, until Tibet was opened by "the powers" so that missionaries could go in under government protection? There is much heart in the question but little logic. Christ does not tell his disciples to wait, but to go. We are not to choose conditions, we are to meet them. The early apostles did not wait until the Roman Empire was "opened" before they kindled that fire that "burned to the water's edge all round the Mediterranean," but carrying their lives in their hands they traveled through the cities of Asia Minor, Greece and finally to Rome, delivering their message in the very centers of paganism. Persecutions came upon them from every side, but nothing but death could hinder their progress or silence their message. They went to glorious martyrdom and being dead they have never ceased to speak. Paul says, "When it was the good pleasure of God * * * to reveal his Son in me, that I might preach Him among the Gentiles, immediately I conferred not with flesh and blood." (Gal. 1, 15-16.) Though he knew bonds and imprisonments awaited him in every city, he pursued his great missionary journeys shrinking not from innumerable perils and even glorying in his tribulations. He was willing "not to be bound only, but also to die at Jerusalem for the name of the Lord Jesus" (Acts xxi 13), and although he did not court death he elected to go to the very gates of the Imperial City and face the judgment seat of a Caesar, because of his desire to preach Christ even at Rome. Instead of waiting till the countries under the sway of Rome were opened, the apostle went forth in the power of God to open them. So it has ever been in the history of Christianity. Had the missionaries waited till all countries were ready and willing to receive them, so that they could go forth without danger and sacrifice, England might still have been the home of barbarians, Livingstone's footsteps never would have consecrated the African wilderness, there would have been no Carey in India, the South Sea Islanders would still be sunk in their cannibalism, and the thousands of Christians found in pagan and heathen lands to-day would still be in the darkness and the shadow of death.

Tibet, like other lands must have the light. The command is "Go preach the Gospel to every creature."

The work is great. So great that beside its greatness any sacrifice involved in its accomplishment is small. Mr. Rijnhart frequently gave expression to his one burning ambition to be of service in evangelizing Tibet—whether by his life or his death, he said, did not matter to him. With David Brainerd he could say, "I longed to be a flame of fire, continually glowing in the service of God and building up Christ's kingdom to my latest, my dying moments." Remembering his consecration I too can be strong and say, as I bring the story to a close, "God doeth all things well—the sacrifice was not too great."

The results of the journey herein described are to me of the most encouraging character. Interest in Tibet has been aroused among Christians of many denominations, and the country and its needs have been brought prominently to the notice of several mission boards. The hope which my husband cherished of seeing many laborers go forth to the field seems nearer realization now than in his lifetime. The seed sown is springing up with bright promise. The trumpets are being blown about the walls of the great closed land. Soon they will fall that the heralds of the Cross may enter in. I see them coming and I exclaim—How beautiful upon the mountains are the feet of them that preach in Tibet the Gospel of Peace!

While at Ta-chien-lu I was much impressed by the possibilities for missionary work all along the eastern border. In the town itself, splendid work is being done by the Tibetan Band of the China Inland Mission, under the leadership of Mr. Cecil Polhill Turner. The

Christian Missionary Alliance have a work at Tao-cheo, while other large border towns, such as Kuei-teh, Tankar, Sungpan and others, offer splendid advantages. Any one of them would make a good center for Tibetan work. Ta-chien-lu is especially advantageous as so many roads branch out from it, and Jyékundo, situated at the juncture of great roads leading to the border and also to the interior, could be a splendid station from which to come into contact with several tribes. In addition to regular evangelistic work there could be established in connection with all missionary enterprise on the border, industrial schools and medical stations.

Meanwhile Kumbum and Tankar, where we labored three years, are without missionaries. Only the worshippers of Buddha now behold the gleam of the Oriental Sun on the golden roofs of the lamasery; the great caravans from the city of the Dalai Lama pass through the border town with no one to tell the pilgrims of the "Heavenly Ruler." From ten thousand tongues amid the flutter of the prayer-flags and the click of cylinders is heard the mystic invocation—*Om mani padme hum,* but there is no Christian altar. The devotees still flock to revere the Sacred Tree and worship the great Butter God, and amid all the host there is not one witness for Jesus Christ! The call comes and it will be answered soon, I feel convinced. And whoever responds will find many who know something of Christianity, who have copies of the Scriptures, and remember with affection the White Teacher who, while he was with them, labored for their good, and who left them never to return. And many will have heard of the lone little grave under the huge boulder at the base of the Dang La.

* * * * *

"To the spirit select there is no choice.
He cannot say, This will I do or that.
* * * * *
A hand is stretched to him from out the dark,
Which grasping without question, he is led
Where there is work that he must do for God.
* * * * *
To the tough hearts that pioneer their way
And break a pathway to those unknown realms,
That in the earth's broad shadow lie enthralled,
Endurance is the crowning quality.
And patience all the passion of great hearts."

—*J. R. Lowell.*

GLOSSARY.

Achi .... Sister.
Ahon .... A teacher among moslems.
Apa .... Father.
Argols .... Excreta of animals.
Aro .... Brother.
Bei-si or pei-si .... Mongol chief.
Chang .... Alcoholic liquor made by Tibetans.
Chang lam .... Long road.
Chen tai .... Military official.
Chong-kuei teh .... Head of a house, shopkeeper
Choma .... Edible root.
Chorten .... Monument.
Churma .... Dried curds of buttermilk.
Dalai Lama .... Grand lama.
Dimo dimo ing .... Tibetan salutation.
Dzassak .... Mongol chief.
Fa tai .... Abbot.
Fen-kuai-tsi .... Dried manure bricks.
Fu-ing-tang .... C. I. M. Chapel.
Fu tai .... Civil official.
Fu yeh .... Living Buddha.
Gelu .... Yellow sect of lamas.
Gimbi .... Controller of Official escort.
Gomba .... Monastery.
Heh-ho-shang .... Black priests.
Ho pen .... Shallow pot for fire.
Huei-huei .... Mohammedan.

Iang-ta-ren .... Foreign great man.
Ie mah .... Wild mule.
Ja-ja .... Sleeveless jacket.
Ja-lam .... Road traveled by tea caravans.
K'a che .... Mohammedan.
Kali .... Slowly.
K'ang .... The hollow heated platform in use as a bed and divan.
Kanpo .... Abbot.
Kao yeh .... Secretary.
Karwa .... Palace.
Khata .... Scarf of ceremony.
Khopa or kopa .... Tibetan from the interior.
Ktang .... Discuss.
Kotow .... Strike the forehead to the ground in worship or honor.
Kuan men .... Official gate.
Kushok .... Gentleman.
Ku tsi .... Trousers.
Lama .... Buddhist priest.
La rong .... Official residence of the abbot.
Li .... One-third of an English mile.
Long ta .... Wind horse made of paper.
Mamba .... Doctor.
Mamba fu yeh .... Medical buddha.
Mang tuan .... Satin given by the Emperor to the Mongol princes.
Mani .... Prayer, rosary.
M'ien .... Vermicelli.
Obo .... Pile of stones on a hill or pass.
Oruss .... Russian.
Panaka .... Nomadic Tibetan of N. E. Tibet.
Pao ren .... A man who acts as security.
Peh Sing .... Subjects, common people.
Peh tsi .... Coolie who carries loads on his back.
Peling .... English.
Pei-lu .... Northern road.

Piao ....Agreement.
Pien shi..Small, boiled, meat dumplings.
Ponbo ....Official.
Ponbo ch'enpo..................Great official.
Puh tsi..Shop.
Pulu..Woolen cloth made by Tibetans.
Sho ....Junket.
Sung Kuan ....Disciplinarian.
Ta ko..Older brother.
Tangut..Tibetan of lake district.
Tao tai..Official of third rank.
Tiao lo..Tower of defence.
Ting..Civil official in small town.
Tong kuan..........................Eastern suburb.
Tsamba ....Parched barley meal.
Tsao ti..Grass country.
Tseh..Thief.
Tung shih..Interpreter.
Ula ....Relays of animals supplied by Government order.
Wang yeh ....Prince or chief.
Wu chai khata ....Scarfs of ceremony in parcels of five.
Yamen..Home and office of an official.
Yesu Ma'shika....................Jesus Christ.

INDEX